A PATRIOT

The Conservative Voice

Jerry Macke

A Patriot, The Conservative Voice. © Copyright 2020 Jerry Macke. All rights reserved. No part of this book may be reproduced in any form or by any means, electronic or mechanical, including photocopying, recording, or by any information storage and retrieval system, without express written permission from the publisher except for the use of brief quotations in a book review. Contact Jerry Macke: domacke2005@yahoo.com. Front cover image © 2020 Fotokvadrat/Shutterstock. Back cover image © 2020 Patthana Nirangkul/ Shutterstock.

Macke, Jerry
A Patriot, The Conservative Voice
/ Jerry Macke – First Edition
ISBN 979-86372359-4-0
1.   Political Science 2. Political Freedom 3. Civil Rights

PRINTED IN THE UNITED STATES OF AMERICA

Dedication

In memory of my parents, Bill and Sally Richard.
Though having passed, they have been a constant
Inspiration in my life to do something creative.

Though they were life-long Democrats,
They were not intolerant,
They did not hate,
They detested corruption,
And were not guided by deception.

Table of Contents

Introduction

The main focus, or point of interest in writing this book, is the destruction of the Democratic Party along with their values and principles. I was a lifelong Democrat who appreciated those values until I began to see them slip away and become replaced by socialism and its radical ideology. I refer to the party of today as the Socialist Democrat Party while their number one admitted Socialist, Bernie Sanders, calls himself a Democratic Socialist. Bernie and the other Democratic Socialists believe that the government should provide a wide range of basic services, such as health care and education to the people, either for free or at least at a huge discount. Whether you put Socialist first or second in their title is unimportant other than, in my mind, it indicates which part has the highest priority. Today, socialism gets top billing.

Unlike Socialists, Democratic Socialists do not believe the government should control all aspects of life, but only help provide the basic needs, and help all of the people have an equal opportunity for success. This is the main focus of Bernie Sanders and his followers. Unfortunately, as we have already seen with the New Socialists that are finding their way into congress, this limited Bernie Sanders' form of socialism will not withstand the weight of an all-out Marxist Socialist attack on both the Party and the Country. As I point out in this book, both the Socialist Party, or the Communist Party, have an insatiable appetite for taking power and control.

Both Socialist Democrats and Marxist Communists will continue to grab more and more power and control over the people once they have their foot in the door. Sadly, as we will see, their foot is already in the door along with a knee and a shoulder. In America, in this conservative's mind, even a foot in the door is unacceptable.

I point out in this book that our 'Founding Fathers' created a balance between government power, and control vs the people's freedoms and liberties. They well knew that a country with a 100% government control – at the expense of the freedoms for the people – would not work, and they also knew that a 100% freedom by the people with no government power would spell disaster. They finally created a balance of 40-60 in favor of freedom and liberty for the people and felt that this balance would stand the test of time.

Our personal freedoms thus granted to us by our Founding Fathers, and protected for us by the Constitution of the U.S. along with our Declaration of Independence, are not going to yield to socialism, or communism. However, the problem with the Socialist Democrats is that they have adopted the policy of 'intolerance' from the Socialist Communist playbook. They have become the party of intolerance and their goal is to shut down the voice of opposition thereby clearing a pathway to a single party system of government. Why else would they, in the name of hate, impeach President Trump but to shut down his voice and destroy the Republican Party? Along with the intolerance they believe that the 'ends justify the means' and they have the perfect right to do anything, say anything they want, in order to achieve their ends.

When a political party chooses the path of intolerance, the ends justify the means, bias evolves as base of their entire decision making and choice making process. A simple bias, out of control and exempt from constraints, will become a fully bloomed bigotry. This is exactly what has happened to the Socialist Democrat Party of today. They have evolved into a party of hate, corruption, deceit, underhanded practices, and behind-the-back tactics. They can do this because there are no checks against them – there is no accountability, or assumption of responsibility – their voice is the only voice; there is no debate, it's our way or the highway. Today they look far more like Socialist Communists than any resemblance to the Democratic Party of yesteryears.

So, I have seen these changes, and I have witnessed the deceit, underhandedness, and the behind-the-back tactics of their leadership. You simply cannot watch or listen to Hillary Clinton, Nancy Pelosi, Chuck Schumer, Adam Schiff, or Jerry Nadler, and miss the obvious intolerance and hate in their messages. Through their dysfunctional beliefs and tactics, they are attempting to close the minds of their followers to act with the same level of hate. It is disgusting and repulsive, and they are an embarrassment to a constitutional Democratic Republic.

It has become clear to this Conservative voice that I am a 'deplorable' (one deserving of censure or contempt, is wretched, and shockingly bad in quality); I am a 'dredge of society' (a group of people you consider are the least important or useful in society). These, in the words of Hillary Clinton and Joe Biden, two accepted Socialist Democrat leaders of the party. I am an 'old White man,' who needs to die before America can be rid of hate, bigotry, and racism. I am a 'racist' because I support national sovereignty and the integrity of our borders. I am a 'murderer' because I support my right to own guns for whatever legal reason I have; I am a 'homophobic' because I believe in the Christian principle of the traditional family. I am 'Islamophobic' because I insist that any Muslim who comes into America must be vetted for the safety of the country. I am a 'woman's rights hater' because I believe in pro-life and feel that the taxpayers should not be held responsible for women's choices. I am a 'fascist' because I actually believe in free speech for all Americans, not just the Republican Party, and because I believe in education in our schools and not indoctrination.

All of these things that I believe in are policy beliefs of our President, Donald Trump, and he works tirelessly to bring about a national support for them. I have honored these ideas long before Donald Trump entered the political scene, or became president, and yet today, the Socialist Democrats hate me personally (actually calling me hate names), because I support the president's efforts on my behalf. I can only conclude that their hate is the measure of who they are. When the Socialist Democrats from the leaders on down to the street workers call me despicable because of my beliefs, it says far more about them than it does me or any other American that feels as the president and I feel.

With all of this negativity and destructive division on the part of Socialist Democrats it has become clear to me that they are not capable of governing anyone who represents over half of the country, and fits into their collective pigeonholes that they hate. You simply cannot hate half of the country that you propose to lead. Barack Obama tried to do that and was a miserable failure as president. He had the greatest of opportunity to do some tremendous good for America but simply could not separate his hate for half of America and his bigotry for the other half. It is for these reasons that I decided to write this book and to be the 'Conservative Patriot's Voice.'

Chapter 1

Conservatism vs Socialist Democrats

I am a Conservative voice for America speaking out against the Socialist Democrat's attempt to undermine our long-standing values, principles, and traditions. I will stand with our fellow patriots, or I will stand alone in support of the liberties and freedoms that our Founding Fathers promised us in their contract with the people. I will stand for our icons that reflect our very foundation and what this country has and will always stand for: The flag, the great bald eagle, the National Anthem, and our Pledge of Allegiance.

Our liberties, freedoms and icons all have very special meaning to Americans, as they represent the strength and resolve to maintain and protect us from tyranny. Mostly they represent the patriotism that has grown from a mere seed of hope for freedom to a fully blown love of a nation that stands solidly for freedom like no other.

We will consider some obvious differences between Conservativism and the Socialist Democrats. We will identify those differences as to their impact on both the people and the nation. As we continue it is important that all Americans ask themselves: "Would I rather have a handout from the government and therefore be controlled by that government, or a pay check from a business that allows you to maintain control over yourself."

I am certain that most Americans would prefer a job which pays good money over a government hand out. Americans need to understand a simple fact: "If government is big enough to give you everything you need for survival, then they are strong enough to take it all away." No human being will work hard for anything unless they believe that they are working for the betterment of themselves.

Conservative Republicans believe that it is important that Americans return to being 'one nation under God,' and to being under the Constitution which the founders based on Christian principles and values. The Socialist Democrats have been doing everything they can to undermine the values of Christianity in America and to weaken or destroy our spiritual life. They firmly believe that to weaken our resolve on our Christian values would weaken our resolve on our nation. To the Christian Conservatives of this country this is a non-debatable issue.

America needs to gain strength in our respect for the Second Amendment. We are clear in our belief that the Constitution protects our right to bear arms. Since 1791, when the first ten amendments were ratified, Americans have been guaranteed the right to own and bear arms. The Second Amendment itself is crystal clear as it reads, "That right shall not be infringed."

Socialist Democrats today are adamant that the free ownership of guns should not be allowed, or in the least, should be severely regulated and controlled. They have long believed that guns in the hands of private citizens stand in the way of their taking control by the state, of the people's liberties and freedoms.

Be apprised that the Second Amendment is the cornerstone, and protector of all of the other amendments, and even the Constitution itself. If the Second Amendment were to fall, as the Socialist Democrats would desire, there would be created a domino effect that would cause all the other amendments, left unprotected, to fall in turn. Each of these amendments represents more of your liberties and freedoms that would be lost. With nothing left to protect any of your once guaranteed constitutional rights – that document would then become worthless.

Understand this about Socialist Democrats: to them, "Gun control laws are based on the assumption that law abiding citizens cannot be trusted with their Second Amendment." They want to stop gun involved crimes by restricting or denying law abiding people their Second Amendment rights. The great Athenian philosopher, Plato, wrote an ancient script that reads, "Good people do not need laws to act responsibly, while bad people will find a way around any law we make." Conservative thought is far more in line with that of Plato, and firmly against the gun control agenda of the Socialist Democrats.

Throughout history socialism – the government that punishes those who are productive through taxation – and gives to those who are less productive has never effectively worked and it will not work now here in America. Some Socialists suggest that it can work in America because we are such a wealthy nation. But those people forget that even Venezuela was once an extremely wealthy nation and is today reduced to the ash heap of other fallen Socialist countries.

Excessive taxation and Socialist regulations on business and industry has caused excessive unemployment and eventually bankruptcy of many of the governments of Europe and around the world. For the individual trapped in socialism it is extraordinarily difficult to rise from rags to riches in any of the European Socialist plans because the taxes produce such personal hardships. Added to this, socialism by its own nature encourages less commitment to excellence and because of this the people simply do not rise up beyond themselves.

In Sweden, Denmark, and other Scandinavian countries socialism is beginning to falter under the decades of extreme taxation, a minimum of deep pocket industries, and the heavy burden of government 'pay for it all' plans, such as government paid health care. Several countries have now gone bankrupt, and others are following closely in their wake. These are countries that have been held as models of how socialism works well, but they, like so many others, are now rapidly following the model of Venezuela.

As a Conservative voice, I know lower taxation that reduces the burden on both the people and business alike, removing the job, killing regulations, and allowing the free enterprise system – coupled with individual and industrial responsibility – has made America the most prosperous nation in history. Socialist Democrats who want to bury business and the people under unsustainable taxation need to open their eyes and clear their minds of the hatred of President Trump and work for continued national success.

Under the guidance of a capitalist approach to our economy with all Americans having the opportunity to experience free enterprise, this country should continue to be the model for success among all nations. America has always been the place where people came to find success and freedom, and to fulfill their dreams of security and a good life. For themselves and their family could only be a place where free enterprise would allow them the chance to partake of its opportunities.

Free enterprise coupled with a limited government that fosters fiscal responsibility and personal responsibility is the ingredient of a nation that can and will flourish. It is certain and has long been established that liberty is unsustainable without responsibility. In the

Socialist Democrat big government plan there is no responsibility, no accountability, and no transparency.

Our Conservative voice believes that the government needs to balance its budget. You and I must balance our household budget, or we create a financial monster in our own homes. The government must not be exempt from this practice. To saddle future generations with the crushing burden of our excessive spending is unconscionable. We do not have the right to force payment of our poor spending habits and practices on our children and their children.

In 2004 the federal debt was $7.3 trillion dollars and the average taxpayer's portion of that was $72,051. Today the national debt is $23 trillion dollars and the average taxpayer owns more than $155,000 of that total. It is unsustainable that in just fifteen years that personal debt has doubled for each American taxpayer. How much higher must it go before the word unsustainable begins to sink in and our legislators and presidents understand that it cannot continue at this pace. Yet the 2020 Socialist Democrat presidential candidates are proposing spending for their pet projects at still a greater record pace.

Socialists, as we saw with Barack Obama, are content to raise the national debt as far as it will go and carry out deficit spending by financing with taxpayer money any welfare program that they can create. It is beyond hypocrisy that in the 2008 election run Barack Obama chastised George Bush by calling him un-American for raising the national debt by $5 trillion dollars and then proceeded to almost double the debt increase of President Bush during his 8 years in office. It certainly makes one wonder just who is the un-American.

Conservatives clearly stand for the Rule of Law principle. We confirm that a consistent, independent, and uniform application of the law is absolutely critical in a free nation. If any part of those ingredients is missing there is no Rule of Law. We do not stand for a legal system that sports a double standard that allows the wealthy, elite, and other specially placed citizens such as government officials to have immunity for their actions while the less fortunate pay the full price for theirs. Socialist Democrats have created a standard that exonerates them while punishing others. This is unacceptable because it undermines our entire legal system.

Accountability is the iron horse of the Rule of Law: It is the principle under which all Americans, institutions, and other entities are accountable to. It is a system that must be publicly promulgated, equally enforced and independently adjudicated. In the hands of the Socialist Democrats, Rule of Law is degraded to mob rule. They are the rule and because they are intolerant of any other person or institution with a different political view, those dissenting views do not have the right of equality before the law. In any system where accountability and responsibility are lost Rule of Law is only an afterthought, and the streets are the home of disorder, chaos, and even anarchy.

There is very little that is dearer to the heart of the conservative thinker than the question of national sovereignty. In America it was not even an issue until the past three decades. Today as our borders are under a savage assault it is not even a question open for debate. Our borders must be protected. America must have secure borders to maintain its sovereignty. For the Socialist Democrats it is not debatable either. Open them up, let them all in, no vetting, bring your drugs, your disease, your crimes, and move right on in. We, the people, will take care of you.

Barack Obama, pushing for open borders brought this issue of sovereignty to the forefront. The Socialist Democrats today are bound and determined to destroy the sanctity and integrity of our borders in order to destroy the identity of this country by not recognizing our national sovereignty. As far as Conservative America is concerned, "A country without borders is a country without sovereignty and is no country at all."

Conservatives also believe that the 'traditional family' is the basis of all civilization. The parents of a family, meaning the mother and the father, have the ultimate responsibility for raising their children. It is the parents who have the right to make choices and decisions for the good and well-being of that family.

As some Socialist Democrats have said, "The children belong not to the parents but to the state." Those Socialists believe that for the good of the state they have the right to make the decisions about where the children go to school, what they learn, and what information they are exposed to – not the parents. Hillary Clinton herself stated, "The president has the right to shape the children." Of course, in her mind the president is the state. This Socialist concept cannot be farther from the reality of the Conservative Representative Democratic Republic. It is only a small step across the pond from the belief of control of the children to that of Adolph Hitler, who proclaimed, "He alone, who owns the youth, gains the future." Socialism has a plan, and that plan is to own the future through the control of the children.

The final point of difference that we will speak of at this time is that of abortion. The difference between two points of view cannot be wider than that of the question of abortion. Obviously, the Conservative Americans are pro-life, non-abortion, disciples, while the Socialist Democrats have always been pro-abortion activists. These two points of view are so separated that they are miles apart even on the age-old question of, 'when does life begin?' It will range from conception to aborting a fetus, and while still alive, laying the body on a table to die of its own accord. Between the two parties there will be no agreement until the question of the beginning of life is agreed upon. In the meantime, the abortion numbers grow at an alarming rate for Conservatives. From 1970 to 2015 the CDC reported nearly 45.7 million legal induced abortions. How horrific. The only bright spot on the issue is a recent decline of abortions over the past decade in some areas by about 24%. But still the number of abortions, year by year, continues to hover around a million.

In the same data from the Center of Disease Control and Prevention, Gaby Galvin reports that Black women accounted for about 73% of all the abortions in 2015. Black women had an abortion rate of 25.1 abortions per 1,000 women while White women had a rate of 6.8 per 1,000 women. Abortion is a curse for Black babies; in 2012 there were 6,570 more abortions of Black babies in NYC than there were live births. These are the numbers that Conservative Republicans have a difficult time dealing with and why this issue needs to be resolved. Unfortunately, the Socialist Democrats do not care about the numbers and the gap will remain wide for generations to come.

Chapter 2

Liberalism to Communism

Liberal values have always been a part of the Democratic agenda. According to the Liberal, one of the basic tenants of the true Liberal is tolerance. They see themselves as the voice of reason and therefore more tolerant of the political views not in line with their own. This may be true of some liberals, but far more often they are the people working the streets and College campus' forcing their views on others and denying Conservatives the right to be heard. Tolerance means that you are willing to tolerate opinions or behavior that one does not necessarily agree with. It would imply that you have a fair, objective, and permissive attitude toward those whose opinions, beliefs, and practices you do not share. I simply do not see Liberals or Progressives as tolerant people. Their view is that their beliefs should be the beliefs of all people and if they are not those other opinions should be shut down and be unheard.

Their philosophy is based on liberty through the consent of the governed. When Liberals speak of liberty, they are referring to that quality that individuals should have to control their own lives, and to have freedom from an arbitrary despotic control by government. To this point you can identify very little difference between Liberal thought and Conservative thought regarding liberty. But, for the Socialist Democrats, from here on, it becomes a hard plan to sell when you are hell bent on creating a big government that is dedicated to eliminating the people's liberties by the very nature of big governments desire to control the people.

On the surface there is certainly nothing wrong with the basic ideals of liberalism. It is not a 'Utopia' as they would like you to believe; far from it. However, it is clearly altruistic, and at the very least, is an unselfish concern for the welfare of others. As good as this sounds, the difficulty comes from controlling the degree with which these values are applied within the framework of the environment they are found. One thing we all know about Liberals, Progressives, and Socialists is that there is no shortage of appetite for power and control. It becomes very easy to act far beyond your foundational views. The farther you move from the traditional liberal views to more progressive and beyond, the more the desire for power and control and less interest in the welfare of the people.

What most people do not understand is that from liberalism to communism it is only a matter of degree. What the Liberal wants in their socioeconomic-political view is the same as what the Progressive wants, and what the Socialist wants, and what the Communist wants. It is only a matter of degree of what each wants in allowing liberty and freedom as opposed to the government control of the lives of the people. As each progress along the road to communism, there are fewer liberties, fewer opportunities, fewer responsibilities, and far more government control over one's life.

Liberalism slides into progressivism far too easily. Progressives are certainly not timid in their desire to gather power and control. Some have said that progressivism is like a cancer on liberalism. They take what is good from the Liberals, such as their desire to be legitimately concerned about their welfare and create a monster that becomes increasingly intolerant, and more concerned, with control of the people rather than their well-being.

It is within progressivism that we first see the strong rudiments of Marxist socialism. They begin to stomp down hard on the voices of opposition as tolerance becomes unrecognizable. We see them begin to call for government control over the health care system, some even to the point of a single payer system with full government control. They begin to use the poor for their own personal and political gains rather than helping the poor. They lose all concern about the high levels of national debt, and become strongly committed to gun control by infringing on the people's liberty for the sake of their own agenda. It is the Progressives that begin to move into educational control and begin to push their agenda's directly into the classrooms and try to take control over the teacher's unions. There is no question that the Progressives are creating the fracture of religious, social class, and racial relationships causing a sharp division of the groups.

With this obvious direction of the Progressives we can see the early stages of political hatred. Historically the dual voices of conservativism and liberalism have largely been a healthy regard for each other's differences of opinion. There may have been some personal dislike but, by in large, the two sides were able to work through the differences. Healthy but respectful debate has always been the cornerstone of a healthy functioning Democratic Government. When the two sides can sit down, debate, and agree to disagree, good work can – and usually is – done in government. There have been, throughout history, exceptions to the rule and they can clearly be traced back to the Civil War and beyond. But for the most part the differing voices of government have been able to share the stage.

Anytime some progressives enter the mix things, issues, and problems seem to build into a deafening battle of words, ideas, and opinions. Name calling and slander become the argument of the day; a time in which the friendly debate on important issues are thrown out the window. Tolerance is a minimum and intolerance borders on radical bigotry. Obviously, when legislators boil to this point their enraged hatred has more power than reaching cooperative legislative decisions.

When intolerance becomes a commitment in politics so that the other side of the isles views should not be heard freely, open debate is at an end. Within this avenue are the first serious attacks on the 'freedom of speech' with attacks directed to the person and the First Amendment. As society resists these attacks on their most precious freedom, the fire of hatred by the Progressives builds to a peak.

While Progressives battle for outright control the Liberals hold strongly to their belief that everyone should get a fair shot, everyone should do their fair share, and everyone should play by the same rules. These are very good Liberal principles, but in the hands of deeper left Progressives reality takes a very sharp 'left' turn. There is no political entity more against the idea of playing by the same rules. Both the Progressive and Socialist will work long hard hours figuring ways to create a playing field that gives them a decidedly clear advantage. The last thing Progressives want to do is compete with their power and control philosophy on a level playing field. We have seen it in the streets, and we have seen it at the ballot box. To the Progressive and the Socialist alike, "Where there is a will to succeed, there is a way to cheat to achieve success."

Progressives claim that their most basic value is freedom, which includes our rights to freedom of speech, association, and religion. Yet it would seem that those freedoms are but a one-way street. They are quick to profess that it is their right, but as their tolerance of other people's rights erode, those freedoms cease to apply to anyone outside of their own political circle.

It is pretty much the same with their view of opportunity. In their mind opportunity prohibits all discrimination against anyone based on race, gender, ethnicity, sexual orientation, religious faith, or anything else they feel necessary to throw into the pot. This is great; there is no question that all men should be free from discrimination. But to these people everything is in total amounts. If the rights of one person interfere with the rights of another person, it is, "Oh well, too bad."

To the Progressives it means embracing total diversity. Wait a minute, when your right to your sexual orientation is in conflict with my religious faith, and I can't stand by the convictions of my faith and have to live by the convictions of your sexual orientation, what the hell happened to my rights? What happened to my right to practice my religious convictions in my way even though you are uncomfortable being confronted by them? Oh, you mean I can't wear a cross around my neck because it is uncomfortable to them? Wait a minute, I find the way they dress is disgusting and I should not have to be exposed to that. It goes very much against the grain of my faith. Oh, it doesn't matter? It is their right to dress however they want, because it is their freedom of expression in their sexual orientation.

So, I have to live with it, but they don't. This is the problem that you run into with Progressives. Everything is a one-way street. I don't care what flavor of discrimination you are talking about, the diversity ends when you are on the side that Progressives do not embrace. Whites vs Blacks, men vs women, Americans vs Islam, or Hispanics, Christians vs Muslims, and on it goes. Soon it will be tall vs short, blond vs dark, blue eyed vs brown, and yes – even old White men vs millennials.

One of the most prominent points of view of the Progressives relates to responsibility. This pertains to the building of personal responsibility and control of one's actions along with that of others in hopes of making things better for all concerned. They profess they believe we must all do our part to improve our own lives by hard work, education, honesty, and integrity. My goodness, what lofty aspirations! How can you not rush to their side and embrace these qualities along with them to help change the world, and to follow these Progressive ideals?

With regard to all of these values – freedoms, opportunity, and responsibility – it appears that the Progressives can talk the talk, but they fail to walk the walk. They say through fostering these values they are trying to achieve a kind of national unity or solidarity among all people. However, by destroying long standing institutions, customs, and values – and a history that millions of Americans are both proud of and enjoy – they are in fact creating division. By trying to replace these tested American values with their own new institutions, icons, customs and values, and rewriting American history to appease their slanted point of view they are creating disharmony, distrust, and even dislike among the people.

Whether it is religion, old long-standing traditions, business practices, or simply family life, it is evident that the Progressives are determined to change how Americans live their lives. It is being done by moving the bar that measures how much freedom the people are allowed by the controlling government.

Progressives are so much closer to Socialists than they are to the beliefs of Liberals that the only way forward for them is towards socialism, which has no interest in the good life and the welfare of the people. The average Progressive is walking with head up, and with eyes wide open, straight into the disillusioned grasp of socialism.

Chapter 3
Socialism to Communism

Socialism follows progressivism down the road to greater government control over the people's freedoms. They believe that individuals should not have ownership of the land, capital, or industry, but rather the community or state collectively owns and controls property, goods, and production. The people work together collectively and share their work, and products, equally.

Unfortunately, what seems to be on the surface, a great socioeconomic plan fails the test when confronted with reality. Socialism always looks good at first but simply cannot succeed without a totalitarian authority telling the people what to do, when to do it, and where it is to be done. All of this requires the creation of a state political police force to oversee that things are done according to the Socialist design. If you want to call it what it is, it is a form of gestapo. Without them the work will not be done. It has well been demonstrated in socialism that, "No man will ever work hard at anything unless they believe there is personal gain."

The history of socialism has deep roots. The first attempt at socialism in America was a dismal and very costly failure. The Pilgrims landed at Plymouth Rock in 1620. They quickly established a community garden where all would work equally, and all would share the fruits and vegetables at the end of the growing season.

Clearly this work and share equally concept was a classic experiment in socialism. Unfortunately, far too many did not want to work in the garden. Most of the Colonists were not interested in either planting or weeding to maintain a garden that was not theirs. As you might suspect, in the very first year the gardens were not maintained well and they suffered with poor crops, which did not meet the needs of the colonists. This led to extreme hunger with deadly consequences. This, coupled with exposure to a very harsh winter, created a horrific start to this heroic colony.

By the end of 1623 the Plymouth Colonists were experiencing greater starvation and disaster. Finally, Governor William Bradford met with the starving Colonists and they decided to take a new direction for the coming planting season. Each family was given a plot of land that was appropriate for them. They would make their own decisions on what and when to plant, they would toil only in their plot, and they would be allowed to keep the fruits and vegetables for themselves.

This new system is credited with literally saving the colony and its resulting success. That fact – plus the nearby Indians who willingly taught these newcomers so much about hunting, fishing, and agriculture in the new world – created a measurable turn of events. This activity was likewise part of the Socialist experiment where fishing and hunting gains were shared with the entire colony, but after the meeting with Governor Bradford, the fish and game were yours to keep. Do not get the idea that the Colonists were a selfish, uncaring people because they were not. Without being forced to share their work, far more colonists were willing to share their products with those in need. This fact is consistent with Americans today. When we are not forced to donate, share with, or help provide for others, Americans are the most generous people on the planet. Being forced to do something seems to elevate the concept that we must take care of our family first and then help others, but when we are free to make out own choices and decisions we are more likely to help others more quickly and generously.

In an article titled, *Why Socialism Doesn't Work* by Johnathan Davis, an economic and wealth manager made a strong point as to why the Plymouth Colony Socialist experiment failed. He said, "When half the people get the idea that they don't have to work because the other half is going to take care of them, and when the other half gets the idea that it does no good to work because someone else is going to get what they worked for, that is the beginning of the end of a nation." It would have been very easy for the Plymouth Colonists to draw the same conclusions about the economic system they were using. Had they continued their experiment there is a high probability that Plymouth Colony would have gone the same way as so many other early attempts at colonization in the Americas. This could have been the beginning of the end.

When you are a Socialist and you finally realize that socialism is a failed dogma you must make a choice. You can stay with it and go down with the ship. You can, since you have come this far, reach up to communism where stronger forces of government will control each and every person to ensure their collective work for the state. Or, like the Pilgrims, you can create a new system that is more democratic; one that gives the people control allowing them to make their own choices and decisions on their success and failure, and that they alone would reap the rewards of their own labor.

Long before socialism gained a foothold in America numerous European countries were very much aware of its faults. In speeches during 1947-1948 Sir Winston Churchill, the Prime Minister of England during WWII made this observation about socialism,

"Socialism is a philosophy of failure; the creed of ignorance; and the Gospel of envy. Its inherent virtue is the equal sharing of misery."

Later, another Prime Minister of England, Margaret Thatcher is given credit for this statement about socialism, "The problem with socialism is that you eventually run out of other people's money." She was a deeply moral conceptualist who believed very strongly in the moral superiority of the free market. Any system like Marxist socialism in which decisions affecting the people's lives are taken from them is an immoral system at best. This as opposed to the free economic system of free enterprise which not only guarantees the freedom of each individual citizen, it is also the most certain way to increase the prosperity of the nation as a whole.

You don't have to survey many Socialist governments to conclude that both Winston Churchill and Margaret Thatcher were quite correct in their conservative thought. Well before either of these two thinkers was a great French Lawyer and Statesman named Maximilien Robespierre, one of the best-known and most influential figures of the French Revolution. He stated the following, "The secret of freedom lies in educating people, whereas the secret of tyranny is in keeping them ignorant."

Robespierre was speaking about the unbending control over the people of the 18th century by the many tyrannical monarchs and oligarchs spread out across Europe. His words describe communism to a T, and he could have easily substituted socialism for the word tyranny as they too rely on keeping their followers ill-informed at best and ignorant at worst.

Someone once said the leaders of socialism and communism would make better mushroom farmers because they keep their people in the dark and feed them bulls***. I would call that a Conservative concept and it could well have been me that said it.

My favorite observation of socialism and communism alike is, "Beware of those who seek to take care of you, lest your caretakers become your jailers." In my point of view socialism and communism are closer to economic and social slavery than they want to admit. It is beyond comprehension why anyone searching for a better life than what they have would walk with eyes wide open into this kind of slavery. There is no other way to look at it; you walk away from economic and social systems that offer you choices and decision making power over your life, and forego the opportunity to reach out and make yourself a slave to socialism and communism that is based on control and power over your decision making rights.

The fostering of socialism and communism in America today, by Barack Obama and his Legislative Socialist Democrats is the return of slavery in America. Slavery just does not want to die, it is like a cancer on society and every time, everywhere you get a hold on it, it just keeps coming back. In America it is creeping back in, piggy-backed by Socialist Democrats waving their flag in support of old Socialist Communist tactics and politics. After centuries of slavery around the world in any place that experienced expansion it became a normal part of society. Places like Rome, Greece, the Ottoman Empire, and most places in Europe all expanded their boundaries by adopting slavery as part of their system. Eventually most slavery was ended in the 1800's, and by 1900 most of the civilized world had abolished it from their midst. But, like the proverbial bad penny, it just keeps taking on a new life and today in America the Socialist Democrats try desperately to revive it.

Chapter 4

The Doorstep of Communism

Stepping over the boundaries of socialism you enter the 'twilight zone' called communism. As we have observed, in some respects, communism is a similar concept to socialism in that ownership of the land, capital, and industry is either greatly limited or, it cannot be owned or controlled by the individual. In communism control of these things is not by the local community but by the state. Since they control all the goods and services the individual citizen is at the mercy of the state. You have no rights except those that are granted by the state.

There is a photo taken from the International Space Station that is a nighttime look at the difference between a Communist state and a free country. It shows that North Korea is totally black at night whereas South Korea is a bustling country, well lighted, and obviously busy with nighttime activity that free people enjoy.

Even in the daytime the difference in activity between the Communist State and the Free State is compelling. The lack of automobiles is obvious with only an occasional car passing on a boulevard that should be busy; mostly the streets are empty with an occasional person or two strolling by. Freedom of travel in North Korea and other communist countries is restricted by the state because they control who gets automobiles, and where they can go. Daytime activity in South Korea is opposite as people, cars, and other modes of transportation are everywhere, taking advantage of their freedom to come and go as they please.

Another marked difference between the two systems is the ever presence of soldiers in the Communist state. No matter where you go in those countries there are soldiers with rifles intimidating the people to stay in line. You seldom see this in a free country. You will always see a police presence, but they are there to protect the people, not to restrict them from exercising their lawful freedoms and rights.

In the United States the Communist Party is deeply rooted in the American Labor movement. The Party played a major role in the early struggles to organize American workers into unions. Later they became active in the Civil Rights and anti-war movements of the 1930's through the 1940's. However, they and their tactics and policies were not popular with the government as well as the vast majority of the American citizens.

The Communists were eventually expelled from the AFL-CIO in 1948 and organized labor's influence on economic and political development slowed, dried up and soon plummeted. At this time the Communist Party in America suffered greatly under McCarthyism in the government. It was then that the government carried out a mass repression against Communists and at the same time nurtured a national propaganda campaign that fueled the Cold War against the Soviet Union. It was this direction by the government that dictated the American foreign policy for the rest of the 20th century. For most Americans, the Soviet Union was clearly considered to be the enemy and not to be trusted. They had only one plan; to destroy America.

With this attitude of the people and the pressure of the government communism was just not acceptable and by the mid-1950's, membership of the Communist Party had dropped from its earlier mid-1940's peak of about 80,000 to an active base of approximately 5,000 die-hard Communists. Records show that some

1,500 of those members were actually FBI informants. The party was surviving but was badly wounded by the close surveillance of the remaining members. The FBI under director J. Edgar Hoover kept a tight lid on their membership and activities.

By 2000, the party's top priority became supporting the Democratic Party in elections, gain their trust, and to defeat the 'ultra-right.' Many Socialist Communist leaders and supporters began entrenching themselves in the Democratic Party and pushing their philosophies on to the old hard-core Democrats. For the first two decades of this 21st century it has been a constant and steady assault to take over control of the party.

During this time the new leaders of the American Communist Party, specifically their new chairman Sam Webb, were beginning to review the older policies of communism that were related to the core of Marxism. They were beginning to soften the old 'Marxism-Leninism' as too rigid and unrealistic for application to the American citizens. It was now becoming clear to the new order that the old, former language of communism was in and of itself unacceptable to the people. There was a strong move by Webb and his followers to interject a new life blood into an old boogeyman.

The fact is that this new awareness of communism has caught on in America and many people are moving away from the stagnant and non-productive voice of liberalism/progressivism. They are, in fact, reaching out past progressivism and into the Socialist Communist agenda. Make no mistake about it that even though the Communists are using make-up to disguise who they are, it is still their intent to overthrow America and its Capitalist way of life. It is still their intent to follow the old Saul Alinsky way of turning this country into a complete Communist state.

I take great pains to spell out the progression from liberalism to communism because there is such a steady march going on in America today that has become an overwhelming part of the Democrat Party. The Socialist Democrat Party today is full of pseudo-intellectual and ill-informed followers who have left behind the principles and values of the common place Liberals and Progressives. As the old Democratic Party has died, this new surge is actively engaged within the party in transforming this country into a Marxist Socialist Communist state.

When Vladimir Lenin and his Communists took over Russia in 1917 he used many young, semi-educated college students to protest and be on the streets, flag waving for support of their cause. Lenin himself called them 'useful idiots,' because they would mindlessly do what they were told, and mindlessly create chaos and anarchy in the cities. No matter what they were instructed to do, there were no questions asked when the Communist leaders called them to action. Lenin recruited this special corps of propagandists to spread the word throughout Russia, the Empire and the world. Lenin was the fanatic who was simply not satisfied to carry on the Revolution throughout Russia, he wanted communism to take over the world – to carry out the dream of Karl Marx – that the workers of the world unite.

His new corps of useful idiots were the foot soldiers that would drive his revolution into every country, and of course America was a prime target for his revolution. Their object was to subvert the democratic processes, foster strikes and create secret armies to interfere with the Democratic process wherever they were. A Russian historian Dmitri Volkogonov wrote in 1994 that these special propagandists, "Became a cover and a tool of the Russian Communist Party's activities in the International arena." Obviously the same would be true of their work today.

"The Communist Party will only be able to fulfill its role if it is organized in a totally centralized fashion, if its iron discipline is as rigorous as that of any army, and if its central organization has sweeping powers, is allowed to exert uncontested authority." These are the words of Vladimir Lenin on how he presupposed the success of his Communist world-wide movement. In the end, when the Communists of Lenin and his corps of propagandists had overpowered the Czar, and he and his family were forced to flee the work of the useful idiots was minimized, many were cast aside as no longer needed. In time, left forgotten, they with the rest of the country sank into the endless poverty that is the child of Marxist communism.

Today in America the Socialist Communist Democrats are again using semi-illiterate, pseudo-educated college and non-college students as their useful idiots on the streets of our cities. They are fulfilling the same role as that prescribed by Lenin and the early Communists. They march and protest and chant the phrases they are taught by the Socialist Democrats, and today they follow the instructions mindlessly – no different than a hundred years ago in Russia. They confront and intimidate anyone that represents a point of view different from their slave master, The Socialist Communist Democrats of America.

This same young useful idiot corps wants and chants for justice, just as we all do, but it will not be coming from their Socialist, Communist, Fascist, or Islamic friends. They are being played the sucker, or the village idiot, and they too will be cast aside as no longer needed and all promises will be summarily dismissed whether the Communist Democrats are successful or not.

Make no mistake about understanding the intent of the Communists in America. Make no mistake in underestimating how well they have learned the goals, tactics, and methodology of the

Marxist tide that had designs on overthrowing this nation. It is clear in their mind that to take over the control of this country's operation and transform the way that its very foundation operates three things must happen: American Patriotism, our morality, and our spiritual life must be destroyed. These three American values are the heart and soul of the people who love America and what these values stand for.

Marxists have long declared, "If we can undermine these three values, America will collapse from within its own structure." They are very likely right, and it is probably true of most any country in the world, if they can get past the hidden quality that has been built within the people of this country – resolve. The resolve to stand firmly against any attack on the principles and values of Americans has historically been underestimated.

In John F. Kennedy's inaugural address that I spoke of earlier where he warns the world, "Let every nation know, whether it wishes us well or ill, we shall pay any price, bear any hardship, or oppose any foe to ensure the survival and success of liberty." He was warning the world of our resolve. He was warning those who would target either our external or our internal framework.

Our Founding Fathers knew that these attacks would come, and they structured a government that they felt could bear the weight of an internal attack on our system of government and the liberties that it protected. They created a government with just the right amount of personal freedom. From their past experiences they knew that the more control the government has over the people, the less freedom the people have.

In the end, after much debate, the Founding Fathers felt like a balance that gave the people 60% personal freedom and the government 40% control would be a balance that both forces could be happy with and could be sustainable into the future. They had come from countries where monarchy's had 100% of the control over the people and they fled that life seeking the opportunity to live under a better balance. They knew that would not work and they also knew that 0% control in the government was a recipe for chaos and anarchy and was 100% destructive for a nation.

The shrewdness of the Founding Fathers to create enough balance to have lasting effect is seen in the documents that lay at the foundation of this Democratic Republic. One of the great Liberal documents of the world is the Declaration of Independence. One of the great Conservative documents of the world is the Constitution of the United States. One to get it all started is Liberal; and the other to give it stability to maintain its structure over the many years ahead, with the many bumps in the road awaiting them is Conservative.

One of the most important parts of the balance measured in the documents is the balance of church and state. The Socialist Communist Democrats in our government are fully aware that the Christian faith provides a moral framework for our society. They know that if they can successfully attack that moral fiber and minimize or undermine it in the hearts of Americans then they can destroy the church and our society's moral attachment. They know that at that point they would have a much easier road to impose big government controls over the people throughout the country. This because they will have destroyed a large part of the necessary balance that provides stability for the nation at large.

Our Founding Fathers were quite united in their feeling concerning the relationship between church and state. They fully understood the importance and meaningfulness that the Church had in their lives and they were aware of how potent and toxic as a source of conflict it could be on the society. This knowledge was the basis of their creating the First Amendment to our Constitution. Its opening sentence says, "Congress shall make no law respecting an establishment of religion or prohibiting the free exercise thereof." That statement is the balance in this issue and makes it quite clear just how important this balance is. This, in and of itself, allows religion to exist without fear of persecution or oppression but does not unduly promote religion – it makes it very clear that the government must not be in the business of religion. The strength of this commitment by the government and the resolve of the people provide the balance that makes it stand the test of time and assault.

It must be understood that when communism is in power the church exists only when granted certain marginal freedoms. In such a regime there is no balance between the church and state. The state holds the power and the church only exists so long as it maintains a peaceful coexistence. The early Communist communicators like Karl Marx had only a disdain for the church and if they could not be kept in their place the government could clearly do without them. With this, it is easy to understand why undermining the spiritual life would have a primary importance for a Communist take-over of any country with a spiritual base. Today's Socialist Communist Democrats have worked hard to create a split between the numerous religious groups in America. In their bid to create big government beyond American expectations they are prepared to divide the religious entities to the point where a crisis would require government to take greater control over the church so that the balance overall moves closer to the favor of government.

Chapter 5

Enter Barack Obama – Marxist

We have seen over the past eleven years, since the coming of Barack Obama, a constant assault on the very foundation of the values and principles of this country. We have witnessed his behind-the-back political tactics to change the bar of balance between the control by the government and the freedoms of the people. We have suffered through his Marxist tactics to divide the country to weaken it, creating a vulnerability to his design for change for America. He was more than clear on his intentions after winning the first election in 2008 when he said, "We are five days away from fundamentally transforming the way this country operates.'" Following that declaration by Barack Obama, his wife, Michelle said, "We are going to have to change our conversation – we're going to have to change our traditions, our history – and we're going to have to move into a different place as a nation."

We can only read these statements one way. Barack and Michelle Obama – with the backing of their Marxist Socialist Communist advisors and their Democrat supporters – fully intended, from that time forward, to transform our constitutional Democratic Republic into a country much more to their liking, such as a Marxist controlled government state.

From the first day of his administration everything Obama did, everything he proposed, directed, or eliminated was designed to transform this nation. In every category of government America came under attack to undermine our patriotism, our love of this country and our undying commitment to our belief in American exceptionalism. Most Americans, who truly love this country, believe that it is inherently different from all other nations. This is not a belief held by Barack Obama. In its earliest form, exceptionalism means that a nation is different in its inherent national credo, ethnic diversity, and its uniquely developed history. Obama spent eight years criticizing our national credo (from the Latin word meaning I believe, but is generally applied to any guiding principle, or set of principles) both at home and abroad. He chastised America for not being diverse enough, even though America is easily the most diverse nation on the planet. Furthermore, he has painfully taught his followers to forget the history of this country, to change that history and make it free from being offensive to them.

In less than one hundred days Barack Obama finished the second leg of his international confession tour where he apologized on three continents for what he viewed as the sins of America and his predecessors. He told the French that America, "Has shown arrogance and been dismissive, even derisive," toward Europe. He travelled to Prague and London, and then Latin America, and in all of these places the message was the same. It is America who has let the world down and has failed to take the steps necessary for the betterment of mankind. We were selfish and more concerned with our own well-being than for the good of the world.

It was on his way to Latin America that Obama said, "We have been too easily distracted by other priorities, and have failed to see that our own progress is tied directly to progress throughout the Americas." This, by the country who fought not two but three, not three but four, and not four but five wars around the world for the betterment of mankind to stop in their tracks the cancers of Communist, Fascist, and Imperialist forces from engulfing the lives of people of the world. This from the country who suffered the loss of

622,000 military servicemen from WWI to Afghanistan fighting in wars while answering a call for help, and from where hundreds of millions put their lives on hold to aid in those calls for help.

This tour was his strongest effort to attack the patriotism and exceptionalism of America and to show the world that America has flaws. Certainly, we have flaws, but what country does not? He repeatedly ranted his disapproval of America and cited that we, as a nation, have done many things wrong that have probably injured many people of other nations. To which we probably have, but no nation can claim otherwise. And no nation can balance that with the massive amount of good we have done for the world. The world today is a much freer, safer, and wealthier than at any time since WWII, and it is much to the beholding of the efforts of the United States. Where there were but a dozen democracies, today there are over a hundred. Billions of people around the world have been lifted from poverty. Unfortunately, there are many who take for granted the way the world looks today and fail to see the world as it really is, but only see it as they want to see it.

The problem is that Barack Obama does not share the love of this country that Americans have for it. He clearly and simply does not love America. No man, nor has any president before Barack Obama, ever come into the Oval Office announcing that he will fundamentally change the country into something completely opposite to every value and principle under which that country was founded. You do not love a nation while professing that it must be completely changed. If he loved this country, he would not have been compelled to travel the world and apologize for who we are. He would not feel the need to stand on foreign soil to chastise, mock, belittle, and ridicule the United States of America for past deeds. If you love a country, why would you take such great pains to make her look bad in the eyes of others?

His distaste for America was no better standing on his own home soil. He said on numerous occasions, "America's Constitution and its separation of powers make it hard for America to adapt to the changing times." Obama has always objected to the Constitution and has said that it stands in his way of making the fundamental changes he wants for the country. He was thinking of such new ideas as the new open society and open borders, his fondness for extreme regulations on industry, business, and the people, as well as his revolutionary treatment of climate change.

Not missing an opportunity to demonize America, he made other criticisms and ridicules as he traveled the world. On one occasion he said, "America has not done enough to promote equality." I would be pressed to name a country that has done more in such a short span of time. The very fabric of our nation defines in our Constitution, "All men are created equal." That, in and of itself, does not make it so, but America is head and shoulders above all other countries in mandating equality as a purpose of man. At another time he said, "America has failed to reduce oppression and discrimination, and needs to do more." Everyone needs to do more, but to single America out as villains with a bad track record of oppression and discrimination is gross shortsightedness on his part.

To even suggest that America is an oppressive nation is beyond absurdity. In this world there are more than 1.6 billion people, literally 23% of the world population, that have no say in how they are governed, and face severe consequences if they try to exercise their most basic rights such as expressing their views, assembling peacefully, and organizing independently of the government. Citizens who dare to assert their rights in those repressive countries most always suffer harassment and imprisonment, and often are subjected to great physical or psychological abuse. In these truly oppressive countries the government controls the public life and the people have little, if any, recourse to justice for crimes committed against them by the government.

In a report called the *Worst of the Worst,* nine countries were identified as being the world's worst human right abusers in 2011. This was late in the first term of Barack Obama. How can you, having this information, compare oppression in America with that of the worst of the worst? We are talking about places like North Korea, Saudi Arabia, Somalia, Sudan, Syria, Turkmenistan, Uzbekistan along with China, Cuba, Laos, and Libya. These are all countries that Obama is well aware of how they are operated. Yet, he proudly declares that America has failed in improving oppression and discrimination. Sometimes one's bias interferes with their ability to reason.

According to Barack Obama, America suffers from political polarization. This is the creating or causing a group to be divided into opposing groups. This is division. He is complaining that America is a divided nation socially, economically, racially, religiously and even worse, sexually. Wow, no president has done more to divide this country than Barack Obama. It is as though he intentionally divided the people into smaller opposing groups so as to subdue them more easily. Could that be? Is that not a major tactic of Marxist communism on how to subdue a nation? If he in truth wants unity of America's groups, perhaps he should foster healing rather than revenge.

Just considering our racial divide it is clear, had any other Black man or woman with a unifying agenda had been elected, the race issue would have been today only incidental rather than essential to their governing approach. This was never true of Obama as the racial divide exploded to new heights during his first term. From the beer summit to 'punish our enemies' to the two different occasions of pop editorializing about Trayvon Martin, and from Eric Holder's 'my people' to 'nation of cowards,' the Obama administration has literally sought opportunity to emphasize racial differences, and mobilize those differences with hate rather than take advantage of those differences to push a positive agenda of healing.

The result of Obama's efforts is that race relations have become more polarized than at any other time in the last fifty years. Obama said, "We suffer from political polarization." If we do, Barack Obama has no one to blame for the severe uptick in negative racial relations but himself, his advisors, and his hand-picked administrative leaders. Under Obama's leadership celebrities, political analysts, and his Socialist Democrats traffic more in racial divide than at any other time in our recent history. Obama possesses a great ability to energize the Black Caucus to voice horrifically inflammatory charges against the other side of the isle, the people who they see as their enemy, and America at large.

President Obama's goal has been largely to divide, not unify. But we ask ourselves how did he create this so quickly? We have reached a climate that can only be described as chronic. We have daily reports on Black-on-White crime in the news, reported by politically correct reporters who dare not report the facts or the truth. Television news networks that were once responsible to reporting the news have fallen in lockstep with President Obama and now present their version of the news as pundits rather than journalists. They have become the new Socialist media working only for the views and agenda of President Obama. Journalism is out the door as the once sacred Journalist Code of Ethics has no place in how the pundits gather and disseminate their stories. There is less than no truthfulness, accuracy, objectivity, fairness, or impartiality. These once prized guidelines were the hallmarks of good journalism in the not so distant past.

When a news network is locked into a single political party and treat that party as the guiding principle that Americans should follow, they often sell their stories to the public, slanting them to fit that single narrative. They do this at the total expense of the second party to which they are principled to give equal attention to which causes that network to do a great disservice to a constitutional Democratic Republic. They should remember that it is that Republic that protects the free speech of their reporting. It is not socialism that protects them.

So, how did it happen so quickly? There is a tremendous transferring of associations between the Obama Administration and the mainstream media in this country. Obama placed numerous people – who were spouses or relatives of mainstream media staff – in his administration, and conversely hand-picked many of his people to take jobs in mainstream media. When they are all in sync they all sing the same tune; the lyrics of that tune by Barack Obama. And, make no mistake about it, the Marxist Socialist Communists have not, over the past five decades, been just sitting back twiddling their thumbs. They are organized and well prepared for the day that one of their people could come along and be groomed to bring their ideas, policies, and philosophy into the White House.

Another attempt at division by Obama is in regard to the slavery issue. This of course is the stirring pot for his creating a divide between the races. Just look what the White man did to you, slavery is the cause of why the Black man has struggled and failed in America for so long. One of my all-time favorite psychologists, Dr. William

Glasser, made this observation about the past, "What happens in the past that is painful has a great deal to do with what we are today, but continually revisiting this painful past can contribute little or nothing to what we need to be doing now." I could not agree with this observation more. In all walks of life to spend your time reflecting on the past at the expense of working positively for your present and future is nothing but a waste of your time. This is one of my biggest issues with the Socialist Democrats today, that they spend far too little time working on today to prepare for a positive and strong future, and far too much time re-examining the past to create issues for today.

Country Western singer and song writer George Straight penned a lyric that jumps out at why the past can be a dangerous place to focus on. He wrote, "If you don't leave the past in the past, it will destroy your future. Look what's in front of you, not what yesterday took away. The best is yet to come." I've seen so many people who went through various painful times in their youth spend too much time reliving that pain while robbing themselves of a well-deserved good life and future. The past was there. You lived it once, now move on. Living a life burdened by the pain of the past makes a man too weak to challenge his future. Barack Obama understood none of this. To him the slavery issue and the past were preeminent, and it was his duty to continually dig them up and through them in the face of America.

I can tell you with complete assurance that I have never seen the man who would change his opinion or attitude about anything while being repeatedly slapped in the face. No people should understand this better than African Americans or Barack Obama judging from his complaints of how he has been abused by White men for simply being Black. It simply does not happen. The fact is more likely the attitude will become deeper and more difficult to remove by one's own efforts.

Barack Obama also complained that America has too much money in politics, and he is probably right. But, it is a bit hypocritical when he joins with George Soros, a multi-billionaire ally to create Organizing for Action which is a tax-free fund with billions of dollars at his disposal while serving as president, and today, while he travels the world chastising President Trump and this country. While he has amassed millions of dollars from his association with George Soros, they push their agenda to redistribute the wealth. I think they need a better plan because while Obama was president the poor became poorer, and the middle class became the working poor, while he and all his cronies quietly amassed their fortunes.

These complaints and criticisms of Obama do not exactly sound like a man who is proud to be an American. He can and will continue to try to embarrass the country with his shortsightedness. He will never love this country until it is more like a Socialist Communist state, nor will he ever admit that this country is an exceptional place in the world.

I would say to Obama there are millions of reasons why we consider America to be an exceptional nation. Every complaint that he has made can literally be found in any country of the world. No country has made more corrections more quickly or effectively than has the United States of America. And as such, this is the place where people from truly oppressed countries want to come. I cannot remember the last time someone said, "If I can just get to Venezuela, or Cuba, or North Korea, or Russia, or China, or any one of a hundred other places that are oppressed and discriminative, everything will be just fine."

The idea of liberty was joined to the idea of equality in America when only a few philosophers, statesmen, or educators thought about such ideas. For your personal information, Mr. Obama, this alone qualifies America as a very exceptional nation. This country is, indeed, the birthplace of constitutional democracy. It is a Republic unlike any other.

Americans can be proud to know that throughout our history we have done more good for the people of this country, and allowed more to reach up beyond themselves to experience the kind of life that the people of other nations only dream about. And if we have caused problems for other countries, as Obama complains, the good that we have done for them far outweighs the bad. When America has been called to stop aggression our people put their lives on hold, absorbed the pain, and responded with blood and life to answer that call. There has been much of that kind of good. We only need to cite the two world wars that were not of our making, but we were called, and we went.

Any time any country has suffered a national emergency the first country called in to help is America. It does not matter if the problem was a great war, fire, hurricane, earthquake, or a tsunami. If a country called, America was the first to arrive with men, machines, and technology. Americans are quite proud of this fact, and we believe in our true importance and value to the world. We will always understand that our heritage has made the country an exceptional place, and that exceptionalism is for the world, not simply for our own self pleasure.

In spite of the fact that this country has been – and remains today – the strongest most successful nation on this planet, Obama has tried to change and minimize our success. In my mind as a

Conservative, Obama's greatest shortcoming is he deals with America as he sees it, not as it actually is. The country must reflect his view, or he is prepared to change it until it does reflect his view of what we should look like. And his view is one of Socialist communism.

At the base of his view is an all-controlling big government mentality where there is no accountability and no fiscal responsibility; where federal spending and national debt would become unsustainable as would the taxes on the people. Half of the country pays no taxes now, so the remaining half will pay for all of the increases through both open and hidden taxation. The Socialist Democrats will tell you that only the top 1% will have to pay. That is their pledge; to carry out a redistribution of the country's wealth. But the reality is that the middle class will be hit so hard that, as it was with the Obama years, they will in short order become the working poor again.

We have all seen the early Obama efforts to move health care under the control of big government where literally 16% of the national economy would be under their control rather than the public sector. They sold the idea to the public with lies, deceit, underhanded tactics, and behind-the-back politics so gross, even the Niccolò Machiavelli would roll over in his grave. In the dark of night in a nonpartisan vote, the Affordable Obama Health Care passed and was a nightmare even before it rolled out of Congress. Some say it was doomed to failure from the start while others claim it was programed to fail intentionally.

The lies that were fed to the people were everywhere. "You can keep your Doctor," "You can keep your insurance," "You can join if you want, or not if you don't want," "The average household will reap an annual savings of $2,500." These are only a few of Obama's most glaring and disturbing lies to the public about what Americans can expect in their new affordable, big government health care system. He stood before you, looked you in the eye, and told you bold faced lies. We are still listening to the next group of Socialist Democrats using their flimflam training to sell us their snake oil designed to control our lives.

You know, it is easy to lie if you are lying to convince someone, or a group, who has the IQ of a snapping turtle. I'm afraid that this pathological lying is a pretty bad reflection on Obama's radical followers who are so desperate to hear something to cheer about that they will accept anything he says.

Chapter 6
A Socialist by Any Other Name

"Arose by any other name would smell just as…" Nothing much has changed in the application of Socialist ideas and tactics from Obama to the presidential candidates on the eve of the 2020 elections. Today Bernie Sanders, Elizabeth Warren, Joe Biden, and Pete Buttigieg – along with the myriad who have dropped out of the race – are the poster people of the Socialist Democrat Party. Their philosophy between truth and dishonesty has not changed; dishonesty is only recognized when they see it in the other party, and truth is nothing but a word in a polite conversation. Tell the people the big lies frequently and they will be believed. The Socialist Democrats are successful with these lies because they are aimed at the least intelligent of those whom they seek to reach. They know that if the lies are attached to the people directly enough even a snapping turtle will believe in them while among their own people they will never be held accountable.

From Barack Obama to all of today's Socialist Democrat leaders it seems that they all come from the Adolph Hitler school of mind control. In 1936 Hitler set the stage for the Socialist Democrats of today when he said, "By a skillful and sustained manipulation of propaganda, one can make a people see even heaven as hell or an extremely wretched life as a paradise." When you watch and listen to the Socialist Democrats selling their snake oil you can readily see that they have bought into Hitlerian tactics lock, stock, and barrel.

It is their mindless faith in the Socialist Communist agenda, and their unfortunate ignorance of the facts of the world that makes Obama and his new Socialist Democrats the pathological liars that they are. It is their bobblehead mentality caused by intellectual starvation that makes these people so insanely self-destructive. It is their inability to prioritize based on what is most important and what is least important that causes them to be so inept in the decision and choice making process. It is their bigotry that flows from an unimaginable hatred that renders them both helpless and hapless in the legislative process. To put people like Lenin, Obama, Sanders, Warren, or Biden, with their totally unmanageable arrogance and ego in front of the ill-informed, the result is a painful denial of reality.

These people lie as naturally as most people change their underwear. With regard to Barack Obama, remember that he was early trained in Islam in Indonesia. He was taught as a young boy that lying is often an accepted behavior. If you read the book, *Spirit of Islam* by Afif Tabberah, he explains that in Islam, "Lying is not always bad; to be sure; there are times when telling a lie is more profitable and better for the general welfare, and for the settlement of conciliation among people, than telling the truth." This means that it is okay to lie if that lie helps to settle the dispute in your favor.

Tabberah says that the Prophet Allah said, "He is not a false person who through lies settles conciliation among people, supports good or says what is good." Of course, what is considered good is in the mind of the beholder. This is largely the mentality that Barack Obama brought to the White House, and underscores why he is such a pathological liar. He is one who lies out of a long habit of doing so. Lying to him is a normal and reflexive way of responding to any questions. Pathological or compulsive liars bend the truth about everything, large and small. For Barack Obama telling the truth was, and is, awkward and uncomfortable while lying feels right. Like most pathological liars, there is evidence that his lying developed in his early childhood. Most pathological liars are not necessarily manipulative or cunning, but Barrack Obama is. He clearly uses the lie to manipulate the mind of the people.

It is clear that the Socialist Democrats who follow Obama's lead have learned the lessons of manipulating through lies. Add to the mix Hitler's skillful and sustained manipulation of propaganda and lies, and you have created the perfect mentality of the Socialist Democrat. If you couple their training with their long penchant to lie their way through points of differing views it is easy to understand why Socialist Democrats are not to be considered as credible or forthright. In short their ideas, concepts, and views should never be considered as honest unbiased appraisals.

Barack Obama, through the use of lies, turned himself into the world's most prestigious flimflam man. He travelled the world, and still does today, selling his snake oil to ill-informed and unsuspecting people. He assures them, in his slick talking way that his snake oil is the cure for all the evils of the world, and if you will just try it you will see that it will make the world better. Consider climate change, consider globalization and a world with no borders, all controlled by a central government like the UN, and controlled by a majority of Socialist Communist tyrants and Muslim Autocrats. His snake oil is not a cure all for a New World Order, it is a destruction of the Old World Order and its Nationalism and Sovereignty.

The Socialist Democrats desire to create a world with no borders is a potential devastation to America. Conservatives believe that a country with no borders is not a country at all. With no borders a country is robbed of its Nationalism and its Sovereignty. One's National Sovereignty is the fact that an independent nation which has declared its independence, has an organized government, and is self-contained with the unspoken right to exist without other nations interfering. Take a nation's borders away to allow uncontrolled entry destroys all meaning of an independent self-contained country. To destroy our borders serves for the Socialist Democrats many purposes. The most underlying reasons for them are self-serving. Sinister at the least and evil at best.

Flood the country with uneducated, ill-informed, untrained Hispanics, and Muslims who speak no English and have no means to support themselves above the level of poverty and you have a major socio-political-economic national problem. Couple this with the fact that the vast majority are not interested in assimilating into the American culture and would rather wave their home flags in defiance of America than wave the American flag in support of the country that gives them a new life, and the problem is greatly magnified.

It is taxpayer dollars that support these people, often from cradle to grave. We pay for their housing, clothes, food, health care, transportation insurance, and very heavily we pay for their education. This, like the $23 trillion dollar National Debt, is an unsustainable economic drain on the taxpayers, yet our leaders of the Socialist Democrat Party continue to propose trillions of dollars for new expenses to these programs. In both cases it is exactly what the Socialist Democrats want, and who they are.

Socialists also feel that in due time, if not now, these migrants will be the voting base of the useful idiot, flag waving followers of their Party. With them they hope that they can dislodge, perhaps forever, the GOP from power. If this is successful it could certainly pave the way for the completion of Obama's transformation to Marxist Socialist communism.

The migrant attack on our borders is clearly a Marxist threat to increase the level of poverty in America to a crisis level. Socialist Democrats know from their experience and knowledge of Marxist Russia that poor people are easier to control and will not fight back if you are providing them with everything they need to survive. Who else would you support but the very hand that keeps you alive?

Barack Obama and Attorney General Eric Holder opened the flood gates into America to tens of thousands of children. There is no question that many were sexually active, and many others had open ties to gangs and the activities that gangs are a part of. This action by Obama and his Socialist Democrats is a major part of their fundamentally transforming of this country. It is beyond reproach that our elected legislators stood by and simply let it happen. They hold a large part of the blame. You cannot look past the deceit and underhanded tactics of Barack Obama and Eric Holder to start the ball rolling in this migrant invasion, but there are others fully to blame. A great philosopher in the golden times, Thucydides, wrote an ancient script that goes straight to the heart of the question, "When one is deprived of one's liberty, one is right in blaming not so much the man who put the shackles on as the ones who had the power to prevent him, but silently stood by and did not use it." The legislators hold much blame when those who misuse their power are not stopped from their evil actions.

There is no question that Barack Obama knew what to say and do and how to say it in such a way that you don't even know that you have been bamboozled. This means to be fooled or cheated. There are many ways to fool or cheat someone, but when they stand up before you, look you in the eye and tell you something good without the intention of following through, that is the height of deceit and underhanded politics.

Consider these examples of what I mean by bamboozled. During his Chicago victory speech in the 2008 presidential election, he mounted the stage, looked America in the eye and said, "To those American's whose support I have yet to earn, I may not have won your vote, but I hear your voices, I need your help, and I will be your president too." For those whose vote I did not win? I hear your voices? I will be your president too? This from the man who was just a day away from announcing that he will, "Fundamentally transform the way this country operates."

At another time during the victory celebration Valerie Jarrett, Barack Obama's senior advisor, offered this toast to their supporters, "We thank you so much for your efforts in getting us to this place, you will be rewarded; to those who fought against us, you will be punished." You heard our voices, but we will be punished? They had no intention of working with the voices that voted against them. Valerie Jarrett made that crystal clear. They will be our president too? I do not believe it was in their plan to be the president of those whose vote they did not win. The only ones they were interested in were the followers of the Socialist Democrat Party.

One month later Obama made this statement, "To ensure prosperity here at home and peace abroad, we all share the belief that we must maintain the strongest military on the planet." He then proceeded over the next eight years to decimate the leadership, ranks, and equipment of the entire military to the weakest point it has been in generations. He never intended to maintain the military to a level necessary to keep the piece or prosperity. His only concern was to create a military that would follow his will and do his bidding without making waves by questioning his agenda.

Initial criticisms of the Obama Administration were that they wasted little time in beginning a complete purge of the military leadership. It is suggested that up to 197 officers were fired over a period of five years. It appears clear that officers suspected of disloyalty to, or who were in disagreement with the Administration on policy were summarily discharged. Many of these officers who had long and prestigious careers under other presidents found themselves forced into retirement.

It certainly is not without precedence that presidents fire military officers during their term in office. They are the commander-in-chief and it is their right to discharge and change leadership as they see fit. But, when nine senior officers are fired by Obama in one year it is baffling and one has to wonder about the state of the National Security at that time.

General Carter Ham, Commander of the U.S. Africa Command questioned the Administration and disagreed with orders not to commence with a rescue mission on September 11, 2012 on the attack of our Embassy compound in Benghazi. General Ham had been in command for only a year and a half. He was good enough to appoint to the command based on his prior service and leadership, but not qualified to make decisions pertaining to missions of rescuing Americans under fire. Who would know better than General Ham what the probability of a successful mission into Benghazi would be? Just perhaps, had they listened to him, our people in Benghazi could have been saved rather than left to die.

Rear Admiral Chuck Gaouette, who commanded the John C. Stennis Carrier Strike Group followed General Ham's expulsion in October 2012 for disobeying orders. On September 11th when General Ham, ordered Admiral Gaouette and his group to assist and provide intelligence for forces ordered into Benghazi he found himself between a rock and a hard place. He followed the orders of the General but disobeyed those of President Obama. He was fired.

Many others were handed their pink slips with a complete laundry list of reasons for their release from command. It would seem that dismissing the services of officers in high command, such as Generals and Admirals, might suggest that Obama was intentionally downgrading our leadership as a superpower. It is perplexing and very difficult to understand why so many of our most talented military leaders, who came into disagreement with Obama, would so quickly suffer the same fates.

What we know for certain is when President Obama's term of office was over the great and powerful military that was the envy of other leaders around the world was but a shadow of itself. It had fallen on hard times with men going into battle less than fully prepared and equipped, pilots flying planes with recycled parts and often grounded because parts were not available, and men operating machinery that were not on a par with what a super power should have to perform successfully.

Yes, Mr. President, for there to be peace around the world it must first require that America have the strongest military on the planet. I could not agree with this statement more, because it is obvious that the world is a safer place when American strength as a military power is clear in the minds of world leaders. You said it but you certainly had no intentions of seeing it through.

In another statement by Barack Obama in 2008, after winning the election, he announced this about his up and coming administration, "Transparency and the Rule of Law will be the touchstone of this Presidency." For a president to come into office behind the cloak of a secret life and identity, whose entire life from grade school to college is secretly hidden away and protected from public view, it is almost laughable that transparency would suddenly become the touchstone of his administration.

Transparency was not the flavor of the day, at any time, during the Obama administration. His entire term of office was characterized by hiding behind deceit, and behind the back tactics to cover up what his administration was doing. Transparency in government means that they are operating in such a way that it is easy for others to see what actions are performed. Transparency implies openness in communication and accountability. His entire term of office was characterized by his responses. When questioned about something that would affect him directly, he would say, "I don't know anything about that, I only learned of it this morning on Fox News just like most of you folks." Or, when he was questioned about his associations with unsavory people such as Bill Ayres, "Oh he was just a guy I would see riding his bicycle in the neighborhood once in a while." Wrong. Reverend Jerimiah Wright, "Oh he was like an old uncle who would come to the family diner and tell wild stories to the kids." Wrong. Frank Marshall Davis, his Hawaiian Communist mentor, "Oh he was just a sort of a local poet I used to visit with my grandpa." Wrong.

The life and times of Barack Obama is filled with these types of explanations and understatements. They always seem to be hiding his questionable policies, associations, and methods that are the background for much of his personal beliefs that guide his choices and decisions concerning this country. Transparency? I think not. Some things in the Oval Office are just not cool. One of those things is a display of ignorance on the part of the president. There is no gain of trust or credibility when your leader is pleading ignorance. Though he promised an open, transparent government he, and it, actually became more secretive as it progressed. His words in referencing the Freedom of Information Act were, "A democracy requires accountability and accountability requires transparency." Mr. President, one more strike and you are out.

Early on, the two people who are the most responsible for fostering the values, principles, and political views of Barack Obama are his good friends Frank Marshall Davis (a card carrying Communist) and the Reverend Jerimiah Wright (a radical anti-American, anti-Semitic, Racist). Together they gave him their views and shaped his priorities as a socio-political Black man.

If I tell you that Barack Obama was an anti-American, anti-White, anti-Semitic, anti-constitution, anti-Capitalist, and anti-Rule of Law president you would probably say, "There is no way he could be that, and be the president of a constitutional Democratic Republic." Well, considering that he was not wanting to be president of a constitutional Democratic Republic, but rather a different government more to his liking, you would be wrong. He was all of these things as president and still is today. What is worse, following in his footsteps, it is not by accident that the current radical Socialist Communist Democrats of our government today are anti-all of these same things. And why not, they are things that all Socialist Communist thinking people would embrace.

We are all the product of our relationships, our associations, our mentors and teachers, coaches, and religious leaders. I used to tell my students, "Today, you are the products of all of your experiences you have had in your past and those experiences bring you to where you are and who you are today. You are who you are, and why you believe and don't believe is because of the positive, or negative, influences on you as you pass through each level of life to manhood or womanhood."

It is no secret that Barack Obama is a prejudiced anti-White man. You need not look farther back than to the Reverend Jerimiah Wright's anti-White, anti-American, anti-Semitic church. You do not go to a church for twenty years unless you are in general accord with the pastor delivering the sermons. You do not sit in a pew week after week for twenty years listening to the ranting of hate spewed forth by a man full of hate for the White man, America, the Government, and the Jews without adopting some or all of these points of hate as your own. You do not sit there for twenty years, nod your head in agreement, and not be negatively influenced by the hateful ranting of Jerimiah Wright and then walk out of that church with a heart and soul full of hate while professing to be a man of reverence let alone a Christian.

If Barack Obama, or his wife Michelle, found the unhinged ranting of this racist to be wrong, or even distasteful, just walk out, and don't ever go back. They were adult, free Black people, and they could have stood up, shook their heads in disgust for what it was and walked out of that house of sin.

They could have, even though they enjoyed his old uncle stories, cancelled his invite to the family dinner. Could they actually believe that this man could have a positive influence on their children? Was this the influence they wanted their children to have as they would grow into adulthood? Is it possible that the Obama's wanted their children to grow up with their hearts full of the same negativism and hate that lives in the soul of the Reverend Jerimiah Wright?

Unfortunately, as we all know from history, they did not walk out of that church, until Barack Obama launched his political career and discovered that it did not bode well to be associated with this kind of evil and hatred, while passing yourself off to the voters as a God fearing, Christian man with the belief that reverence, not hate, was by far the most important thing.

Chapter 7

All Birds of a Feather

In his memoirs, *Dreams from my Father*, Barack Obama was laying the foundation for change. As we have noted earlier Obama never saw America as it really is, only as he saw it and thought it should be. From the time he came to the mainland to start his college career he was never happy with America. Following his high school graduation, he moved to Los Angeles at Occidental College in 1979 and studied there for two years. He was enrolled there under the name of Barry Obama and remained at Occidental through his sophomore year in 1981.

After leaving Occidental behind Obama enrolled in Columbia University where he attended for two more years, and graduated in the class of 1983. Apparently, it was a very uneventful two years because there has been much discussion concerning his presence at the University. Many people who attended Columbia at the same time as Barack Obama have said they knew nothing of him, though sharing the same majors never had a class with him, and do not ever remember seeing him or hearing of him. Others have come forward with knowledge of him being there and in spite the tag later of, "The man who was never there," it seems that he may have been. At any rate Columbia University celebrates their celebrity president as the man who indeed was there.

As everyone knows, after graduation from Columbia, Barack Obama enrolled in Harvard Law School to finish up his college work. After leaving Columbia he went to Chicago to work for some time before continuing his education at Harvard. In 1985 he was given a job as a community organizer in Chicago and he remained there until he arrived at Harvard at the age of 27, in 1988. During this time, as a law student, he met professors and students who would prove to be helpful to his future political rise to the presidency of the United States. Probably his biggest accomplishment at Harvard was in 1990 when he was elected the first Black president of the Harvard Law Review. In his new capacity he became one of the most active students on political issues. As a leader on campus he also became quite vocal on the matters of social and political disputes. It is noted that he spoke at one protest rally, but largely he preferred to stay in the background and lead by example. This is the Obama of later years as president of the country. Seldom was he out in front stirring the pot; but on any issue in his agenda he was behind the scenes ensuring that his views were being activated by his street people.

By the time Barack Obama graduated from Harvard in 1991, and returned to Chicago, he was already a committed Liberal/Progressive with threads reaching to Socialist communism, thanks to his mentor Frank Marshall Davis. During his high school years in Hawaii, Obama befriended Davis through his grandfather Stanley Dunham. Mr. Dunham, a leftist, regularly took young Barack to visit with Frank Davis and the three would have long conversations. As we will see, of all the associations Obama had along his path to the White House, no other man had more of an impact on him than Frank Marshall Davis.

Paul Kengor, in his book, *The Communist,* about Frank Davis and Barack Obama puts together a tale of a lasting permanent relationship between the two that played an integral part in Obama's early years. He talks of how Obama's grandfather took this naïve and impressionable boy to this man to be mentored, and how Barack took to Frank Davis as a father-like figure. He tells how Davis and

Dunham spent hours drinking and conversing on social justice or injustice, race relations, oppression, and what he called limitations of White tolerance. A young Barack sat and listened to the tall tales and personal feelings and opinions on these subjects, but rest assured that he was absorbing the words, the emotions, and the suggestions.

Paul Kengor makes a strong point that you would have to be extremely naïve to think during those many conversations Frank Marshall Davis would never speak of the Communists and their goals and aspirations for change in this country. Communist politics was a subject that lay deep in his heart and soul. Considering that he was such a strong political activist it would be amazing that the politics of communism did not enter their discussions. As a mentor for Obama he certainly was going to do all he could to teach Barack about the great values of communism and plant the seed that would one day be the basis to his entire political thought. There is no question that his grandfather Stanley was not disappointed.

Certainly, with his associations in the colleges he attended, and his friendship with Frank Davis by the time he reached Chicago, he was ready to test the water of his Liberal/Socialist ideas. Chicago was a hot bed for left-wing politics so it was fitting that Barack Obama would enter the fray as a community organizer. Chicago was also a hotbed for the Communist Party of America, to which Frank Marshall Davis was a big part and for whom he advocated. As we will see, many of Barack Obama's new associates will have very tight ties to this Communist Party of both the Communist youth group and the adult Communist activists.

Obama makes it clear in his memoir just what activist path he wanted to take. He said he went to Chicago to 'organize Black folks.' With little to no experience, and the personality of a flimflam man, he was still a good fit in the all Black neighborhoods that he wanted to organize. He was given the job as community organizer. He went right to work and set a goal to retrain workers in order to restore manufacturing jobs in his area, and to enlist an alliance between the community and the Catholic priests to help in the redevelopment of their communities. He recognized that there was an overwhelming amount of work to be done and in much of it he was aware that a lot of it was improbable.

Obama, wishing to actually find out how to go about this job and what it was all about, turned to the writings of Saul Alinsky, a well-known Communist community organizer, writer, and activist. Alinsky was considered an authority on the subject and had written a book called, *Rules for Radicals*. Most certainly this book became a prized possession of Barack Obama. This book is a playbook of methods, guidelines, and rules for how to bring about social change. It has been the driving force behind Progressive leftist politics and media for nearly fifty years as he outlines for radicals the tactics needed for success.

Alinsky speaks of how an organizer must be an "abrasive agent so as to rub raw the resentments of the people of the community." He is saying that organizers must intentionally inflame the people to cause them to rise up against their enemies. He insists it is not their purpose to lead the people to rise up, but to show them why and how they should do it on their own. These are exactly the tactics used by Barack Obama to bring about change as he came into the White House. He taught, he showed, he manipulated, he inflamed; and with this the people were expected to rise up in protest causing mayhem, chaos, and even destruction and anarchy.

It is no small wonder that these tactics are the very tactics Barack Obama used to inflame division among the races, the sexes, the politics, and the religions once he was in the Oval Office. So many times the leaders of the Gay Pride Movement were brought to the White House, time and time again, for meetings with Obama and his new community organizers to teach the Alinsky methods of radical tactics to picket, march, and to create havoc in the streets. Do you wonder why his chief organizer, Al Sharpton was a guest at the Oval Officer eighty or more times during Obama's administration? Training, teaching, indoctrinating all take time if you are going to get it right and have a maximum effect on your target. Why were the leaders of the Black Lives Matter group so often guests of Barack Obama? Did he have some special use and plan for them to serve his administration? Is it any wonder that the most vocal of the Hollywood leftist elite met with Obama behind closed doors in either the White House or in Hollywood? A good organizer never lets up; he always reworks the group so that their inflamed mentalities never had an opportunity to relax and forget what their goals were. It is no small wonder to me that the new radicals of Barack Obama were such frequent visitors of their mentor.

For eight years it was the work of Obama activists, like Al Sharpton, to fan the flames and bring out the hostilities to the point that they were unafraid to challenge, confront, and attack. It was the work of the Obama organizers to inflame the Black Lives Matter group to march the streets of Baton Rouge chanting, "What do you want? Dead cops! When do you want it? Now!" This at a time when tensions between police officers and Black civilians was high because of a confrontation in Dallas just three days prior in which five officers were killed and several others injured. Following the march, a week later three more police officers were shot and killed, and conditions quickly worsened. It is fair to say that Black men in Dallas and Baton

Rouge were inflamed, and much of this revenge seeking, hatred mentality can be attributed to the marching of the Black Lives Matter under the leadership of Obama's organizers.

It was during this Obama period, as a beginning community organizer, that he also was drawn to the Reverend Jerimiah Wright. Obama had attempted to enlist pastors from local churches to come and assist in the movement of organizing the Black community. Rebuffed because he himself was not a church going man, he turned to Reverend Wright to get his foot in the door. He joined Reverend Wright's Trinity United Church of Christ, began attending sermons, and created a relationship with the Reverend. He stayed with the Reverend until political pressure caused by the Reverend's anti-American rantings along with his passionate racist and anti-White sermons forced Barack Obama to distance himself from his so-called old friend. Obama never repudiated the words of Jerimiah Wright, but simply minimized his association with him and his bigotry.

If the Reverend Jerimiah Wright and Frank Marshall Davis were not enough radicalization in the life of our future president, it was in the mid-1990's that Barack Obama, now a respected and reasonably successful community organizer in Chicago, was hired to be the chairman of Bill Ayers brainchild, the Chicago Annenberg Challenge (CAC). From 1995-1999, he led the CAC and remained on the board alongside Bill Ayers until 2001. Under their leadership the CAC poured more than $100 million dollars into the laps of community organizers and radical education activists. The Annenberg Challenge was founded by Bill Ayers and Walter Annenberg to provide grant funding for reform to about half of the Chicago elementary schools.

Bill Ayers, good God Almighty! This is another of Barack Obama's early Chicago associates that was as questionable as having direct ties to the Communist Party of America. Ayers was another of his associates, his birds of a feather, whose background was far too questionable to defend honestly, but with whom he worked closely, and in the end Obama was forced by politics to minimize their friendship.

When questioned about Bill Ayers Obama said, "Oh, he was just a guy in the neighborhood who I would see riding his bicycle once in a while." Imagine this; a radical Barack Obama, reader of Radical Saul Alinsky, friend of Communist Frank Marshall Davis is now the Chairman of an organization fathered by Bill Ayers, a radical underground domestic terrorist and he's 'just a guy.' That's like saying, "Oh, Allah is just a guy in a book about Muslims."

Bill Ayers was the founder of the Weather Underground in the 1960's; he was a terrorist who was in bed with a radical group of other terrorists who raised hell, havoc, chaos, and destruction around the country. He was not a good person; more like a radicalized moron. His group was founded on the Ann Arbor campus at the University of Michigan. The Underground was organized in 1969 and by 1974 its expressed political goal was to create a revolutionary party to overthrow what it viewed as American imperialism. Their founding document called for a White fighting force to be allied with the Black Liberation Movement to achieve the destruction of U.S. Imperialism and to form a classless Communist world. The FBI classified them as a terrorist group and several of their members were listed on the FBI's most wanted list. But, "He was just a guy in the neighborhood." As a self-described Communist he had and has a violent hatred of America.

After the Charles Manson murders in Beverly Hills, in 1969, Bernadine Dohrn, later Bill Ayers wife and a member of the Weather

Underground said of Manson's horrific slaughter of human beings, "Dig it! Manson killed those pigs, then they ate dinner in the same room with them, then they shoved a fork into a victim's stomach." It was as repulsive as an act can be; and her feelings and report of it is as inhuman as can be. I am sickened to just write about it. This story is not new; it is a take on horror that has been reported since the Manson family went on their rampage. These people thought it was beautiful. Bill Ayers and Bernadine Dohrn, still married, broke bread with Barack Obama and Michelle Obama. Barack and Michelle were married in 1992, at a time when Bill Ayers and Barack were so-called neighborhood acquaintances, and a time later when they worked together on the Chicago Annenberg Challenge. Don't insult our intelligence by suggesting that Bill Ayers was just 'a guy,' when it was at Bill Ayers and Bernadine Dohrn's home that Barack Obama launched his political career. He broke bread and shared in the wine – with Monsters – I'm guessing that Barack Obama and Michelle Obama were not sickened by the past behaviors of these two terrorists at all. It is easy to see why J. Edgar Hoover called Bernadine Dohrn "The most dangerous woman in America," and "La Pasionaria of the Lunatic Left."

Ayers is a retired college professor now, but in the 2008 Obama presidential campaign Obama had to dismiss any relationship because Ayers was and still is such a radicalized Communist. But when the pressure was not on them, they clearly remained birds of a feather. He is not a reformed old college professor. Not even close. On 11 September 2001 – the same day Al-Qaeda attacked and killed thousands of Americans – an article in the The New York Times by Dinitia Smith began, "I don't regret setting bombs," and Bill Ayers said, "I feel we didn't do enough."

What follows is another excerpt from The New York Times article by Dinitia Smith in 2001. She reports that Bill Ayers is said to have summed up the Weatherman philosophy this way, "Kill all the rich people. Break up their cars and apartments. Bring the revolution home, kill your parents, that's where it's really at." At the time of the NYT's article he was a distinguished professor of education – education? – at the University of Illinois at Chicago. He says that he doesn't actually remember suggesting that rich people be killed or that people kill their parents, but as Dinitia Smith suggests, "It's been quoted so many times I'm beginning to think he said it." His only reply was, "It was a joke about the distribution of wealth." A joke? If this qualifies as a joke it is a sick joke by a sick man.

Another dastardly deed by Bill Ayers and Bernadine Dohrn was the bombing of the Pentagon. When asked many times about this incidence neither of the two ever expressed any regret, or remorse for their terrorist assault. In his memoirs he wrote that, "Everything was absolutely ideal on the day I bombed the Pentagon." I have to say that sometimes when you hear these Communists speak the best thing for you to do is just shake your head and walk away. To argue with them is like giving medicine to a dead man. Neither will wake up.

Working together, Obama and Ayers created some very radical plans for funding education around Chicago. They worked out a plan where they did not fund the schools directly, as you might expect, but rather required the schools to get together with external partners, who actually received the money. Proposals from the schools for use of the money for math and science programs were generally dismissed from the funding. Instead the CAC dispersed the funds through various far-left community organizers, such as the Association of Community Organizers for Reform, or Acorn. This name should sound an alarm, as they were involved with one controversial act after another.

Barack Obama was very close with this group as well, and once conducted a leadership training seminar with them. Later, in 1995, members of Acorn were side by side with Obama and served as volunteers for his first campaign. Acorn is another of the very far-left voices that Obama partnered with in his early years that lasted well into his first term of office as president and beyond. Once again, he was forced to minimize his relationship with the group.

During the 2008 presidential campaign the McCain-Palin Republican ticket claimed that Acorn was involved in massive voter fraud. They claimed that Obama had a long and loyal relationship with Acorn and that many members of the group were deeply involved in voter fraud in favor of Barack Obama. Some hold the claims to be true, but others claim that they were involved in voter registration fraud. In fact, several Acorn canvassers were found guilty of faking registration forms and others were being investigated as well. The McCain-Palin side was convinced that their actions were for the sole purpose of stealing the election.

Clearly Acorn, as a community organizing group in the mold of Saul Alinsky and Barack Obama, were guilty of unsavory practices. They engaged in bullying banks with intimidation tactics to force the banks into issue risky home loans for the Blacks in the Obama district that were the same types of loans that caused the financial crisis that followed. It is no wonder that the Obama officials were trying to distance themselves from Acorn, by saying, "Barack Obama never organized with Acorn." But the fact is that Obama himself taught classes for Acorn where in all likelihood they were learning first-hand about the Saul Alinsky tactics for social change. Overall, there were at a minimum eleven investigations across the country involving thousands of probable fraudulent Acorn actions.

While running for the presidency, any time Bill Ayers' name or the Acorn name popped up the Obama campaign cried, "Foul, guilt by association," but in reality it is clear that it was no less than guilt by participation. Barack Obama was a leading moral and financial support to Bill Ayers and his radical circle of anti-American and anti-Rule of Law minions.

As Obama attempted to distance himself physically from Ayers and his radical circle he makes no attempt to shut down any thought that he still maintains the emotional political bond that he shares with him. In 2006 they were as thick as thieves. This is the year that Bill Ayers and his cohorts penned a book called, *Sing a Battle Song*. This was a collection of intensely radical writings from the days of the Weather Underground which in the end has Ayers painting a picture that as Stanley Kurtz describes, "Makes a point of hoping that their old writings would be of some use to new generations of militant activists and organizations." Nothing has changed with this man; he remains a vile and disgusting anti-American, anti-government terrorist. There is little to no remorse for their past or present, and there is no remorse on the part of Barack Obama for sharing their views and breaking bread with such evil people.

Valerie Jarrett had been Barack Obama's closest and longest standing advisor during his entire presidency. Born in Iran, her father Dr. James Bowman had extensive ties to Communist associations. According to FBI files in 1950 he was in communication with a paid, card-carrying Communist named Alfred Stern. Stern had fled to Prague after being charged with espionage. Dr. Bowman was also a member of a Communist-sympathizing group that the FBI described as having a long and faithful following with the Communist Party line. They were noted to engage in numerous un-American activities. Bowman was born in Washington D.C. and had deep ties to Chicago where, in his younger days he was often known to collaborate with fellow Communists.

Vernon Jarett, Valerie's father-in-law appeared in the FBI's Security Index, and was considered to be a potential Communist saboteur who was to be arrested in the event of a conflict with the Soviet Union. His FBI file shows that he was assigned to write propaganda for the Communist Party front group in Chicago. They would then disseminate the propaganda to the middle class. This material was brought to light by the efforts of the Judicial Watch. The Jarrett family Communists were also very involved in the Communist Youth Movement; this making good on their goal to win over the youth to communism to fulfill their plans of taking over the U.S. and replacing its democracy with communism. Their ties go even deeper to Vernon Jarrett's maternal grandfather, Robert Rochon Taylor, as he is found to have ties to the same Alfred Stern, the Soviet agent associated with Valerie Jarrett's father.

My goodness, the birds of a feather has turned into a flock of the same feather. Valerie Jarret has always remained faithful to her roots and still has connections to many Communists and extremist groups, including the Muslim Brotherhood. She and her family had strong ties to Frank Marshall Davis, Barack Obama's personal political mentor. It is from the teaching of Frank Marshall Davis that Barack Obama had developed a special feeling for Marxism and later in his memoirs described himself as leaning towards communism.

When Barack Obama became president, it was Valerie Jarrett who was given the task of appointing the presidential Czars to their operative positions in the government. Staying true to her loyalty to Socialist Communists who served the campaign well she appointed many to Czar positions. The vast majority of them brought extreme to radical political leanings. They would range from very Progressive, to Socialist, to Marxist Communist. Long time Communist Van Jones was one of those Czars appointed as the Green Jobs Czar.

Appointed to Barack Obama's first Administration, Van Jones – an America bashing Communist extremist – was forced to resign his appointment after findings showed that he was a 9/11 Truther who believed that George Bush may have been behind the 2001 terrorist attack. His radical and extreme statements were not something new. The Administration and Valerie Jarrett must certainly have known of his arrest record and his disturbing Communist past. They had to have been aware of his involvement in the 1990's with a group called Standing Together to Organize a Revolutionary Movement. The group was a grass roots anti-Capitalist, anti-war organization committed to achieving solidarity with direct militant action from the Judicial Watch. Surely, they had to know who he was and what he stood for, and what an embarrassment to the Administration he would be. But Valerie Jarrett was loyal to those who got them to the White House, and Barack Obama had learned to cover his tracks and distance himself from people like Van Jones. It is not that either Valerie Jarrett or Barack Obama would disagree with anything Van Jones said or did. Not likely at all. Does any of this about Van Jones remind you of the unhinged mentality of Bill Ayers? There are so many people like this surrounding Barack Obama there is barely enough room for him to stand there. Who could ever imagine so many birds of a feather?

There were numerous Czars in the Obama Administration who, because of their extremism, were clearly unfit for their positions.

Their appointments were largely out of a reward for their support and allegiance to the campaign. They were presidential appointees, many of whom were taking positions of elected people. Many were not confirmed by the Senate and none were accountable to anyone but Barack Obama. They were free to do their work with no pressure from Congress, as long as they carried out the agenda of President Obama. Van Jones was only one of many who should have been forced out of those positions.

It does not seem to be far out of line to suggest that the political Barack Obama is the product of all of his life's experiences and the associations with vile and unhinged extremists along the way. One of the great things that my father passed on to me is this, "Consider the source. There are many people who will pass through your lifetime and some will try to impact you in positive ways, while others will clearly have a negative influence on your opinions, your attitudes, values, principles, and even the very core of your character. It is up to each one of us to filter those associations by considering the source. Take with you those learnings that you feel comfortable with and that you know will resonate with you in your future in a positive and constructive way; take that and move on. Those associations you encounter that will leave you with a negative feeling, leaving you with nothing constructive. Leave it lay and move on to the positive side of your life. You must filter the good from the bad, the upstanding from the evil, the honorable from the dishonest and the right from the wrong. If you cannot do that you will find yourself in your later years surrounded by evil. There will be so much evil that there will be no other recourse for you than to become a part of it."

We have all engaged many friends, teachers, coaches, pastors and just plain acquaintances that have impacted our lives. We have had to filter these people and use the best that they had to offer, discard the worst, and make ourselves the best we could be. I believe that Barack Obama has a failed filter and is not capable of considering the source. Because of this he is perpetually bombarded by negative influences. What must a man be thinking when he engages a people like Bill Ayers, Rev. Jerimiah Wright, Bernadine Dohrn, or George Soros, and Frank Marshall Davis, filters them, and allows them to pass through and become a part of your life, a part of your values and principles system, or make their opinions your opinions and be responsible for the development of your basic attitudes.

Chapter 8

The Ends Justify the Means

The idiom 'the end justifies the means' is a hallmark of the Socialist guidelines for furthering their agendas. It is used to say a desired result is so good – in their mind – or so important that any method, even a morally bad one, may be used to achieve it. Socialists believe that the ends justify the means and because it is so, they will do anything to achieve their goal. It may be a goal of simply getting their point of view before the public or doing whatever is necessary to get their candidate elected. In the Socialist Democrat Party in America this same idiom is their greatest guideline for achieving their goals and in organizing their tactics.

To the Socialist Democrats a good outcome excuses any wrongs committed to attain it. An example of this, which we have seen numerous times, would be a Congressman campaigning with illegal funds on the theory that if they win the election, the end will justify the means. The practice of applying this idiom to your tactics for achievement may seem, on the surface, to be a simple and insignificant thing, especially since it is today becoming more widespread around the country. However, it is probably more like opening Pandora's Box with meaning and ramifications that are far reaching and dangerous to the maintenance of ethical values.

The first thing you need to understand about this idiom is that it is not necessarily what one thinks it is. As an ongoing practice it is clearly impacted and more readily understood by such words as deceit, behind-the-back, and underhanded behaviors. As a concept it can be traced back to Prince Niccolo Machiavelli, a diplomat, historian, and politician of the

Renaissance period. There are some who say it may go further back, but more often he is given credit for its inception. He was a man of clear political thought, and he would raise questions about the way this idea is treated today by Socialist Democrats and others. In one of his writings he said, "Power defines political activity and therefore it is necessary for any successful political leader to know how power should be used." He would argue that the use of deceit and behind-the-back tactics to enrich their power is wrong.

So, when the means used to reach the end includes deception, lies, stolen ideas, slavery, or serves to harm others in the process, the end result cannot and should not be justified. Obviously, one's character level must enter the equation as it relates to one's moral and ethical compass. All things have rules and our actions are guided by sets of laws that tell us what is acceptable to do and what is not. To claim that they do not matter is to nullify a significant part of the balance between man and government, the Rule of Law.

In a baseball game there are rules which control the integrity of the game and provide the game with meaning. If the rules are sidestepped and replaced by one's own idea of what is right and what is wrong in playing the game integrity and meaning are lost. If I electronically steal the other team's signals it is okay, because the ends justify the means. In a foot race you do not trip your opponent in order to win the race. If that's allowed, what is the meaning of the race? The winner is the one who trips the most opponents. Or, you don't use performance enhancing drugs because the rules of the game say that you will have an unfair advantage because they make one faster, quicker, and stronger. The rules of the game should apply to all performers, politicians and citizens alike. Altering the playing field to give you the advantage in politics, or anywhere else, is simply unacceptable. It is a universal acceptance of this idiom by the Socialist Democrats that renders their politics, tactics, and even their victories questionable.

It is one thing to say, "I won the campaign," or, "I won the race," but it is quite another reality that says, "You won but you cheated to do so." If you win by deception, deceit, or other underhanded tactics you show the world the level of your character. Socialist Democrats are notorious about bending or outright ignoring the rule of the game, and replacing them with their own interpretation of how they see the game should be played. More times than not the rules are interpreted to be applied to the Socialist Democrats differently than how they are applied to others. They seemingly ignore Rule of Law as it applies to them, but fully expect and insist that others adhere to the strict application of the Rule of Law.

Socialist Democrats have a very loose relationship with ethics. As with their lack of a moral compass they equally lack an ethical compass. In reality these two values overlap considerably. It should be our job to make our choices and decisions based on our ethical values. These are the kind of values that have to do with being good and doing the right thing according to the norms of society. The most common positive ethical values are justice, honesty, respect, self-discipline, responsibility, and accountability along with integrity. If a politician has strong, positive ethical values in all of these categories he is someone I would vote for, however, if I see flaws in any of these values they are not someone I want making decisions and choices affecting my future or that of my family.

Politicians should be honest and truthful in all of their dealings with the citizens, and they should not deliberately mislead or deceive the people by misrepresenting themselves, or using partial truths to hide the real truths. They should also refrain from using overstatements that the Socialist Democrats call misspeaking, and they should not use selective omissions of information in order to slant or bias their actions. To apply this to Socialist Democrats one only has to look at the godforsaken impeachment trial of President Trump, concocted and carried out in a total void of honesty by the leaders and the entire partisan Socialist Democrat Party.

On the political scene integrity, as an ethical value, is seen as the courage of one's conviction to do what they believe is right even when there is great pressure to do otherwise; they will be principled and honorable and they will fight for their beliefs. They will not sacrifice principle for expediency, be hypocritical, or unscrupulous. Integrity is all about doing the right thing in every situation, whether it's convenient or not. This is where you separate the fish from the bait when it comes to Socialist Democrats. They want you to believe that they are honorable and what the right thing dictates, but they fall very short when it comes to their own actions.

It is characteristic of someone who lacks integrity to do the right thing while giving the appearance of having integrity, but when they do it only for an audience – or obviously for their personal reasons – they are not truthful in the matter and therefore lack integrity. This could be Mitt Romney going before the public, giving a speech on why he will vote for the impeachment of President Trump, and proclaiming, "I will suffer for this, my entire family will suffer for this, but my conscience tells me it is the right thing to do." He justifies his reason for acting contrary to the entire Republican Party (my conscience tells me I am right and they are wrong), with an, "Oh poor me, I am the martyr," even though he very likely did what he did for personal reasons, or to look good before the press or an audience.

It is also obvious of the Socialist Democrats that they lack integrity because we see, all the time, that to them if it is legal it's ethical. Just because something is legal does not make it the right thing to do. It does not make it the honorable thing or the moral thing to do. You might think it's obvious, but it's not; most forms of lying are legal but not ethical. Breaking a promise is generally legal, but widely thought to lack integrity. Cheating on your husband or wife is legal, but it couldn't be more unethical or lacking in integrity. In government we see evidence of lying, breaking promises, and cheating all the time. There certainly is no lack of appetite in the Socialist realm for these infractions of integrity. Anyone who tells you or simply implies that whatever is legal is also ethical is most likely indulging in self-serving rationalizations, and the Socialist Democrats are hugely guilty of these kinds of rationalizations.

It goes without saying that the little white lies Socialist Democrats engage in while carrying out their job of governing is considered to be acceptable behavior, and may well be another part of their rationalizations to justify their political decisions and choices. These little white lies may seem superficial because we see them happening all around us in the general public all the time. But, no one has said that lack of integrity is just a part of politicians. But it is what they do in government that I am interested in here. For the Socialist Democrats little white lies are their cover up for jobs poorly done. Adam Schiff is a master of not only the little white lies, but lies of all kinds that are designed to prove a point that lacks provability. Barack Obama was the master of the little white lies to conciliate an issue in his favor. Where otherwise something may look bad for them, it can be cleaned up with a little white lie. When challenged on her performance Hillary Clinton, who had been caught in a laundry list of little white lies said, "Obama made the policies, I just carried them out." When someone soft peddles their own behavior, which is known to be significant, they generally use little white lies. Obama said, "Selma got me born." This is very strange because Obama was born in 1961, while Selma occurred in 1965 with no possible effect on his birth. This could go on all day, Elizabeth Warren said, "I'm 1-1025th Cherokee Indian." Bill Clinton said, "I did not have sex with that woman." Oops, that was a big white lie.

Far too often the Socialist Democrats are wrapped up too tightly in their own agendas. It is a clear lack of integrity that they hold true to their goals and plans even though they may be hurtful to the people. It is a lack of integrity to believe that your behavior does not hurt others. There is, built within this framework, a level of selfishness that does not allow many government officials to see the effects of their choices and decisions. I have long been an exponent that the greatest gift a president can have is the gift of being a visionary. It could be said of legislators as well. One of Donald Trump's strongest qualities is that he is a visionary. It is clear to me that he can look into the foreseeable future and understand the impact that his decisions and choices have. I cannot think of one Socialist Democrat in today's government that has the visionary power to understand the impact of their decisions and choices on the future. It would be wonderful if the Socialists could legislate their laws in a way that they could see what impact those laws have on the people. They cannot do it because bias blocks vision.

Perhaps the most disgusting quality in the Socialist Democrats armor is a point of view that seems to be prominent in their belief system, "Do as I say, not as I do." This is probably the most exasperating, frustrating, and irritating behavior they have that causes extreme annoyance in most people. I can fully remember my dad telling me that same thing, and I was beyond simply annoyed. Preachers say it in church, and it is equally exasperating. It is clearly one of the Liberal/Socialist platitudes that the world can do without. Socialist Democrats pride themselves on being committed and selfless and seem particularly confident of the purity of their motives and the evil nature of their opponents. They exude themselves in an air of moral certainty that they are, by their nature, people of high moral standards and it is their job to make others understand that it is in their best interest to do as I say, not as I do. For them it is not necessary to say it, because they imply it in their very interaction with people. It is often an expression used to call out hypocrites, including environmentalists with private jets – like the Hollywood elite – and politicians who send their children to private schools while opposing measures to give other kids the same chance, or those who accuse others of racism while not hiring minorities.

The world's biggest hypocrite in this measure is Hillary Clinton and is the basic proof of the Socialist Democrat's philosophy of do as I say, not as I do. Although well aware of her husband's philandering history, Hillary backed his squishy denials, and famously denied his exploits on national television saying, "I am not some little woman standing by her man like Tammy Wynette." As far as she was concerned the women were of questionable character and cannot be believed. This, while claiming to be an advocate for women's rights and how women, with their stories of assault, should all be believed. That policy has become the hallmark of the Socialist Democrat Party as was clearly demonstrated by the Judge Kavanaugh confirmation hearings where they backed their witness' against Brett Kavanaugh with no realistic or supportive proof presented. Their idea was clearly the same as Hillary Clinton's, women are to be believed, supported, and encouraged; even while lacking any clear-cut supportive evidence.

Hillary Clinton has had these kinds of problems her entire political career because of her loose relationship with truthfulness. Her treatment of Gennifer Flowers and Monica Lewinsky was beyond brutal as she flatly denied their involvement with Bill Clinton and claimed that their stories were untrue. Her involvement in Travelgate was a disaster and a plethora of innuendoes, misinformation, and understatements. Her improper handling and removal of sensitive documents from the office of Vince Foster following his suicide bordered on criminal behavior. Her claims were lies and she later had to fess up to her behavior.

In my eyes, as a conservative, the Socialist Democrats are among the most unscrupulous people you will find for no other reason than they believe any end justifies the means. They are the most hypocritical people for the same reason. William Hazlitt stated, "The only vice that cannot be forgiven is hypocrisy." In my mind it is better to be a sinner than a hypocrite. At least a sinner can be forgiven. True hypocrites, like Socialist Democrats, are the ones who cease to realize or understand their deception; the ones who lie with sincerity. We all know who these people are who can stand up, eyeball to eyeball, and never flinch as their hypocrisy explodes from their mouths. These would be some of the Socialist Democrats who would cut down a Redwood tree, mount the stump, and lecture everyone else about conservation.

I would expect that politicians should have respect for others as their key ethical value. I cannot imagine a productive legislature if the parties do not have a healthy respect for each other. I cannot imagine the value a party might have by disrespecting the other side of the isle. Having respect for others doesn't mean respect for just those who think like you do. Considerably, more broadly, it means having respect for human dignity. It means having respect for autonomy. In government it means possessing the capacity to make an informed, un-coerced decision and allowing others to do the same. It means to respect privacy and not spying, or invading one's privacy. It means respecting the rights of others, to have a view which you do not share, and having interests in all of those who have a share in their decision making powers.

If one has respect in humanity then one should be expected to be courteous and treat all people with equal dignity and respect regardless of sex, race, national origin, or different political and life views. In the question of respecting others, when I am thinking of the leadership of the Socialist Democrat Party, all I can do is shake my head and walk away. The quality of being tolerant is based in one's respect for humanity. If you want to consider yourself the party of tolerance then you must demonstrate that you have respect for humanity. In the 2020 State of the Union address, Nancy Pelosi tore up President Trump's speech. What a shameful disgusting episode of disrespect for the president, his office, and all of the comments he made regarding the little children, the Tuskegee WWII Veteran, the man dying from cancer, the war hero who comes home by surprise to see his family, the single mom who can now send her daughter to the school of their choice, a two year old living and breathing after a twenty-one week pregnancy, and more – all Americans, Madame Chairman – all Americans. I have never witnessed a grosser display of lack of respect in the People's House. You and the other hateful legislators of your party, that applaud your childish immature behavior and overall lack of respect for humanity, are a disgrace to this nation.

This display by Nancy Pelosi is not an act in isolation by the Socialist Democrats. This is who they are. This is what they do. For the past three plus years this party has conducted themselves in a selfish, uncaring, sometimes vile, and certainly ugly manner with regard to President Trump, the Republican Party, the followers of that party, and the nation as a whole. Chuck Schumer, Nadler, Schiff, the entire reporting staff of CNN, and MSNBC are particularly guilty of disrespecting the president on a regular basis. When the leadership of the party shows no humanity and disrespects not only the president of the U.S., but the office itself, they are buried in their own bigotry. Bigots need not be in Congress and I would suggest that the Socialist Democrat Party would be more in line with the principles and values that this country most admire by doing away with this brand of leaders.

One's own accountability to their behavior is, or should be, an integral part of one's ethical values. One's capability to be fair and just in their dealings with people is a significant quality to success in leadership. Good people are found, not hanged. I recently read a headline that said, "We don't teach our people to be nice. We simply hire nice people." Wow! What a clever shortcut. It is too difficult to fathom that the voters might hire nice people instead of the ones they know will never be changed, and once resistant to accountability they only grow worse with their new power. We have certainly been through the mill on this one. I won't go much further than to cite Mob Rule. Someone once asked, "What is the difference between the Democratic Party and a mob? Nothing." The Socialist Democrats act like an angry mob as opposed to a well-oiled political machine working for positive constructive change in America.

David Harsanyi wrote, "Former Attorney General Eric Holder believes that Michelle Obama was wrong when she famously advised, "When they go low, we go high." Rather, he told Democrats at a gathering in Georgia, "When they go low, we kick them." There is certainly nothing wrong with fighting in politics, it is indeed part of the process; but a line must be drawn that requires all combatants stay in tune with their actions and be accountable to them. If you cannot be fair and just in your dealings you are lost in the blindness of bigotry. Accountability is sadly lacking in the Socialist Democrat Party. They surely are a party that has lost its ability to defend their policies in reasonable and honest debate, so they turn quickly to slander and personal attacks. The honorable Greek philosopher Socrates was first credited with pronouncing this concept, "When the debate is lost, slander becomes the tool of the losers." The debate for the Socialist Democrats must surely be long lost, because it seems there is not a Party member around who doesn't wear the mantle of slander. They are clearly the masters of making false and damaging statements to harm a person's reputation. I will only say one word: Kavanaugh. And so many others in line.

Socialist Democrats must learn to discipline their disappointments. And with that learning they must find a way to hold themselves accountable to their feckless and irresponsible political behaviors. If they are fair and just they do not try to exercise their power over others arbitrarily, and do not use overreaching and indecent means to gain or maintain a political advantage. Fair people who are accountable manifest a commitment to justice, and equal treatment of all people including their adversaries. 'Just' people have tolerance for and the acceptance of diversity; they are open-minded, free of bigotry, and willing to admit when they are wrong. When was the last time you heard a Socialist Democrat admit to being wrong?

These people have lost much of their reasonable attachment to good, strong, positive and constructive ethical values. They seemingly have lost their ability to distinguish between what is right and what is wrong, what is just and what is unjust, what is good and what is evil in terms of human behavior. This is caused by their failure to balance their moral compass. Once your compass is out of balance you have lost your ability to think objectively and rationally about issues that have emotional meaning and value. When one has turned their back on reason, they have committed themselves to a single line of thought that destroys their ability to think with an open mind. A closed-minded person, like most Socialist Democrats, create for themselves an intolerance to any other line of thought, and gives them a clear path to bigotry. This is the path that Socialist Democrats have willingly decided to follow. This is the path they have chosen, believing that it is the path that will energize the people to rally to their cause. This party in America has lost their ability to think constructively and to reason.

The failure to maintain a positive and productive moral and ethical balance system has destroyed the integrity of their party. Their reaction to anyone from the president on down to the common working man, who supports what the president is trying to do for the country, is one of intolerance, hate, and an attack of slander. One's moral and ethical values are not something you are born with; it is learned. It has been the direction of their leadership for decades and, like a cancer, it continually eats up and destroys the good while leaving the ugliness and evil that it has created. Once their moral values have been impacted by the bombardment of negative learning it is a long road back to the sanity of being able to reason.

In Little League baseball we teach children many positive moral and ethical values that hopefully they can take with them into their adult life to be a positive, constructive thinker. Among the most important of which is, "Win with grace, lose with dignity." We teach them that when you share an important event with others you count on everyone to do their level best. Whether it is your job, family, friends, church, or just a baseball team, always give 100% to an honest effort for success. Sometimes we will win the game, and sometimes we will lose. But win or lose, if you gave 100% to your effort you have played with integrity and you can and should be comfortable with the outcome. It is significant that our young people learn and understand that whether you win or lose to always conduct ourselves with grace and integrity.

I genuinely believe that Socialist Democrats should have to spend three to four years, depending on how far they have regressed, playing Little League baseball. I will admit that the boys and girls on the teams carry this learning off far better than the parents in the stands. Much of the time parents seem to have regressed to the level of politicians. But can an adult and politician recover what they have lost? Certainly they can recover and the easiest way would be to have a parent to child conversation, and they may be amazed at what they can learn about winning and losing. I remember years back when I was coaching high school baseball and we would take a long bus trip to another city, play the game, lose under difficult circumstances when we probably should have won. I was in the front of the bus going over the score book to try to make some kind of sense about what had just happened to us, poring over my notes, feeling the frustration and just not quite getting it. Meanwhile, the players had long forgotten the game, they knew they had given 100% but what the hell, sometimes you win and sometimes you don't. They were happy and simply enjoying the three-hour ride home on that bus. What a great teacher I was; they had learned what I wanted them to learn and I didn't even know I had taught it.

Another value that coaches work hard on teaching their young athletes is about respect. In my view respect is also about esteem. Because you are sharing a common relationship it is important that you share a common positive feeling towards someone that has value in your relationship. It is important for them to understand though the players on the other teams are their adversaries you must respect them as people and players. I remember, way back, when I was coaching my own son in Little League that our home was a common gathering place for boys around the town. It was where the boys from the different schools, churches, and other ball clubs gathered to decide on what mischief they would get into on that day. They were not always from the same team, far from it, most of the time there was a mixture of different team jerseys and ball caps. Oftentimes in the previous week they had been our opponents, half of which had won and were now showing that they can win with grace; the other half having lost were on this day showing they have learned to lose with dignity. I doubt that I will ever see this in the chambers of our legislators ever again. Hate prevents this from happening.

Socialist Democrats cannot win with grace; it always seems that it is necessary to rub their enemy's noses in a Socialist victory. It always seems that they must take their win to the level of revenge. They are not proud of the win because they won, they are happy because they were able to exact revenge on a mortal enemy. They also cannot lose with dignity. They have been demonstrating their lack of dignity for the past three years since their horrendous defeat at the hands of Donald J. Trump. They announced from the very first day of his administration that they would block anything that President Trump tried to get passed. That would be like a Little Leaguer saying, "I'm not going to play against that team anymore because they beat us." How childish, how immature; their emotional development is certainly not fully developed. I'm not speaking of the Little Leaguer's; I'm speaking of the Socialist Democrats. They have tried to block every effort in creating a new direction for the American people simply because they hate Donald Trump. For three years they have called him a racist, a homophobic, an Islamophobic, and a white supremacist, simply because he would dare to not share the Socialist

Democrat point of view. He is not a racist or any of the other slanders any more than those who follow his views. His crime and his follower's crime are that they do not believe in socialism and the agenda of Socialist Democrats. So, we are racists and deplorables and dredges in society, considered to be a group of people who are immoral and of no value, from the mouth of Joe Biden. Let's just call a spade a spade. That is a lack of integrity. That is intolerance. That is bigotry. That is who they are.

I shouldn't even put into print what the radical Socialists from Hollywood have said about President Trump and his followers, or what the radicalized media talk show pundits have said and done. Most of it is disgusting, vile, despicable, or abhorrent. But then, they follow the mandates of the Socialist Democrats in Congress and the words of Barack Obama so you would expect nothing more from them, but the same lack of integrity as that their mentors. These people, in their ignorance, very often are more offensive and objectionable in their use of despicable and filthy language in their slanderous rants. Barbara Streisand rants on President Trump whenever possible. She says, "He is a man with no manners, he doesn't see his own flaws, he doesn't know what he doesn't know. He has no humility." This from a woman with no integrity, humility, and doesn't see her own flaws. This from a woman who is so bigoted and intolerant she doesn't even understand that a broken clock is right twice a day. In 2017 Madonna said, "Yes, I have thought an awful lot about blowing up the White House." This is the rant of a Socialist Democrat, with a total lack of integrity, and the mindless equivalency of a bobblehead doll. It is beyond the pale of humanity that someone would make such an ignorant, vile statement that carries unheard of destruction because they hate so intensely. How would one defend this kind of statement? "Oh, I was just trying to be funny." That wasn't funny, it was sick. The joke was sick, the person saying it was sick. Barbara Streisand would be better off challenging Madonna's poor humility and failure to know what she doesn't know.

Socialist Democrat comedians today are something far different from what they were in the past. There isn't even a fine line between humor designed to make people laugh and the political humor of today's standup comics. It used to be that a comic was attempting to make all who watched laugh at their material; today in political humor the comics are only interested in making half of the audience laugh and the other half feel uncomfortable. So, while you appeal to part of the audience the rest not only think you are not funny but in actuality you are a moron. What is funny about a comic holding up a replica of the severed bloodied head of President Donald Trump? That's not funny, it's sick, and it shows a vile lack of integrity and character. Point of fact is that anyone who would use this type of prop to illicit a laugh should be drummed out of the profession. Businessmen should black ball them, and audiences recognizing the despicable nature of the act should refuse entry into their dark sadistic world. The ends justify the means? Wow! How far will they go to seek those ends?

This was an act taken against not only the President of the U.S. but all the people of this country. Someone raised the question that if the Socialist Democrats would go this far to impugn the President of the U.S. how far will they go to shut down the common folks. What steps will they take against me, a Conservative voice, as I impugn their attacks against our voice? As a comic or a politician you must take three considerations to your proposed actions: Before you even start the action, ask yourself what is the intent of this action? Is the intent positive or negative? Then you carry out the action and hold the bloody head up high for all to see and admire. Now ask yourself again: Is this action positive or negative according to the social norms? Or, is it just the norms of Socialist Democrats? Finally, after your action was executed – holding the head up high – what were the consequences or the outcome of that act, positive or negative?

Red Skelton, Jonathon Winters, Bob Newhart, Bill Cosby, Robin Williams, Dick Gregory, Phillis Diller, Joan Rivers were the greatest of the great comics, and what they did, gig after gig, was funny; it was positive and they were universally humorous. Everyone laughed at their material, not just Conservatives, or 'just' Socialist Democrats, because their jokes were generally a fair treatment of any political nature. They did not have to rely on political bias, or sexism, or vile and vulgar material to sell their humor. When hate loving Socialist Democrat comics take the stage comedy goes out the door. What rises to the surface is hate, morbidity, vulgar, vile, and sexuality all wrapped up in a grotesque immorality that is characteristic of who they are; an amoral, unethical collection of comedic frauds who are not interested in the rightness or wrongness of their material, only the end result, which in their mind justifies the means.

Who has written the rules that it require vile and lewd behavior to make people laugh? Who has decided that vulgarity in its most personal and intimate form is necessary to make people laugh? Who has written that morbidity and hate of those you detest is what makes comedy? Funny. It is the liberal, progressive, socialists of the left-wing writers union, or the group of performers who have a love for the morbid, vile, vulgar, and sexist jokes on humanity.

If these comics really want to illicit some good ole fashioned belly laughs they should study the Socialist Democrats with the closed-minded antics in Congress.

Where did this all start? Oh yes! With the Socialist concept of, 'the end justifies the means,' all wrapped around the concept of moral values and morality in general. Morality as a basis of man's means to an end is not just some far-fetched topic in a psychology book, but is close to, in my view, man's conception of life. Moral goodness is what gives each of us the sense that we are worthy human beings. If our moral goodness lines up with our behaviors regularly we are pretty happy and satisfied people in our lives. And I would suggest that those who would exploit, minimize, or twist moral values to meet their own ends probably find in themselves that they are not so worthy as human beings. When you have the answer you will probably find that the moral values that guide one's behavior towards others and the community is based on a simple little thing that we all call truth. Plato said, "Truth, justice, and what is good are the highest principles in life." I say, "Do not waste your precious time failing to do what is right by failing to answer the search for truth, justice, and good.

The following is a poem that I have written in free verse style to illustrate the direction of Socialist Democrats in America as they move the bar closer to Government control at the expense of the freedoms of the people. Free verse is a form of poetry that is free from limitations of regular rhythm and does not rhyme with fixed forms. This form of poetry will show that where the Socialists want to go and is not where Americans want to be.

PICTURE YOURSELF IN THE R.S.F.S.R

Picture yourself in the R.S.F.S.R.
Of America I mean,
It used to be the U.S.A.,
But division brought a change of scene,
We lost our grip to socialism and now we are enslaved,
And our country is now devastated,
By a cruel and ruthless enemy from within
We are now despised and hated.

Picture yourself with your freedom destroyed
With all your precious liberty suppressed,
As you friends and neighbors disappear,
You learn that they have been taken away.
Care must be taken to what you say,
No one knows who one dares to trust,
Many were arrested their views not allowed,
And things they had written are disavowed.

Picture yourself being told where to work,
And where and how you must live.
Now gone are the hopes we have dreamed for,
Compliance for a new way now imperative.
You go to church in some secret place,
But your heart is a throb with fear,
For worship of God is now forbidden,
And the punishment is severe.

Picture yourself as a virtual slave,
No vote – and to strike would mean to jail,
Travel of course must be approved,
And the right of assembly severely curtailed.
Your children they claim now belong to the State,
And can be taken from you at their will,
The life of a robot is now your fate,
Mind controlled, and your spirit enslaved.

Picture yourself with this kind of life,
It could happen, so beware!
You are being lulled to sleep by Socialists,
Are we too apathetic to care?
What can we do to change this fate?
Could it be that we've waited too long?
We can stand up with a Patriot's pride,
And fend off the assault of socialism.

Chapter 9

Socialism: The Future of the Democratic Party

You simply cannot be any more direct about the direction of the Democrat Party than this statement by Tom Perez, "Socialism is the future of the Democratic Party." This clearly confirms what the American people already knew about the Democrats in spite of their repetitive denials over decades. In 2017, on the eve of the 2018 mid-term elections, the Democrats have finally come out of the closet. It is now more than obvious that a vote for the Liberal-Progressive candidates is a vote for socialism in America. It should be understood conversely, a vote for the Republican candidates would be a vote to stop this country from becoming a Socialist nation.

Tom Perez won the race for the Chairmanship of the Democratic National Committee (DNC) in February of 2017. He had been in a very hard-fought campaign for the leadership position with Keith Ellison of Minnesota and several others. Representative Ellison was the first Muslim ever elected to Congress and was the prime adversary to Tom Perez. While Perez had the support of numerous well-positioned Democrats such as Joe Biden, Tom Vilsack (former Agriculture Secretary), and former Attorney General, Eric Holder, Keith Ellison was supported by Senate Minority leaders, Chuck Schumer, Bernie Sanders, and Elizabeth Warren, along with New York Mayor Bill de Blasio.

It is interesting that both of these candidates were heavily backed by Socialists and Communists in the Democratic Party. Both are clearly pilots of the riverboat on the course to socialism and communism with designs to complete the journey that Barack Obama had set in motion in 2008.

On the eve of the final balloting there was much activity to solidify and redirect the votes. Well into the night, for several evenings, what appeared to be a party time filled with booze and food was in reality a last ditch effort for the champions of Perez and Ellison to capture support from the "also rans" who were dropping out of contention.

Other candidates vying for the chair were Sally Boynton-Brown, the executive director of the Idaho Democratic Party, Raymond Buckley, chairman of New Hampshire's Democratic Party, Jaime Harrison, the South Carolina chairman, and Pete Buttigieg, Mayor of South Bend, Indiana. Mayor Pete dropped out of the race early and was not included in the first ballot. Likely he quickly discovered, in his first exposure at the National political level, he was simply not Socialist enough to win against this serious Socialist competition.

That is one scenario, but another one is that Mayor Pete was recruited during this foray, or he saw the light that it may be time to prepare for a run at the office of the President of the United States. In any case it was only about two years from announcing his choice to run as a presidential candidate for the Democratic Party. It was clear that he could not get his message across to the DNC that "the Democratic Party is an aging party and very much needs to build up its millennial base." Perhaps he would be ahead of the game by taking this message straight to the millennials by running for the Oval Office.

So, Tom Perez, clearly a Socialist as we learn from his coming out of the closet statement, is elected Chairman of the DNC. In an effort to bring together the fractioning sides of the party he appointed Keith Ellison as the Deputy Chairman. He then called for unity and for all to stand together as a team working to make the party stronger. Early on it was clear that the members were receptive to this message of solidarity with numerous key players in the party rallying for his support.

As the new Chairman, Perez was replacing Donna Brazile who was the interim chairperson. Brazile had replaced Debbie Wasserman Schultz who had during the previous summer stepped down as chairwoman. She had resigned amid extreme backlash from the hacks into the DNC which was said to be part of a campaign by the Russians to meddle in the 2016 election.

With the campaign over and the election vote finally solidified, by capturing the commitment from Jaime Harrison who convinced his supporters to change their support to Perez, the battle was over. With the final tally recorded Vermont Senator, Bernie Sanders, was among the first to endorse the new head. Even Bill de Blasio, who strongly supported Keith Ellison was quick with his congratulations, and his willingness to work with the new Chairman. But why not, Socialist to Socialist and Socialist to Communist, there is not that much difference.

As Tom Perez worked to unify his party there were still many who were not so quick to come to his side. It could clearly be seen that from the beginning of the campaign, through the grueling four month battle to the election, that there was an improbable thread that they all knew. They could agree that whoever won the chair position needed to be able to heal the discord between the party's establishment wing that supports Tom Perez and the anti- establishment group who was rallying around the clear-cut Socialist ideas of Keith Ellison.

Barack Obama weighed in with support of Tom Perez, who had worked for Obama, in an effort to help with the solidification among the split groups, by offering his congratulations to Perez. He said, "I know that Tom Perez will unite us under the banner of opportunity and lay the groundwork for a new generation of Democratic Leadership." Obama had not been in the forefront during the campaign, but remained behind the scenes, while appearing to remain neutral, but was directing others in bringing out the results that he wants.

There are some who say that Tom Perez was Barack Obama's handpicked candidate to guide this Socialist Democrat Party into the future that Perez had claimed was the Socialist future of the Party. During the final few days of the campaign, while leaders were jockeying for support, it was Valerie Jarrett, former President Obama's long-time advisor and front man (woman) who was busy with the phone, convincing DNC members that Barack Obama likes to support Tom Perez.

At any rate Obama congratulated Tom Perez for a job well done, and went on to state his party's track record of growing the economy, creating new jobs, keeping the people safe with smart foreign policies, and expanding the people's rights that were guaranteed to all Americans. He thought he had just the right Socialist to carry this legacy forward. Now all they had to do was introduce the Marxist tactics ensuring the government would gain control over the production of the hard work of the people to ensure that the people would march forward into this Socialist world in lockstep.

You must give credit where credit is deserved. Tom Perez came up, in very short order, with a plan that would energize the state level Democrats Party. He himself was energized by some early successes in states and quickly surmised that they were a good sign for the party. He went to war with the state Democrats and literally forced them into action where many were already convinced they were lost. He made sure that the DNC's of the states that he would settle for no less than a party majority and he launched an all-out fifty state strategy to do exactly that.

His plan breaks with the traditional practice for parties to concede in states where the opposition is strong in order to pour resources into states where seats were up for grabs. It was clearly a gamble, but Perez felt that considering Democratic wins in the Alabama Senate race and gubernatorial contests in Virginia and New Jersey, there was a great opportunity to open a challenge in other states where the party would not ordinarily commit resources.

Needless to say, gamble or not, this fifty state attack was extremely productive, and in places it did catch Republicans resting on their laurels and not planning ahead as they should have. A fact is a fact; the Democrats were able to take control of the House of Representatives by a solid margin. This fact had made the political life of President Trump a living hell for the next two years. There was a flood of new people who picked up the banner of socialism and began operating the House like a body from a third world government. They refused to budge, and they remained united against the president, his policies, and his followers. They pledged, as a war tactic, a policy of obstruction in which they would block any efforts on the part of the president to carry out his purposeful and positive agenda for this country. The systematic across-the-board obstruction of the president's policies was considered unfair to him and to the American people. It created a stagnant Congress that had very little positive and constructive legislative activity, and allowed processes like the massive migration assault from Latin Countries to create massive negative and destructive damage to Americans.

Just suppose that this fifty state strategy was a bad gamble and the Republicans had maintained a balance or control of the House. Nancy Pelosi would simply be an afterthought in our government rather than a constant thorn in the side of President Trump and a productive government. Just imagine how productive this country would be today. President Trump has made tremendous inroads in his first term in office; almost four million new jobs created with more Americans employed than ever recorded in history. This after taking over for Obama where 40% of the working age citizens were not working.

More than 400,000 manufacturing jobs were created since President Trump's election with manufacturing jobs created at the fastest rate in more than three decades. The unemployment rate standing in early 2020 was at a forty-nine year low. African American unemployment has recently reached the lowest rate ever recorded. The same can be said of the Hispanic-Americans. The median household income reached the highest level ever recorded in American history. Women's unemployment reached the lowest rate in sixty-five years. Almost four million Americans have been lifted off food stamps and youth unemployment has recorded their lowest rate in nearly half a century. Just imagine what these numbers could reflect if the Socialist Democrat Party was a cooperative party rather than an obstruction.

The Socialist Democrats have major problems and at the top of that list is the fact that their plan of obstruction will, in the end, backfire into their astonished faces. It is evident just one year before the 2020 election that the Trump train is rolling down the tracks of success at a higher clip than the Socialists could have ever imagined.

The crowds at the Trump rallies are livid at the tactics that the Socialists have used, which are reminiscent of Nazi Germany's all out attempts to shut down the GOP, President Trump, and his dredges. As we have noted intimidation, assault, and slander are the norm of their tactics. This has prompted even reporters of CNN and MSNBC to take note with one saying, "I have never seen such excitement and commitment at these rallies in all my years of reporting. The deplorables are definitely on the march and preparing to bring it back in the face of the Trump derangement Socialists like they have never seen before. Many pundits are reporting that the 2020 election may well be the most one-sided and stunning beating any political party in America has ever had.

So long as the Socialists continue to propose their outlandish ideas for our future, they are bound to pay the price at the polls for their failed vision. A recent poll in the summer of 2018 by the Hill-Harrisx poll showed that an overwhelming majority of respondents, 76%, stated that they would not vote for a Socialist political candidate, while only 24% said they would. Another poll clearly showed that 37% of all Americans surveyed have a positive view of socialism, while 58% hold a very negative view. These reports are bad news for Socialists and clear evidence that the tactics of the Socialist Democrat are not working in their favor.

The American people, as a whole, are reacting negatively to the half-baked plans that the Socialists are offering. The Elizabeth Warren proposal plans to weaponize the IRS again, by targeting a certain percentage of the country a tax with a mandatory audit quota every year. When questioned about how much that percentage is, she has no idea. And worse, no idea about the future impact on the people by politically weaponizing the IRS as Obama tried to do directly against the GOP. Senator Kamala Harris of California – while a candidate for the presidency – told a town hall meeting that she plans, "To abolish private health insurance and enact a government- funded, single-payer healthcare system." This is blatantly taking 16% of the national economy out of the hands of the private sector and handing it over to the Federal Government to run and control. Do you really want the government to control your health needs? The National debt is already at an unsustainable $122 trillion dollars which includes unfunded liabilities, which includes Medicare, Social Security, and federal employees and veteran benefits.

These are the people of a 'free everything' in life. They want to give free college and free healthcare and one has even gone so far as propose a universal basic income which is nothing more than free money. Lord, I thought Obama was bad wanting to give free cell phones to his street people so they could rise up and protest in an instant, but compared to these new Socialists Obama was a penny-pinching Grinch.

Free stuff is one thing, but these people have been itching to spend your money in a thousand different ways. The guiding light of the Socialist plans that would have a price tag of trillions of dollars with far more negative return with little to no positive results is the ridiculously outlandish Green New Deal. This idea was the brainchild (no pun intended) of Ocasio-Cortez and Senator Ed Markey of Massachusetts. It would bring in carbon taxes that would disproportionately impact the lower income households by costing as much as $25 per year in higher energy prices. For those who are wealthy, the tax is not a problem, but for the middle class, the working backbone of this country, and those of even lesser income this could be a devastating problem. There would also be major challenges in the manufacturing, shipping, and transportation businesses by increases in the cost of operation. Do you think that Ocasio-Cortez even considered the impact that these increases would have on the working people who are the backbone of our economy as those businesses passed their new overhead on down to the common people? I think not.

Because of all of these poorly thought out proposals and the tactics of the Socialist Democrats, people are abandoning the party in huge numbers and they comprise all races and ethnicities. They are rapidly coming to the realization that these ridiculous expenses will be coming out of their pockets just as much as out of the pockets of every other American. Hell, one of these said, "We have to tax the poor." Now that is striking right where the bullet hits the heart. Tax the poor? Have they no mercy? Have they no common sense? For a long, long time the people have understood that in government common sense is not so common. But the Socialists will get it and take it wherever it is found just lying and waiting for them to take it.

From this Conservative voice, the actions and proposals of the Socialist Democrats is not politics, it is the work of ignorant fools with no visionary powers and a total inability to use reason. Reason is the capacity that we all have in various levels, to make sense of things, to apply logic to problems, and to adapt or justify one's beliefs that are based on either new or existing information. Failing to possess these qualities goes a long way in explaining why the Socialists are so inept in using rationale to solve even the most obvious problems.

Offering opinions and ideas is a wonderful thing; it is something that clears the path for a productive future, and it is something that we all do. But Socialists do not seem to understand that opinions and ideas are the medium between knowledge or facts, and ignorance. When one continually offers ideas void of knowledge or facts, those ideas are based solely on ignorance. When I make a statement on ignorance and knowledge, who comes to my mind but Representative Alexandria Ocasio-Cortez. The newest (2018) of the radical Socialist Democrats in the ever developing House of Representatives, who learned her trade as a bartender listening to the make or break stories of a drunken clientele.

One of Ocasio-Cortez's interviews taped from The Daily Show went viral and with good reason. In the interview she was asked, "How is the government going to pay for all the free things that the Democrats are now promising?"

She replied, "This is an excellent question and, in fact, there's a lot of back-of-the-envelope stuff based on our values. So, for example, I sat down, ummm, with a Nobel Prize economist last week. I can't believe I can say that! It's really weird. But one of the things we saw is, if people pay their fair share – share. If corporations and the ultrawealthy – for example, as Warren Buffett likes to say – if he paid as much as his secretary paid, 15% tax rate, if, uh, corporations paid – if, uh, we reverse the tax bill but raise our – our corporate tax rate to 28% which is not even as high as it was before. Um, if we – if we do those two things and also close some of those loopholes, that's $2 trillion right there."

Uh, ummmm, okay. Well, there is an outside chance that I underestimated her, but I don't think so. If all of that makes clear as mud sense to you, you are probably in the right (left) party. Now here's the kicker. Tom Perez, Chairman of the DNC says Alexandria Ocasio-Cortez is the future of the party. Let me tell you what this Conservative voice thinks. If she and the other think-alikes of the freshman class are the future of the Socialist Democrat Party, then happily the Socialist Democrats have no future in this country. And, if Tom Perez actually does believe that they are the future he should take a job as a bartender, because that will be her future.

Tom Perez seems overjoyed that he has gathered around himself so many new Socialists that have an abundance of motivation. And, we must admit that there is no shortage of motivation on the part of these Socialists. In fact, one of Perez's close associates proudly pointed out that they have fifty to sixty highly motivated new recruits at all levels – federal, state, and local – ready to move forward in the 2020 elections. Now this is scary, not because of the numbers but because they also are highly motivated like Ocasio-Cortez and her close freshman associates.

Here are words of wisdom for Tom Perez, "Motivation alone is not enough. If you have an idiot and you motivate him, now you have a motivated idiot." In which case you and your Socialist Party would be ahead of the game rounding up the drunks Ocasio-Cortez left behind; at least they are not motivated.

Make no mistake about it; the takeover of the Democratic Party is very real. Cortez came from nowhere to defeat the House Democratic Caucus Chairman Joe Crowley. He was entrenched, but this one case shows how the Democrats have lost control of their own party. Ocasio came along singing a song of 'free this, free that, and free all the other things,' plus the abolition of ICE, the redistribution of wealth, Liberal drug policies and – wait for it, wait for it – forcing business owners to give up control of their companies to the workers. Folks, it just does not get any more Socialist than that, and for those millennials who don't want to do anything with their lives but suck the helium out of a balloon so they can sound like a chipmunk, all this free stuff sounds a little like heaven. All she had to do was sing the right (left) lyrics to the pampered and ignorant 'it's all about me' spoiled brat millennials, and with her motivation she was half-way there.

It is clear that the Socialist Democrats will go all out, full steam ahead, and stop at nothing to gain federal control over our energy, healthcare, income, your life, the elections, and even your freedom of speech. They are not bluffing; it is exactly what they believe and what they want to do. Remember that bar that the Founding Fathers used to measure the good balance between power held by the government and what you control of your liberties and freedoms? They thought we would be okay with a 40% government and 60% freedoms by the people balance.

That bar is on the move my friends. The Socialist Democrats do not believe in the 40%-60% balance. It is no longer at 40%-60% and they have not even gained full control of the government yet. If they have their own way it could easily turn to 60%-40%. If the Socialist Democrat Party in America continues to grow their numbers, and they are elected to the government leadership, according to their plan this country could return to the 100%-0% that our patriot Founding Fathers ran from to find a better balance to their lives. If they are allowed to put into play all of their agenda of socialism/communism this country could, in your life-time, be faced with the totalitarian rule of another Adolph Hitler. Nazism was and is a form of socialism. Germany was a country before Hitler that enjoyed much of the freedoms that we enjoy in America today.

We will complete this chapter with another poem to illustrate the need to stand strong against socialism and the Socialist Democrats. Americans should all benefit from the writings of patriot Thomas Paine who said, "Those who expect to reap the blessings of freedom must, like men, undergo the fatigues of supporting it." If you do not support our freedoms by rejecting those who would take them away, in truth, you are not worthy of freedoms at all.

SAVE THIS LAND

The time has come when people who love this land…
Must speak as one, and to the Socialists say…
You have not treated us well, and the truth is this…
Our basic values you fail to understand.

In place of peace we view your threat as war
The substance of our toil you are draining away
Vast sums of wealth that would make us strong
On foolish projects you choose this gold to go.

And now the folly of these thoughtless acts
Have brought this nation to disaster's brink
Or, are all your actions…errors, not at all
Is this all in your plan…Is this the fact of facts?

You are constant sapping of our country's strength,
Strange rules and regulations that quell it all.
The senseless plans that stress and confuse,
That knows no end and goes to endless lengths.

The doles that sadly beggar our patriot's pride,
The programs ill-conceived and doomed to fail,
Your debts on future generations laid,
A trend that spells financial suicide.

A change must come, we've been duped by your words far too long.
Endangered are out freedoms we have known,
And while there still is time, if there still is time,
We must demand you admit that you are wrong.

By your actions from within this great nation could fall,
As history so vividly portrays,
This fate we must not let our land befall,
This must not be the tale our children tell.

Chapter 10
Socialism Reminiscent of Nazism

During a speech in 1927 Adolph Hitler said, "We are Socialists. We are the enemies of today's capitalist system of exploitation, and we are determined to destroy this system under all conditions." To this Conservative voice, it is clear that Hitler saw his movement as one of Socialist concepts, and their goal was to implant those concepts into the Germany society. It was probably not Socialist in the true sense of the word because it implied nothing about workers ownership of the means of production, but when Bernie Sanders says, "I am a Socialist, and my followers are Socialists," you tend to understand that, at the tactical level, there is certainly socialism in the air. Hitler was not so much interested in the class so much as the race but the applied tactics to elevate his super race were much the same as the Socialist of Bernie Sanders to elevate the level of the workers.

In Germany the Weimar Republic had been the government from the end of WWI in 1919 to about 1933 when Hitler gained control. That fourteen year period was, for Germany and the people, a difficult time since coming off of a war that they had lost. The National economy was at best unstable and there was much chaos throughout the land from the new political forces. But at least the new government had created a Constitution that was generous to the people with many freedoms and liberties. It was not a Socialist country, or a Communist one, though both were hard at work building their base and doing all they could to gain as much control as possible from the chaotic country. A climate of national chaos is always a bad thing as it creates a pathway for tyrants to take advantage of the crisis. In point of fact Germany was during this time more of a Republic, though a weak and faltering one, and a Republic in trouble.

As with our Constitution, the German Weimar constitution guaranteed all Germans to be equal with the same Civil Rights and responsibilities. It assured them the right to freedom of expression, and the right of peaceful assembly, religion but with no state church, and a state run education system that was free and mandated for all children. It included the right to private property, equal opportunity and earnings in the workplace. These freedoms were clearly quite inclusive in the Weimar Republic of Germany and they should indeed look very familiar to people of the constitutional Democratic Republic of the United States of America.

By 1932 the Nazi Party had become the largest political party in the Parliament. The chaos had worsened and the people feared a takeover by communism. They turned to what they considered to be lesser radical parties like the Nazi's who professed protection and social amendments for the people. In January 1933 Adolph Hitler, the leader of the Nazi party, was named Chancellor and the transformation of Nazi power was complete. Within weeks the German people's freedoms were gone. Just that quickly Hitler invoked Article 48 to the Constitution and simply squashed most of their, once protected, Civil Rights and suppressed all members of the Communist Party in the Parliament. The Communists enjoyed the second largest position in the government, but that was not to last long.

In March 1933 Hitler introduced the Enabling Act to allow him to pass laws without the approval of Germany's Parliament or president. To ensure that the Enabling Act was passed, Hitler forcibly prevented Communist Parliament members from voting. From the time that it was passed, Hitler was free to legislate as he saw fit and his dictatorship was complete. All liberties and freedoms of the German people were wiped out, and they were allowed only those freedoms that Hitler of the Nazi Socialist Party would allow. This was just two months from the time that he was made Chancellor to when he assumed full dictatorial powers over the people. That quick.

As time went on from 1933 all the freedoms mentioned above were quickly eliminated. Those same freedoms of gun ownership, speech, assembly, and religion lost in Hitler's Germany are under attack in America by the Socialist Democrats. The tactics of suppression in both cases are much the same as each use intimidation, slander, and physical attacks as their weapons. The attempt by Hitler to divide the country by race is not unlike that of the Socialist Democrats in America today, by dividing Americans by social class, politics, religion, sexes, and by freedoms such as gun ownership, patriotism, free speech, and assembly.

Nothing says Hitler like his own words drawn from his speeches from 1931 to 1938. Nothing says socialism like the very actions of Socialist Democrats right here at home. Hitler said, "Demoralize the enemy from within by surprise, terror, sabotage, and chaos." He was perfectly comfortable having *Schutzstaffel*, otherwise known as the SS , and *Sturmabteilung* – meaning assault division – also known as the Brownshirts using intimidation, fear, and hostility to keep the people under his control and dare not step out of the prescribed Nazi narrative. Socialist Democrats are perfectly comfortable using the same tactics in their way to squash any narrative offered by the right at any level. Hitler's Brownshirts are not much different from the Antifa who are activists involved in the movement trend to be anti-capitalists and subscribe to a range of ideologies, typically on the left. And when they are at their best, they are intimidating, and causing fear and hostility among any group from the right. They are anarchists, socialists and communists, along with some liberals and Socialist Democrats. Their jobs are the same, to demoralize the enemy – Conservative Republicans – by causing relentless chaos.

The Hitler Youth was a logical extension of Hitler's belief that the future of Nazi Germany was in its children. The Hitler Youth was seen as being as important to a child as school was. In the early years of the Nazi government Hitler made it perfectly clear as to what he expected German children to be like, and they were indoctrinated to his cause. The children were organized into groups called 'cells' and met in their groups with adult leaders several times a week. They were instructed in the beliefs in Nazism and their responsibilities to the National Socialist Party. By 1933, when Hitler took full power, the membership of the Youth movement stood at 100,000 strong, and he was well on his way to ensuring the future of Germany through their youth.

In the U.S. the Socialists follow in lockstep the advocacy of their mentor Saul Alinsky, and his Marxist Communist playbook, to take over the youth and their minds as with Hitler, and to ensure the Socialist future in America through the youth. The education system in America has, in the past two decades, been flooded with not only left leaning Liberals and Progressives, but by scholars that are clearly Marxist Socialist Communist. In their efforts to capture control over the thinking of the youth, they are taking control over the reading material and what the youth hear in their classes. The rhetoric of Socialist communism is free flowing in the universities, and it is becoming impossible to recommend schools where a balanced education is available. In the past ten years, because of programs started by Barack Obama, there has been much change to a liberal educational format that pushes an agenda of progressivism and socialism.

Another quote that is attributed to Adolph Hitler that shows the closeness in his philosophy to that of the Socialist in America is, "It is not truth that matters, but victory." We have already spoken of the idiom 'the end justifies the means.' These two concepts have the same meaning. In the end they say that the only thing that is important is the end result; one does not care how that result is accomplished. Moral and immoral means apply equally to achieving one's goals. Victory is the only thing that matters; if you have to kill to achieve your narrative then that is what is acceptable. The level of lying in the Socialist Democrats Party is appalling. They have no apprehension to achieving even at the expense of hurting others.

There is much more similarity between Nazi's and the Socialist Democrats than they would care to admit. Their philosophies with subtle differences and their tactics laced with deceit, underhanded tactics, and behind-the-back politics walk the same path to achieving their goals. Their insistence that they are the superior people and that their voice is – and should be – the only voice, is the product of an arrogance that only they can understand. They have such an air of superiority that convinces them they cannot be wrong, that their narrative is right, and their beliefs are the beliefs of a people who are possessed of a knowledge that others simply cannot perceive. Which, by the way, would be the same description of Adolph Hitler. Like Hitler, Socialist Democrats have an overbearing manner which makes it easy for them to believe in their presumptuous claims.

At this point I would like to relate a story that demonstrates the life of two young men in Germany under the dictatorship of Adolph Hitler. This is a brilliantly written story by Adam Makos with contributor Larry Alexander from his book *A Higher Call*. It features two brothers from Auberg, Germany who became pilots in the German Air Force, the *Lufthwaffe*, in the late 1930's.

Franz, the younger of the two, was the first to become a certified pilot and he flew four years for a German Airlines. At the end of one of his flights he was met by a German officer who handed Franz an envelope and said, "Your orders; your country needs you." And just like that young Franz was conscripted into the German Air Force and made a Pilot Trainer. He was sent to pilot training school and quickly earned a reputation as one of Germany's most respected and proficient pilot trainers.

"In early 1939, Franz's brother August, who had just enlisted in the German Air Force, reported to the training school and became one of Franz's trainees." Adam Makos reports that, "All young German men were being drafted, and August enlisted in the Air Force to avoid induction into the German Army."

Finally, with training about over, Franz and August took leave to return home for a vacation. "They stayed in their home in Auberg, and while looking for August one afternoon, Franz, wandered into August's bedroom. On August's desk Franz found some letters. He picked one up and read it. His hands began to tremble. The letter was a copy of *With Burning Concern,* the Vatican's secretly composed message to all the German Catholics. On Palm Sunday, 1937, this letter had been read by every priest, bishop, and cardinal across Germany to their congregations. Three hundred thousand copies had been distributed to Germany's Catholic population."

The Catholic Church was a known enemy of The Party and their sermons constantly call out Hitler, his gestapo, and the crimes of the Third Reich. This particular letter carefully described the Nazi government as an evil religion that is based on racism, and was in opposition to the beliefs of the church. It also made reference to 'an insane and arrogant prophet' but did not name Hitler by name.

"Franz was frightened by the discovery of this letter and confronted his older brother, who attempted to downplay it as nothing more than a curiosity. Franz objected and tried to make his bother understand the dangers of being in possession of material of this nature. He asked, "Do you want to go to Dachau?"

Everyone in Germany would understand what that meant. The Dachau Concentration Camp was built by Hitler in 1933 and was to be used as a political prison for those Germans who spoke out or acted out against the Führer or the Nazi Party. Rest assured that this letter had very much angered Hitler and he rounded up as many as possible to be destroyed. The church feared, and the people feared, there would be very severe backlash for this letter, but the heavy reprisals never came. The gestapo had raided several churches and confiscated what they could find, but for some reason Hitler did not follow up with sanctions, and did nothing more than harass some of the clergy. It was, however, for the clergy and the people a difficult time because any person could be labeled a political enemy and imprisoned at Dachau. And hundreds were.

Through fear, intimidation, hostility, chaos, and the systematic elimination of those who by words or actions fought against this tyrant, he gained an absolute stranglehold on the lives of the people of Germany. This story of Franz and August by Adam Makos shows that it was all very real, and that the lives of the people under this Dictatorial Totalitarian insane prophet was going to get a lot worse before it got any better. We all know from our historic involvement in WWII that by the time the end came for Adolph Hitler in 1945, hiding in his bunker, Germany was once again a Holocaust of its own making. Thanks to Adolph Hitler and his National Socialist Party (Nazi's) there was little left for the post WWII people to salvage.

Do not wait, America, to stop the evil spread of Marxist Socialist communism. Look how quickly the people of Germany lost all of their freedom. Look how quickly a ruthless tyrant promising a paradise was able to take control of a crisis and an entire population and own it. Look at the futility of those who had the strength tried to stand up against this evil, yet in the end lay down and died.

The socialism of the Socialist Democrats may or may not be the same socialism of Adolph Hitler, and it doesn't really matter. What is important is the tactics of tyranny that he used to enslave and entire people and eliminate by execution another entire people. Those tactics are one in the same tactics of the Socialist Communist Democrats in your paradise of America.

SLAVERY OR SALVATION

We live in a country in turmoil,
We live in a country where some have gone mad.
I look at the sea of faces,
And the look that comes back is sad.
Distress is the countries affliction,
And our own National Anthem brings fear,
With our people at the mercy,
Of the lies of the Socialists we're forced to hear.

Now under attack are the hopes we lived by,
Now gone missing are the standards of the brave.
O're all is a threatening shadow,
Of those Socialist forces that would enslave.
What chance for a brighter tomorrow?
What way can this evil tide be turned?
An act of God is the answer,
But such acts "We" must earn.

As we can see by this narrative, socialism is the product of more than one brand and color. In the U.S. it has historically been very weak, largely because of the stigma with their association with Marxist communism. Even in the early 1920's under the Socialist Party of America, with candidate Eugene V. Debs they could muster no more than about one million votes in the presidential races. They continued to fail to gain support through six presidential races with candidate Norman Thomas from 1928-1948.

In the mind of this Conservative voice it was around 1944, near the end of Norman Thomas's reign as leader of the Socialist Party in America, that the Democratic Party began its movement to slide in with the Socialist and Communist ideologies. By this time the Communist Party was already fostering many of the policies of the Democrats, such as organizing and lifting up the working man through Union supports, and a strong anti-war agenda. It would not be unexpected that the Socialist Party began to change their approach to gaining future support by masking their goals and supporting the Democrat platform.

It was at this time that Norman Thomas began to realize that there would be no success for socialism as a third party. This country would not recognize socialism or communism, in their present form, with its third party agenda. It was clear that America had a very bad taste about buying into either socialism or communism; for decades they had refused to accept any part of their beliefs. Some have said that Thomas made his thoughts clear that the only way American's would accept socialism was if it was cloaked under the flag of liberalism. He was convinced that under this banner the American's would likely buy every part of socialism and adapt to its cause.

There is much discussion about when, how, and if Norman Thomas actually spoke about this claim, but the fact remains that when the Socialist leadership gave up running a third party candidate they began to infiltrate with the expectation of taking over the Democratic Party. They would work together with the Democrats to beat down the platforms of the Republican Party. We know, from this point forward, the takeover of the Democratic Party by the Socialist Communist ideologies was a gradual and patient effort. It is as though they were content to slowly grow their numbers within the Democratic Party, while awaiting the arrival of their prophet to complete the transformation of the Socialist Democrat Party.

The 1960's seemed to be exactly what the doctor ordered for the Socialists. It was an intense period of chaos involving much racial divide and relations, domestic terrorism by such groups as the Weather Underground, the Black Panthers, and other anti-American and anti-Capitalist groups. Amongst all this mayhem there was a direct assault against the Vietnam War effort. The chaos, mayhem, and protests were everywhere, and the Socialist Communists ideology was in the forefront while continuing to take advantage of the crisis to build strength in the Democratic Party.

Saul Alinsky, the mentor of the new left, in all of his glory wrapped in Marxist Socialist communism, was reaching into the minds of thousands of the discontented and malcontents doing nothing more than throwing more fuel on the flames of chaos and anarchy. Hillary Clinton loved Saul Alinsky, became a close friend, and stayed in contact with him during her early political years. She had written to him and met with him, seeking information for her college thesis.

Saul Alinsky was a heavy hitter for the Socialist movement into government. As we have noted he was a community organizer who spoke the language of socialism and communism. He said, "If you want to change a society, one had to first infiltrate the major institutions; the schools, the media, the churches, the entertainment industries, the labor unions, and the three branches of government and then it would have the power to implement policies."

Just look at his list! It is a list of all the places that have today, just fifty-five years later, been infiltrated in massive numbers by Socialists, Communists, and Muslims, many of which represent extremism at its worst. From Alinsky forward to the mid-1970's it was but a short step for the new left to effectively eliminate their opposition. Does this not sound like Adolph Hitler and his Third Reich? Eliminate their opposition. Their opposition was the centralist Liberals (moderates) who had vehemently opposed any form of Socialist Communist intrusion into the Democratic Party. Once they were eliminated as an effective foe, the new left simply took control.

The Socialist Democrat Party of today is extremely far-left and moving farther left every day with new a Socialist Totalitarian voices. The top levels of the party have been infiltrated by very high numbers. One article that I researched listed and claimed that at minimum sixty-nine to seventy hard core Socialists or Communists have, in the government, long associations or memberships with far-left, Socialist, or Communist organizations. They range from the Communist Party USA, to the Democratic Socialists of America Organization, Maoist-leaning Black Panther Party, The Socialist Party of the USA, and The World's Worker's Party. And there are many others as well. This group does not even include those of hard core Islamic connections.

There is so much socialism/communism in the Socialist Democratic Party that it is, today, impossible to distinguish who is who. We know that the centralist's (moderate) are gone with less than a handful still around. We also know that Debbie Wasserman Schultz, when she was the chairman of the DNC was asked directly by an MSNBC host, "What is the difference between a democrat and a Socialist?" She had no answer and was unable to distinguish between the two. She evaded the question and sidestepped the issue completely.

The Democratic Socialists of America (DSA) is the largest Socialist organization in the United States and they have played a huge role in the creation of the Congressional Progressive Caucus (CPC). This Caucus has the largest membership within the Democratic Caucus of Congress, which at this time stands at ninety-eight listed progressive members. Their founding organization, the DSA, is a principle U.S. affiliate of Socialist International, the world-wide organization of Social Democratic Socialist parties.

The CPC is currently co-chaired by representatives Mark Polan D-Wisc., and Pramila Jayapal D-Wa. The CPC was founded in 1991 by six members of Congress: Bernie Sanders, Peter DeFazio D-Ore., Maxine Waters D-Calif., Ron Dellums D-Calif., Lane Evans D-Il, and Thomas Andrews D-Me. It is noteworthy to mention that an early addition to the Caucus, after 1991, was current Speaker of the House, D-Calif., Nancy Pelosi, and Jerry Nadler, D-NY.

The CPC is the political entity in the Democratic Caucus of Congress (DCC) to keep your eye on closely over the next few elections. They have, since their inception, wrapped themselves in bold and aggressive economic and social justice reforms. As they have grown over the past three decades, their unabashed boldness has evolved as well, taking on the face of socialism as their dominant force. Their advocacy for Obama care, as an inexpensive health care program for the poor, has evolved beyond that to a single payer health care taken over by the Government and disseminated to the people by the will of the state; plus calling for a debt-free college, a universal child care, and universal wages package are all steps up for even the Socialist Democrats.

The 2019 mid-term election was good for the House of Representatives, gathering forty seats from the GOP control. Even more significantly is the fact that twenty House freshman who put Liberal points at the heart of their campaigns joined the caucus. They now represent about 25% of the entire House. Some may feel that in the overall picture of American politics, this is an insignificant change. As a Conservative voice, I vehemently disagree, as it may seem insignificant, it may be a Pandora's Box with severe and far-reaching consequences. These new freshman members are extreme even for the policies of the overall Socialist Democrat Party today.

This new group, headed by the very obtrusive Alexandria Ocasio-Cortez of NY, is radical beyond the dreams of Americans. With them gaining in political maturity, in just two years, they have – for the American people who love this country – as a Representative Democratic Republic become more of a nightmare. Cortez along with three other newly elected congresswoman known as the 'squad' (Ilha Omar D-Minn., Ayanna Pressley D-Ma., and Rashida Tlaib D-Mich.) have quickly become, both within their party and with President Trump, a force needed to be dealt with. Some within the party see them as dangerous to the future of the party, while others see them, as Tom Perez does, as the new face of socialism and the party in America.

We can say with certainty that we are at a dangerous crossroads between socialism and democracy in this country. We must stop taking our freedoms for granted, because if they are lost, they are lost to the world. We simply cannot allow ourselves to stand by while our freedoms are stripped, one by one, by this menace of Socialist communism. We saw earlier how Adolph Hitler stripped the German people of their rights, liberties, and freedoms in just a matter of weeks once he gained totalitarian control. Mark my words that the goal of Socialist communism is the same as that of Hitler. In the end, you are not what matters, but only power and control count. Once they are lost, they will not be coming back any time soon.

Far too many Americans have forgotten the lessons of our past. There are a host of people in America that are false prophets selling the snake oil of socialism as a great panacea. The best I can say of those Socialist Communist Democrats that buy into and push this evil on their fellow citizens is that there is an abundance of ignorance of the past, ignorance of the present, and ignorance of the future among some Americans. These are not sheep in wolves clothing, these are wolves in wolves clothing. They know what they want, they are shameless on how they will go about bringing socialism here, and unabashed about who or what is the collateral damage to their grand scheme. Someone once wrote, "Ignorance is not bliss; ignorance is poverty. It is devastation, and it is tragedy. Ignorance is a mental illness." For those lost in the vacancy of their ignorance the great gift of human imagination is ended. How ignorant are the Socialists? Americans have the greatest chance for opportunity than anyone else in the past six and a half thousand years. Never in recorded history have so many different gifts been brought from all over the world and deposited in one country, with the collective knowledge that they are in a stronger and more hopeful position materially, intellectually, morally, and religiously than is true of any other people at any other place on this globe. And what do the Socialist Democrats want to do about this position? They intend on changing it to one of destitution, poverty, tragedy, and failure.

THE SOCIALISTS

The Socialists are out to enslave us,
And only a fool would deny it,
Yet there's little we seem to do,
But wring our hands, and decry it,
The strength that once was ours,
Has turned to meek submission,
There is no easing from hostility,
From those Socialists who fathered this condition.

Socialists are out to enslave us,
But we've closed our eyes and allowed it,
Though their intent is crystal clear,
We did our best to becloud it,
So now we pay the price,
As allies no longer trust us,
While to protect themselves,
They further from them, drive us.

Socialists are out to enslave us,
But the most we do is resent it,
For it seems we've waited too long,
To take steps to prevent it,
Concerned we rue the thought,
Of the road that lies ahead,
Knowing we face the threat,
Of a nation with freedom ... dead.

Chapter 11

George Soros and the Shadow Party

The prophets of doom have spoken clearly. Their plan to cause the fall of American principles and values from within is easily perceived. They will do the work prescribed by the writings of Saul Alinsky to undermine our political, social, religious, and educational networks to rebuild them in the image of Marxist Socialist Communist ideals. It is obvious how their use of propaganda will allow them to indoctrinate all educators and their students, the media, and the entertainment world to accept their dogma.

We see how the Socialist Democrats have evolved within their own chambers to become not just the flag wavers for socialism and communism, but they have all banded together to build a solid party network within the party to underscore the freedoms and liberties that Americans have long lived by and for.

Within our government, the Democratic Socialists of America is like a huge octopus reaching out with its slithering tentacles wherever it can go to grab ahold of something, or someone, to support its insatiable hunger for power and control. That octopus grabbed the Congressional Progressive Caucus of the House of Representatives, and they grabbed back, causing an inseparable union of Socialist communism to be formed. Little did the Democrats understand that the tactics of that octopus were so inclusive they would be gobbled up by its shrewd, cunning, and underhanded methods. Left without a home of its own, their party would become the party of Marxist Socialist communism. Oh, but they would still retain an asterisk (*), a reference to an annotation, or to stand for an omitted matter once known as the Democratic Party of the United States of America.

Today, there is a party that lies within the Socialist Democrat Party that is called the Shadow Party. It is the brainchild of George Soros and Hillary Clinton. They, along with Harold Ickes, created a network of non-profit activist groups in order to collectivize resources on behalf of the Socialist Democrat Party. The forces they wanted to organize were money, get-out-the-vote drives, and campaign advisories; all for the purpose to elect Socialist Democrat candidates who would help guide the party further towards the left in the 21st century.

George Soros had begun the work on the Shadow Party as early as 1994; starting at that time to put piece after piece together as soon as he could manipulate his way through weaknesses and loopholes in the campaign finance structure. In the mid-term election of that year, the Republicans won majorities in both houses of congress under the Bill Clinton administration. This was devastating and unfathomable to hard core Democrat, George Soros. He knew and understood from this point forward that there must be changes made to campaign financing. He began negotiating for a Bipartisan Campaign Reform Act that was passed in 2002. This Act became known as the McCain-Feingold Act. Soros poured millions of dollars on its support from 1994 to when it was passed.

It should be noted that it was early in this period that George Soros threw his political and financial support behind Barack Obama. It was largely with Soros's financial support that Obama was able to make the run at the Illinois Senate seat. Soros was there in 1995, in Chicago, at the home of domestic terrorists Bill Ayres and Bernadine Dhorn, when Obama announced his bid for the Senate seat. As Obama moved forward with three terms in the Illinois State Senate and as U.S. Senator from 2005-2008, Soros was there bringing Obama along and seeing to his financial needs. He was also there bringing Obama along into his causes leading to the Shadow Party and the Shadow Government after Obama left the White House. With Barack Obama tucked neatly under his financial far-left wing, Soros had the best platform one could have to sell his snake oil.

It was probably not known at the time of the passage of the Bipartisan Campaign Reform Act of 2002, but this bill would have a major role in the development of the Shadow Party. The bill was designed to decrease the role of soft money – a donation to a political party where it is not made to promote a particular candidate in political campaigns – as it places limits on the contribution by interest groups and national political parties. Included was also a 'Stand by your Ad' provision that regarded ads on television and radio as a statement by the candidate that identifies the candidate and states that the candidate has approved of the communication.

Proponents of the act, like Soros, said it was necessary to get rid of the larger contributions from corporations, labor unions, and wealthy individuals so as to return to a system dependent on regulated individual donations. However, opponents argued that it would be a restraint on the freedom of corporations, unions, and the wealthy to express themselves.

Surprisingly George Soros was in support of this Act that would remove soft money and seemingly be unfavorable to the Democratic Party's future fundraising efforts. But remember he had been working on finance changes for some time and was quite prepared to take advantage of changes by putting his own plans to work. His Open Society Institute, along with some other far-left foundations began financing individuals and groups whose goal was to persuade Congress to engulf the myth that millions of people were crying for campaign finance reform. It was largely these foundations that funded the program.

It did not take long for his reasoning to become clear. The McCain-Feingold Act left certain types of groups untouched in their fundraising activities. These were the '527 committees,' the name is derived from section 527 of the Act. They were created primarily to influence the selection, nomination, election, appointment, or defeat of the candidates at all levels of government. It is common practice that the term 527 applies only to those organizations that are not regulated by campaign finance laws.

There are no upper limits on contributions to 527s and no restrictions on who may contribute. This was made to order for the deep pockets of the likes of George Soros, and he has spent the next eighteen years creating massive numbers of non-profit groups that could take advantage of this 527 program.

The Secretary of State Project is one such example. It was founded by Becky Bond, Michael Kieschnick, and James Rucker as a 527 non-profit committee focused on electing reform-minded progressive Secretaries of State in battleground states who, ironically enough, typically oversee the election process. And we should add that George Soros funds this committee along with members of the Democracy Alliance (DA). Members of the DA include George Soros and Tom Steyer. In 2017-2018 alone the DA members spent $100 million on various liberal causes. They state clearly that their purpose is "to fund and build a progressive infrastructure to help counter the well-funded and sophisticated conservative apparatus." Soros, with his new opening, was able to cut off the Democrats and place the soft-money where these evil geniuses felt it would do the most good. It allowed them to hand-pick candidates and throw their support to the ones they most wanted elected.

Ironically, where the new campaign finance Act was intended to control deep pocket money, the opposite effect actually became the case. These people gathered greater power, and since George Soros was the principle deep pocket and funded most of the committees, he amassed greater power over the electoral process in America. The Shadow Party and the shadow government were well on their way to redeveloping government and Soros began using the committees to foster his pet projects. His stealth PAC's and anti-gun group organized a campaign to neutralize the influence of the NRA by targeting any candidate, at any level, for whom the NRA endorsed. Likewise, he used the 527s to campaign for pro-marijuana support in various states, and he spent a lot of money to defeat these issues.

After 2001, and the infamous 9/11 attack on America by terrorists, Soros was grievously angered; so much so that he changed much of his attitude concerning American responsibility toward world problems. Ironically, he was not angered at the terrorist that murdered 2,000 Americans, but rather at the United States. His view now was that the world was endangered by American world domination. He felt that President George W. Bush was taking dangerous steps that were giving rise to American hatred by people around the planet. He cited Bush's statement of referring to our enemies as evil as a danger by signaling America's belief in our exceptionalism.

Soros responded to this issue by launching a global war on poverty and began to send huge amounts of aid to impoverished countries. Just days following 9/11 he gave a speech in which he identified the hallmark of this plan to address social conditions, and a call for terrorist volunteers, who are willing to sacrifice their lives, to be recruited. This was Soros' biggest movement yet, in launching his Global Open Society plan. He was, and is, convinced that targeted action on a global level was necessary to cause America to restructure her priorities.

Many Americans feel that his country is under such a terrific assault from George Soros, and the radical left, that if not stopped now our generation will witness it slipping from our grasp. It is more than clear the forces of the new left, namely the Shadow Party of the Socialist Democrats, are overloading all of our institutions with their anti-American, anti-capitalism, free enterprise, anti-Christian faith, and anti-exceptionalism.

When George Soros launched the Shadow Party on 17 July 2003 at his Southampton estate on Long Island, there would be created a monster intruder to the old Democratic Party. Soros was, and is, a so-called top dog among many well-heeled, far-left strategists, donors, labor leaders, and Socialist activists, and these are the people who he invited to the Hamptons to enlist support for his new project.

His mega wealthy guests included Open Society Foundations (OSI) director Morton Halperin. He is currently a senior advisor to the Soros Open Society Foundation; Emily's List activist Ellen Malcohm, who has a long political career – especially noted for fundraising in liberal, progressive measures; Clinton Former Chief of Staff, John Podesta who owns the Podesta Group, an active lobbying firm and is chair of the Center for American Progress (CAP) a long time Soros Think Tank; Sierra Club executive director Carl Pope, (Sierra Club is an American environmental organization) and Pope is a regular contributor to the Huffington Post, a progressive website. Also included was labor leader Steve Rosenthal, Robert Glasser, Lewis and

Dorothy Cullman, Robert McKay, Peter Lewis, and Robert Reich; all well-heeled extreme far-left activists, strategists, and donors.

It was at this meeting that Soros announced his plan to defeat George W. Bush in the 2004 presidential election. He was so contemptuous of Bush that he collectively blamed him for most of the problems that disrupted the country. In the election year to unseat Bush, Soros spent $26 million of his own money to ensure George Bush's defeat. He funneled huge amounts of funds into the America Coming Together committee in support of its get-out-the-vote initiative. But in spite of these massive funds his plan failed, and George Bush was reelected for a second term. However, a great momentum was turned loose and the Shadow Party, with its 527s and other committees were well on their way to redirecting the Democratic Party into the new Socialist Communist Party.

Today, the Open Society Foundation, formerly the Open Society Institute, can be said to be the flagship of the George Soros' international political financing network. They are organized from the Open Society Foundation down to each and every nook and cranny of the committees that carry the load of their individual promotions.

The following is a list of the various promotions of the Foundations' tremendously variable collection of promotions that the individuals and committees of the Shadow Party are responsible for carrying out.

- Promoting the view that America is institutionally an oppressive nation.
- Promoting the election of leftist political candidates throughout the U.S.

- Opposing virtually all post-9/11 National Security measures of U.S. Government.
- Depicting American military actions as unjust, unwarranted, and immoral.
- Promoting open borders, mass immigration, and negativizing current law.
- Promoting a dramatic expansion of social welfare programs, with massive taxes.
- Promoting social welfare benefits and amnesty for illegal aliens.
- Defending civil rights and liberties of suspected anti-American terrorists.
- Financing recruitment and training of future Left activist leaders.
- Advocating America's unilateral disarmament of citizenry, or steep reduction.
- Opposing the death sentence in all circumstances.
- Promoting socialized medicine in the U.S. with single-payer policy.
- Promoting the tenets of radical environmentalism.
- Bringing American foreign policy under the control of the United Nations.
- Promoting racial and ethnic preferences in academia and business.
- Promoting taxpayer-funded abortion-on-demand.
- Advocating stricter gun-control measures.
- Advocating for the legalization of marijuana.

This is an extremely comprehensive list of the goals and promotions of the Soros plan to change the course of America; it is also a list of all the Barack Obama held ideals that he would impose on America in order to fundamentally transform this country and the way it operates. Likewise, it is a list of today's Socialist Democrat Party as they transform themselves into a Socialist Communist Party with the intention of following the footprint of George Soros, his far-left allies, Barack Obama and his Socialist Communist advisors and allies and the Shadow Party. They had but one purpose in mind; to transform America into a country more to their liking (Marxist Socialist communism).

The previous list of promotions was in the hands of, and were governed and dictated by, a radical gang of wealthy Socialist Communist players, and sympathizers. When, in 2004, the administrative core of George Soros's Shadow Party was in place there were at least seven groups placed in operation, and much of the growth of that early network stems from these early committees.

1. America Coming Together (ACT): This committee is a very progressive political action, 527 group dedicated to get-out-the-vote activities. It operates almost exclusively on behalf of the Democratic candidates. It was, at its conception, funded primarily by Peter Lewis, George Soros, and labor unions, especially the Service Employees International Union, or SEIU. It was led by Steve Rosenthal a former radical director of the AFL-CIO. Their behind-the-back, and strong-armed activities were considered illegal, and by 2005 the Federal Election Commission caused them to close their doors and fined them $775,000 two years later. George Soros jump-started this program with a $10 million grant and it quickly became a huge success in getting-out-the-vote with their questionable tactics.

2. Center for American Progress (CAP): This group was designed to serve as a think tank to promote ideas and policy initiatives of George Soros, for which he pledged $3 million to get the

project started. From the beginning, the CAP's leadership comprised a group of officials from the Clinton administration. The former Clinton Chief of Staff, John Podesta, was selected by George Soros to serve as president. It does not bode well for the integrity of this group when you consider the behind-the-back, underhanded, and deceitful tactics that these people use. From Bill and Hillary Clinton, through John Podesta to George Soros it is, in and of itself, a network of failed integrity. Podesta laid claim to the goals of the group when he said, "We will send out a daily briefing to refute the positions and arguments of the right." He stayed on as president until 2013 when he joined the Obama administration on the White House staff. And just like that another one joins the group. The current chair is Tom Daschle and president is Neera Tanden. She was on both the Clinton and Obama administration. This group through the years has gained much power within the Shadow Party.

3. America Votes group is like an extension of the ACT group and has responsibility to coordinate the efforts of many of the get-out-the-vote organizations using thousands of activists to carry out their activities. Soros, continually during each election cycle, donated millions for their work.

4. Media Fund is the largest media buying organization supporting a progressive agenda in the U.S. They produce strategic political ads in the print, broad cast, and the media. The Media Research Center reports that George Soros has spent more than $48 million, from 2003 to2011, funding media properties, including the infrastructure of news, journalism schools, investigative journalism, and even industry organizations.

Among the beneficiaries of Soros's money to the media entities are NBC, ABC, The New York Times, The Washington Post, the Columbia Journalism Review, Propublica, the Center for Public Integrity, the Center for Investigative Reporting, The Lens, the Columbia School of Journalism, the National Federation of Community Broadcasters, the Committee to Protect Journalists, National Public Radio, the Media Fund, the Independent Media Center, Media Matters for America, and Free Press. To this Conservative voice, this is placing your money in all the right places if you want to control what others read, hear and see in the news. The vast majority of these entities are Left-leaning to far-left media productions.

5. Joint Victory Campaign 2004 (JVC). Focused on collecting contributions and dispersing them chiefly to America Coming Together and Media Fund. Soros gave $12 million to the Media Fund, while the ACT gathered some $38.4 million.

6. Thunder Road Group (TRG) is a political consulting group that coordinates strategy for the American Coming, America Votes, and The Media Fund. The TRG can be said to be the strategic nerve center of the Shadow Party. This group was founded by Jim Jordan, campaign manager for John Kerry and an attorney with a long record as a 'spin doctor' a public relations advisor, pollster, and media consultant who develops deceptive or misleading messages to spin to the public. They engage in opposition research and through the TRG the Shadow Party uses this information to formulate their plans of attack against opposition candidates. This group is among the most underhanded, and behind-the-back entity of the entire Soros network. As a pro-Democratic far-Left 527 committee

they are fully engaged in the support of Democrat candidates in the U.S. presidential election.

7. MoveOn.org is also a political advocacy group for the Shadow Party. They have raised millions for Liberal candidates throughout the U.S. It was originally formed as a response to the impeachment of President Bill Clinton. They have received severe criticism to advertisements which drew parallels between President George Bush and Adolph Hitler. It should be noted that it was George Soros himself who first drew those parallels, and he is the main contributor to the MoveOn.org group.

Fox news criticized MoveOn.org when they successfully encouraged the 2008 Democratic presidential candidates not to attend two debates sponsored by the Fox News network. Commentators Sean Hannity and Bill O'Reilly have also made accusations that the MoveOn.org 'owns' the Democratic Party and George Soros 'owns' MoveOn.org. Because of their radical and highly bigoted tactics over the years they have had many complaints thrown at them, but it does not change their plan of attack and they continue to operate with bias and by deceit.

Though the formation of this Shadow Party belongs to George Soros it is also the responsibility of Harold Ickes, as he had his hand in the foundation of virtually every Shadow Party core group with the exception of MoveOn.org. Ickes is the one who brought the organizational pattern to life so that there was a defined cohesion between the groups. In the early years John Kerry said of Ickes, "He is the most important person in the Democratic Party." Ickes has had a long history of activism coming out of the Civil Rights activists of the 1960's and had been the Deputy Chief of Staff in the White House for

Bill Clinton. He headed up Clinton's primary campaign in New York and he was considered by all to be the Democratic Party's go-to-man.

The Progressive Legislative Plan was designed to furnish state legislatures with a pre-written model; legislation reflecting leftist agendas. They are part and parcel with Soros's methodological campaign to shift American politics and public attitudes left by gaining a foothold inside the halls of the power legislature on a state-by-state basis.

The Health Care for Americans Now (HCAN) is a progressive political group of over 1,000 organizations that joined together in 2008 in a successful effort to bring about the Obama Care legislation. All of the groups of the Soros Shadow Party worked together relentlessly, each doing what they do best to bring this product through the legislature. The HCAN was credited with being the major contributor to its passage. Today they spend much of their efforts defending the law from opposition attacks.

They enjoy very deep Soros and Obama pockets, and the network is vast. They support a single-payer model where the Federal Government would be in complete charge of financing and administering the entire U.S. healthcare system. In 2009, Soros gave the HCAN $5 million to promote its campaign for reform of the health care legislation. There is no doubt that his view of the single payer system would and was platformed by Barack Obama.

Other organizations of the Soros Shadow Party were the Project Vote which is a mobilizing arm of the corrupt ACORN; the catalyst who helped the Progressive Shadow groups to bring about strengthening of their national voter database, and the Brennan Center for Justice, whose aim was to fully restore voter rights following criminal convictions. Supported and fostered by Barack Obama they know that felons would be likely to vote for Democrat candidates over the Republicans; the Progressive State Network that was charged with seeing that progressive legislation was passed in the states, and the Progressive Change Campaign Committee to which George Soros personally donated $8 million. Their job was to help elect the strongest progressive candidates.

Some of the most stunning of the Shadow groups, but lesser known are a number of organizations that promote extreme leftist ideas and world views via the media and the arts. These groups go a long way in showing how the mainstream, or other media, have taken such a strong and biased left turn. The Soros money going to these organizations has been deep and far reaching. The political mentality of these groups range from Progressive to Socialist Communist and their leadership is extremely biased and far-left.

1. The American Prospect, Inc. It is the purpose of this group to counteract the growing influence of the Conservative media. This is a daily online and print quarterly dedicated to American liberalism and progressivism.

2. Free Press is a media reform organization that openly and outrageously calls for a revolutionary program to overthrow the Capitalist system in America and to then rebuild the entire society on Socialist principles.

3. The Independent Media Institute, whose goal is to change the world by projects like AlterNet to reflect the voices of progressivism. AlterNet is a strong Left-leaning political website. Their executive director is Don Hazen, the former publisher of Mother Jones, a heavily left supporting

publication. He has recently stepped down from his position with AlterNet because of accusations of sexual misconduct.

4. The Nation Institute operates with the far-Left magazine, nation, which vows to drive the progressive ideas into the American mainstream. Today, the Nation Institute and Nation magazine are no longer associated together. They still advocate for social justice and civil rights, which is done largely through publishing far-left books and other materials.

5. Pacifica Foundation which owns Pacifica Radio that founded with Marxist Socialist rhetoric of class warfare and anti-capitalism. They flood the airways with an extremist Progressive-Liberal political orientation.

6. Media Matters for America is a Progressive research and information center where George Soros filtered much indirect funds to monitor and correct what they consider to be conservative misinformation in the U.S. Media. They operate as their own biased opinion fact checkers. On occasion George Soros has donated as much as $1 million to this organization.

7. Sundance Institute was launched by Soros as a documentary fund to produce social justice films that would spur awareness and social change. In 2001 the fund became part of actor/director Robert Redford's Sundance Institute. Early on, OSI placed about $5.2 million for the production of several hundred documentaries with this fund. Many of these documentaries were highly critical of capitalism, American Society, or Western culture generally. In 2009, Soros pledged another $5 million to Sundance Institute, directly.

Finally, there are three other Soros connected Shadow Organizations that target the American Judicial system in order to build a strong leftist values system in the judicial branch of government. This is particularly disturbing because we have all seen how, since the Obama presidency; far-left progressive and even Socialist judges have tried to block legislation of President Trump and the Republican Party in power. These judges seem not to care about the Constitution, but rather to interpret its meaning based on their bogus and progressive values. Considerable amounts of money are routed into their funds to give them the opportunity to block passage of rules, laws, and regulations that are conservative in nature.

The Alliance for Justice constantly depicts Republican judicial nominees as radical Right-wingers and extremists whose views range far away from the boundaries of mainstream opinions. The fact is that these Shadow Party members are beyond biased in nature. They are clearly a Progressive advocacy group that monitors federal judicial appointments. The current president of the Alliance is Nan Aron who is a noted opponent of conservative judicial nominees. She repeatedly called for Bill Clinton and Barack Obama to be more aggressive in nominating Progressives to the bench. She acted as a clearing house for recommendations for such appointees.

The two other organizations that are Left-oriented from the George Soros stable of Shadow groups are the American Constitution Society for Law and Police, and Justice at Stake. The former seeks to indoctrinate young students to view the constitution as an evolving, or what they call a living document, and to reject conservative buzzwords, such as originalism and strict constitution.

The latter is designed to promote legislation that would replace judicial elections with a merit-selection system where small committees of legal elites, unaccountable to the public, would pick those most qualified to serve as judges. OSI has spent a minimum of $45.4 million to change the way judges are chosen. Of course that small committee, in their thinking, would be overloaded with Progressive and Socialist people and they would be the ones deciding the merit of those selected to serve on the bench.

Over the past two decades America has nose-dived into a period of racial divide and civil unrest that is unprecedented for the past sixty years. Anti-police marches and behavior in Ferguson, Baltimore, Milwaukee, and numerous other places have created an anarchic mentality that is dangerous to both the police and the citizens throughout the country. At the root of this mentality are such Soros backed organizations as Black Lives Matter, MoveOn.org, International Action Center, ANSWER Coalition, and many other far-Left shadow support groups. They methodically perform their mayhem and chaos on cue, because they are generously funded by Soros and the Open Society Foundation. Did you ever wonder why Barack Obama was so anxious to provide free cell phones to people who could not otherwise afford them? SafeLink Wireless is a government supported program that provides a free cell phone and airtime each month for income-eligible customers. In other words, our tax dollars are being distributed to a wireless phone provider to provide welfare recipients, or people that activists need to contact in a hurry, to go to work with free cell phones. What a deal.

Black Lives Matter is one of the most prominent riot-making machines that receive huge financial funding from the Shadow Party, and their billionaire allies. This organization was founded by Patrisse Cullors, Alicia Garza, and Opal Tometi; three Black lesbian Marxists. They are mesmerized by the Communist terrorist revolutionaries like the Black Panther Party and the Black Liberation Movement (BLM).

Because Soros believes the same as they do, their purse is wide open for his donations. It is note-worthy to say again that these BLM leaders were frequent guests of Barack Obama at the Oval Office. Certainly, he was taking these opportunities to renew his skills as an old community organizer, passing them off to these new rioters. Many of the leaders of other groups along with Al Sharpton were regular timers to the White House.

The BLM involvement in the Trayvon Martin shooting in 2012, and that of Michael Brown in Ferguson, wrapped in the support of Obama and guided by his top riot-master Al Sharpton – along with Obama's AG Eric Holder – did all they could to inflame, by false narrative, a huge racial division. No differently than any of the other Soros funded, Obama supported, and Sharpton activated Shadow groups, they are all collectively creating a huge gap in America between social classes.

As it is clear to see by all, the Shadow Party is not dying; it has an unlimited supply of resources. There are so many deep pockets in this country that forsake the democracy they were born to, forsake the Capitalist economy that produced their wealth, and provide them with the freedoms of choice to throw themselves into the life they wanted to follow. There are thousands to millions that are ready, willing, and able to carry the flag of socialism to the people. They are also people who have – through their ignorance of the past, present, and future – forsaken their birth right to become the useful idiots of those who are making millions from their ignorance.

The flag wavers of the Socialist Democrat Shadow Party today refers to an ignorance of brainwashed Liberals, Progressives, and Socialists who blindly support and follow an idea that they have only limited information about, with no idea on how to translate that information into intelligent meaning. Usually these are college students who aren't necessarily idiots, but clearly misinformed, naïve, and ignorant of the facts. They have suffered from being indoctrinated into the propaganda of the Liberal-Socialist mindset through their public education and an extremely biased media. Many people think that intelligence is simply the gathering of information. If that were the case those who gather the most information and facts would be the winners. Clearly, it is not what you know, but what you do with that knowledge. If you have a little bit of information on a complex subject, and think that it provides all the answers you need to understand the subject, you are in a dangerous place because you will have no idea on how to use that little bit of information in a rational problem-solving manner. Far too many young people and college students, with too much time on their hands, fall into this group. Far worse is a simple fact that these people are easy targets for manipulation, propaganda, and control.

My final words: Beware because as Voltaire once said, "There are far too many people out there that can make you believe absurdities and can make you commit atrocities.

I wrote this poem about the Shadow Party to complete the illustration of how power in the hands of the corrupt and the deceitful, who operate behind your back and take full advantage of underhanded tactics, can rule as though they were totally invisible from your mind and sight. They profess to be working for your ends, but they will do whatever means are at their disposal to reach their own ends.

THE SHADOW PARTY

Beneath an avalanche of words,
The bewildered people tries,
To ferret out the truth,
That the Shadow Party would disguise,
Hidden deals in secret made,
By those whose voice you cannot trust,
The hopes and dreams we've saved for our lives,.
We see the Shadow turn them to dust.
The changes that would make us strong,
Would stabilize our great nation,
Are somehow strangely sabotaged,
And in their place – a shadow lurks.
The life blood of our country,
Daily being pulled asunder,
And all now found in separate pieces,
By catastrophic programs,
That common sense would disobey.
The overburdened middle class,
The backbone of our land,
Are slowly being undermined,
By that Shadow who has long planned,
To saddle this country with socialism,
Communism's other name.
For in essence and in action,
Either one add up the same.
Precious freedoms we have cherished,
Human rights, these too, we see wavering,
Can it be with the Shadow Party the master,
And the people the slave.
Only time alone will tell,
But this we must know and never forget,
A life without freedom is a life in hell.

Chapter 12

Obama Drives the Wedge

If you follow the political and financial roadway of George Soros in America it is inevitable that his path will intersect with Barack Obama. I think it was also inevitable from the moment Obama accepted the Soros money and support, Soros became his Edgar Bergenand while Obama became his Charlie McCarthy. You don't take money from the government and assume that they don't want something in return; and you don't take money from George Soros and assume he is just that kind of a nice guy and that's all he wants.

They are like 'two peas in a pod;' so similar in many ways. They both like the same thing – money and power – and will do virtually anything within their ability to take all they can get. They are each blessed with a super-ego which is the ethical and moral component of a personality that is underdeveloped, and interferes with their ability to make good moral and ethical judgments. To distinguish them from each other would be a Herculean task; while identifying their political similarities and their patriotic identities would be like identifying identical twins.

It was by no accident that George Soros launched his shadow party at the same time that he launched his deep political and financial relationship with a new and upcoming political novice in Chicago. It is by no accident that the 'the twins from different mothers' were at Billy Ayres home in Chicago when Barack Obama launched his political career. After all, Soros had been searching for his stepping-stone into the White House for a long time.

Barack Obama was well prepared by the time the two came together. He had already been well schooled by Frank Marshall Davis in the subject of Marxist communism. He had already identified with Communists and community organizer Saul Alinsky, and he was already well indoctrinated on the evils of American Capitalism and free enterprise with their effects on his Black folks. He made strong political ties with some of his college professors, student relationships, and civic leaders; and he had formulated a plan for change in America. He was ready for George Soros, and George Soros was ready for Barack Obama.

You can research Barack Obama's years at Columbia University (1981-1982) until your eyes begin to tear, but not much information about him or his activities are to be found. He was there to study political science, and he did receive his bachelor's degree upon graduation. But filling in the middle, beyond these two facts, even his contemporary students with the same major can report little to no information about Barack Obama at Columbia.

On the teaching staff at Columbia University were two professors that Obama would have surely engaged in classes. Assistant professor Richard Cloward of the Columbia School of Social Work was the spouse of Frances Fox Piven of the Political Science department. The two had worked out a strategy and plan that was called the Cloward-Piven Strategy. The principles of this strategy were the ground floor of much of the political science curriculum. It was understood that if you were enrolled in the political science program you were likely subjected to this plan, and it would have been the subject of discussion for much of your time at Columbia University.

The Cloward-Piven Strategy had multiple facets but was very detailed in principle theory. They proposed overloading the U.S.

welfare system to the point that the overload would precipitate a crisis that would lead to a replacement of the welfare system with a guaranteed annual income and thus, an end to poverty. Clearly Obama had been there and studied this plan, soaking up the principles of the plan. We are acutely aware of Barack Obama's efforts to overload the welfare system when he was president. We are acutely aware of his efforts to increase the number of people who received welfare by the millions. It is clear to this Conservative voice that if Obama had one more term of office, or if Hillary Clinton won the 2016 election, this part of the Cloward-Piven Strategy would have been completed, and America would today be a full blown Nanny Nation.

During the presidency of Barack Obama, 660,000 Americans were removed from the job rolls at one point. Over 90 million working age, able-bodied Americans were no longer in the work force. The work force participation rate dropped to its lowest level in forty-three years. For men alone it became the lowest since post-WWII, 1948.

About fifty million Americans went on food stamps (20% of all eligible adults); fourteen million more were on disability, and yet millions more on welfare, unemployment, housing allowances, and for dependent children, and many more on other subsidiary programs. You can add to these figures free health care, plus twenty-two million government employees. We quickly reached record numbers of Americans who emptied their retirement accounts to survive. Student loan debt was a national disaster with defaults up 36% from just the previous year. Sixteen million Americans lived in poverty, just in the suburbs. Every day with Barack Obama was the same story that the private sector was shrinking, while the democratic government was growing at an insatiable rate.

This Cloward-Piven Strategy had its sights set on bringing down the American way of life by this overloading tactic. Obama was confident that this would bring such a crisis; the people themselves would clamor for change. Obama knew that capitalism was at stake, which he despised, and it would be destroyed and replaced by the state run Marxist Socialist economic system. In combination with this plan they did follow the Saul Alinsky plan that America must be destroyed from within for social change to be successful. In the Marxist mind, America could not withstand the overwhelming debt, welfare, and entitlements; and capitalism would falter and crumble and the economy would be destroyed. The crisis would be complete, and under this enormous weight the people would call for change.

Barack Obama was at Columbia – he learned the lessons well on how to fundamentally transform the way this country operates – and he had the tools and the resources to put it all into action, along with the Soros plan for a Shadow Party. Everything that Obama did in his eight years in the Oval Office, every presidential action that he took, every law he had passed, every regulation he imposed, and every speech he made were each another step in his plan to transform America to a Marxist Socialist state.

The Obama presidency was in a state of total disorder. I can think of few presidents who have promised more, delivered less, or did more damage to the country. Certainly, we recognize that he inherited an economy that had been through a steep recession, but by the end of the mid-term of his second term in office his economy was being called the slowest recession recovery in the history of the U.S. There have been forty-seven such recessions in America since the Articles of Confederation and historians cannot cite one recovery worse or slower to return to a normal economic state of health than that of the 2007 recession.

The Obama answer to the recession was rising taxes, suffocating regulations resulting in loss of jobs, soaring domestic spending that produced some jobs but few that were more than part-time work, and an exceedingly avid growth in entitlements. All of these things further burdened the economy and the people creating a slowdown in growth, innovation, and the creation of new jobs. Their crisis seemed to be coming. By the first quarter of 2014 the economic numbers were so bad that the experts – Wall Street and financial planners – were wondering just how far this slow down economy could go before there was another recession.

The damage, destruction, and the devastation that was America during the Obama second term was not something that could be explained as simply as a coincidence that followed the backside of a recession. This was the leadership of Marxist Socialists taking advantage, once again, of a crisis to put their policies into place of a damaged nation. It was their opportunity to point their 'fickle finger of fate' at the previous administration as the cause of it all, and we are doing the best we can to clean up their mess. In the meantime, they would continue to deceive the American people with their lies that all was well, and the economy was flourishing. They were masters at 'cooking the books' so they could cite numbers that clearly showed progress where none existed.

It was ironic that the unemployment numbers, which would be a huge issue in the election cycle when reported by the Bureau of Labor Statistics (BLS), were a bit of a mystery. When the numbers were reported a month before term two of the presidential election for Barack Obama, nearly unprecedented employment growth was reported. After experts dug around it was found that the unemployment rate had dropped from 8.1% to 7.8%, a huge decline. However, the economy only added 114,000 new jobs. Research pointed out that for this much of an unemployment drop to take place we would have had to experience 873,000 new jobs for that period. Keep in mind that the BLS is a federal agency and reports directly to their boss, Barack Obama. And he knows that those good numbers on unemployment – at the time of a very tight election – would certainly make him look good. Cooking the books is an art form of the Socialist Democrats. Simply understood, cooking the books is an extension of another art form of the Socialist Democrats called lying, or is it like the means to an end? Whatever you call it, it is Marxist socialism at its best.

No president ever came into the Oval Office with a better opportunity to do some great things for this country than did Barack Obama. The country was wobbling in so many ways. We all well knew that the economy was bad. Millions of Americans were desperate and needed help; they needed a rebuilding of the confidence in themselves and in the government. Most of all, millions needed a rebuilding of their trust in a government that would make better decisions for the country. No president failed more completely than did Barack Obama in meeting the needs of his people at a most critical crossroad. Instead, this president launched his Cloward-Piven Strategy and his plan to fundamentally transform the country.

It was a purposeful attack against an already devastated economy. It was designed to take us down, to collapse the middle class who were already nothing more than the working poor. It was intended to wipe out small businesses that had become the walking wounded facing bankruptcy on a month-by-month basis.

There was little to no recovery for the millions who had been damaged by the loss of their homes. There was no rebuilding of confidence, and to be sure, there was no regaining of trust for a government that was failing to show good faith they were working for all of the people. Quite the contrary. The people were developing the mentality that their government was inept, not being accountable, and not assuming responsibility for their job. Americans were beginning to believe that the onus was on the people to take charge. The people would need to overcome the damage Obama had done to the country. It is time to make ready for battle. This is the stepping-stone attitude of the people that in 2016 returned the power of government back to the Republicans and Donald Trump.

Obama had failed to keep his promise on health care that 'you can keep your health care.' Instead, millions were forced to buy coverage, the funds of which were used to finance this unsound, unwise, and inept piece of garbage that was doing far more harm to the medical system than any good it may contrive. The promises of great, yearly family savings. Nothing. The promise that you can keep your doctor. Nothing. The promise that you can keep your insurance. Nothing. These lies to the people did not relieve the suffering, nor did they rebuild trust in the government.

What the people did see were the record numbers of people not working, the outrageous growth of homelessness, the higher and higher unemployment numbers, the closing of businesses, while millions were being spent on many projects used to foster the growth of socialism. T was the destruction of these people's integrity, sense of worth, and desire to take responsibility for their own success in the future.

Dr. Booker T. Washington once wrote, "Character is power," and, "Nothing ever comes to one, that is worth having, except as a result of his own hard work." Nothing can raise one's character like a feeling of dignity, and nothing can support one's dignity like a feeling of self-worth. Nothing gives one a feeling of power like a strong feeling of self-worth. Those with an open-mind have long known that what the government gives you as so-called free stuff is paid for in freedoms. This is but one more way that Obama broke the backs and the spirit of the people and divided the country by social class.

No man ever came into the presidency of the U.S. that was more divisive than Barack Obama. This is a man who presented himself well and is extremely well spoken. This is a man who people that were starving for help could rally around because they could feel comfortable that he would honestly, intelligently, and pointedly attack the problems of all the people, and we could build trust in his word and return that trust to our government.

I can remember so well, on the eve of the 2008 election, my wife and I were in our living room with my Mom and Dad discussing how we were going to vote. Mom and Dad had both, for most of the summer, been riding the fence between John McCain and Barack Obama. My wife and I, both Conservative Republicans, were leaning toward John McCain and Sarah Palin. We were living in Arizona, and both had a trust in his decision-making power and his vision of the future. We were confident that his make-up could get us through the recession and put America back on the track to prosperity. Obama had said a lot of things that I felt were counterproductive to regaining a strong economy. Most of what I was skeptical about had to do with the placement of money in Nanny projects that would have little to only temporary help. I liked Sarah Palin; I was raised in Alaska, and familiar with her work as governor, and I thought she would make a very good vice-president. I thought, as the first female vice-president, she would represent the women of the country well.

Mom was pushing ninety-one years of age and she announced that evening that she would support Barack Obama. She was a democrat, but not a strong one. She told us this, "I think he will help with the economy, and in his speeches, he talks a lot about race relations and division among the people. I think, being a Black man, I can trust that he will bring some unity between the people of the country." I couldn't argue with that, they were good points. Mom and Dad didn't have a whole lot left in their retirement; they were living in a small house at my ranch to save expenses and they lived quite frugally. So, the economic problem was not number one on their list of issues, but the people coming together as a nation was a very important issue.

Dad surprised me some when he confirmed that he would vote the same as Mom. He had been even more on the fence than Mom was, and since John McCain was a war hero, I fully expected him to throw his trust and support to McCain. Dad had been a war hero himself, as he had flown B-17's out of England, North Africa, and Italy during WWII and was very proud of his war effort. Yet, in the end he bought into the same ideas that had drawn Mom to the Obama vote.

I wasn't too happy that my vote was going to be cancelled, but this is what America is all about, and no one knew that more than my depression era surviving Mom and my WWII surviving Dad. He passed away in 2009 so he would never know he had bought into a narrative that never delivered. Mom died in 2015, but from the end of Obama's first term to her end she suffered from dementia and would never know that Obama did not only fulfill his promises of solidarity and unity among the races, but in fact, made things a hell-of-a-lot worse.

With regard to all of the ways division among Americans was made worse during the Obama years – racial, class, and political – there is a clear track record that from the start to the end of his administration there was considerably more division in America. Did he start it? No! Did he do anything to make it better? No! Did he make it worse? Yes! When I speak of the divide between groups then I am actually speaking of the tolerance for people's differences that exist. In the mind of this Conservative voice, the tolerance between political views is non-existent, between the social classes is intolerable, and between races and their views toward each other is as low as I have seen in my life time.

The level of intolerance has opened into full bloomed hate between some of the groups. At the federal level of Congress, hate overrides good sense and reality to the point that they are left against right, or right against left; incapable of working together to solve problems and serve the country with integrity and honor. To my way of thinking open mindedness does not, and cannot, exist in the minds of Socialist Communists in government. Open-mindedness tells us it is okay to disagree with the thoughts or opinions expressed by others. It means it doesn't give you the right to deny my position or opinion; nor does it give you the right to slander me or call me names such as racist just because you don't like what I am saying. I believe that a person who is open-minded and tolerant has learned to recognize good thoughts when they hear them even though they may be in conflict with their own thoughts. This requires one to overcome their own pride and open their mind beyond what is comfortable. Barack Obama never learned this and was always one of our most intolerant presidents.

In racial matters Barack Obama had no interest in healing what divide already existed between the Black Americans and White Americans. He had no interest in trying to reconcile the problems between Black and White America. He had no interest in bringing the Black and White Americans to a better place, or even a mutual coexistence; nor was he interested in that of other races. He could have had unity and solidarity among races had it been his agenda. But it was not. He was only interested in seeking revenge. To Obama, it is what it is; the Black man has been held back by the prejudiced and bigoted attitude and actions of the White man throughout our history. Now, it is time to make them pay, The White man brought us here, enslaved us and stole our dignity. Now, it is time to make them pay. This is a country that is oppressive to the Black man, destroyed our feeling of self-worth as a people. Now, it is time to make them pay.

As a candidate running for the presidency, Obama made clear his intentions if elected. He said, "We need to reckon with race and with America's original sin – slavery." He was always too quick to reacquaint with the past and bring its history to the forefront while maligning those who took part in the slavery issue; while at the same time letting Islam off the hook for their part in the Trans Sahara and East African slave trade. Certainly, slavery anywhere is a bad thing, but to allow an entire planet off the hook for trade practices – most of which were far worse than American involvement – is shortsighted and ignorant. So, it makes one wonder why America is singled out as the villain when even the Muslim slave trade was horrendous. Booker T. Washington has a quote that approaches the same question, "Not with-standing the cruelty and moral wrong of slavery, the ten million Negroes inhabiting this country, who themselves or whose ancestors went through the school of American slavery, are in a stronger and more hopeful condition, materially, intellectually, morally, and religiously, than is true of an equal number of Black people in any other portion of the globe." And he is right, any place you choose to look, the conditions and life was far more horrific than those living in, not just the Americas, but on the continent of North America that would become the U.S.

In the Muslim slave trade, most that were destined for the Muslim Middle East were for sexual exploitation as concubines, in harems, or military service. In the Trans Sahara and East African slave trade between 80% and 90% died in route. Most of the male slaves destined for the Middle East were castrated, and most of the children born to the women in slavery were killed at birth. An estimated eleven million Africans were transported across the Atlantic, of which 95% went to South and Central America, mainly to Portuguese, Spanish, and French possessions. Only 5% of them went to the U.S. However, at least twenty-eight million Africans were enslaved in the Muslim Middle East. As most died in transportation on the continent, it is believed that the death toll from the fourteen centuries of Muslim slave raids into Africa could have been over 112 million.

To continually revisit America's involvement in slavery, but to pay no attention to his beloved Muslims slavery activities is wrong. To chastise America as immoral while giving Islam a free ride, and to demand revenge for past deeds that indeed the entire world partook of while remaining silent to the fact that in the Muslim world today there is still slavery, is wrong, shortsighted, and intolerant. The Quran justifies slavery. "Prophet, we have made lawful for you the wives to whom you have granted dowries and the slave-girls whom God has given you as booty." (Quran 33:50).

Revenge was Obama's answer to racial issues, and the tactics that he used was to throw slavery back in the face of today's America. To repeatedly slap White America in the face with a constant reminder of how evil the White man has been in their treatment of Black Americans is, at best, a futile tactic. Nothing will be accomplished. How often have you witnessed a man change his attitude while being repeatedly slapped in the face? Sometimes? Seldom? Never? I have never met a man who would change his attitude about anything while constantly being beat up. Black Americans and Barack Obama, more than most, should understand this.

One thing you can be certain of is that the Republican Party is unified that Barack Obama was the most divisive president of our time. In 2012 Marco Rubio said, "We have not seen such a divisive figure in modern American history." During the next four years of the Obama administration Rubio did not change his mind, but instead in 2016 confirmed that he still maintained that Obama was among our most divisive presidents. Senator Ted Cruz complained after one of Obama's State of the Union addresses that "He lectures us on civility yet has been one of the most divisive presidents in American history." Another Republican Congressman, when interviewed said, "There probably has not been a more racially-divisive, economic-divisive president in the White House since we had presidents who supported slavery." And I say, "There has never been such a racially motivated president in the Oval Office since the time of the slavery Democrats of the Civil War era." I guarantee that you will not find very many Republicans who will disagree with these statements.

In one of Barack Obama's last State of the Union addresses he stated, "It's one of the few regrets of my Presidency that the rancor and suspicion between the parties has gotten worse instead of better. I have no doubt a president with the gifts of Lincoln or Roosevelt might have better bridged the divide." I am certain that on this point he is correct. The difference being that those presidents, and many others, both Republican and Democrat, would have entered the office with a better agenda than did Barack Obama. They would not have been professing to tear down a country that those who came before had just built. They would not have entered the White House with malice and revenge as their shining star. They would not have entered the Oval Office with a hatred of the White Americans who had founded this land. They would not have even run for the office of President of the United States unless they had reverence for the nation in their heart and soul. So, to this Obama conclusion that others could better have bridged the divide, I have to say, "Right on brother."

Nothing speaks to the Obama mentality more than his remarks made to the Congressional Black Caucus just before the 2016 election. Trying to push support behind Hillary Clinton, who he had been stumping for during the entire election cycle he encouraged the African-American community to vote for her by saying, "I will consider it a personal insult – an insult to my legacy – if this community lets down its guard and fails to activate itself in this election." He felt that much of his legacy was tied to his accomplishments with the African-Americans. In this case he is saying that he feels his legacy was one of success and that his legacy of success and accomplishment must be preserved. At the time he made these comments they were met with much scrutiny by both the Republicans and the public. The public sees his legacy much the way we described it as the creation of division for the country, concluding with far worse relations than before he arrived in the White House. Obviously, his view was decidedly different, which tells me he is either blind, or accomplished exactly what he intended. This Conservative voice is convinced that the latter is the truth.

OBAMA'S DIVIDE AND RULE

Divide and Rule – is the Obama goal,
To weaken the Nation and seize control,
Race against Race – Creed against Creed,
Brother against Brother, Father against Son
Divided now he must defeat just one.
Suspicion and Hate – Planting the Seed,
Using the Schools – To brainwash and confuse,
Our Freedoms and Rights - Obama will flaunt and abuse,
Creating the Lie – Twisting the Truth,
Grim tailored Bigotry – Aimed at our Youth,
Aimed at the public – Subtly spread,
Into Frustration – So subtly lead,
Grave is our Danger – From forces within,
God help this Nation if Obama should win,
If as a people we fail to Unite,
We'll feel the Cruel Heel of socialisms might.
He learned his lessons well,
Divide this country and drive it to hell.
The Obama goal for all – To divide this nation,
To beat him at his game – We must rely on Education.

Chapter 13

Deceit: It Is Who They Are

I think it is fair to say when your guidelines to gaining what you want are based on hook or crook tactics, and you use deception to gain your results, you are likely a deceitful person. If this is true of your entire political party, then your party is one of deceitful means. If your leaders thrive by means of twisting the truth, using inappropriate innuendos, half-truths, and entirely false statements and narratives to make their point, then they are likely deceitful leaders and can care less about truth in any form.

We can define the leadership of the Socialist Democrat Party as being deceitful with actions that are based in deception, and statements designed to mislead and hide the truth in order to promote their beliefs, concepts, and ideas that are not true. They are the worst of deceptive people because mostly they do it for no other reason than personal gain, or to create an advantage. Their deception involves the use of propaganda, behind-the-back and underhanded forms of distraction, camouflage, and concealment. Socialist Democrats never tell the truth because they have learned that the truth will never sell their product. The intelligent and informed will see through their deceit, while the less intelligent and ill-informed cannot see through the propaganda and are too hapless to resist a free lunch.

There is no doubt in my mind that what all of the Socialist Democrat leaders today want is what Barack Obama wanted. What Hillary Clinton planned on doing was, and is, all the same thing, "To make America a Socialist nation by eliminating our constitutional

Republic." They all play a major role in the deceitful practices of the Socialist Democrat Party.

This group of wealthy, arrogant, and underhanded politicians uses their power to bring about a political coup in our government. For no other reason than they hate President Trump because they are embarrassed they were rejected when they believe they should have won, they have colluded to bring this president down. By a massive undertaking of deceit and underhanded tactics, the Socialist Democrats colluded to circumvent the Constitution of the U.S. to change the outcome of the 2016 election of President Trump. They colluded in the House and the Senate to collectively obstruct any, and all, measures by the president, rather than work together with the Republicans to carry out some productive legislation for the good of the nation. For the first three years of his term in office President Trump worked tirelessly to put America back on a non-Socialist track, while the Socialist Democrats failed to support a single measure of his efforts.

Their attempt, as a last-ditch effort, to impeach the president was the most outrageously, disgusting, and collectively inept attempt at governing I have ever seen. They have clearly shown and proven to all they are incredibly inept, so mindless, intolerant, and bigoted by their hate for the president that they cannot work within the framework of reality to govern effectively.

Their obstruction had nothing to do with illegal immigration or phony tears while children were being ripped from their mother's arms and thrown into a cage in a dungeon. It had nothing to do with health insurance for the poor, nothing to do with discrimination, and the fact the president was a racist, homophobic, or Islamophobic. It had nothing to do with what he did, 'bad guy that he is,' or what he said; Lord knows, they have said and done far worse. It was all about hating President Trump for personal political reasons that they simply were not grown up enough to move beyond.

In the mind of this Conservative voice, the Socialist Democrats are just simply people with low character levels who possess a set of principles that even the most illiterate of third world countries would find offensive.

The anti-Trump demonstrations follow a pattern that we have seen over and over. Supported by Obama and Hillary, carried out under the supervision of Al Sharpton, funded by George Soros, and followed with dancing in the streets by Socialist Democrats in our own government, they are an abomination of where their mentality lies. From the protests of Occupy Wall Street to Black Lives Matter, to Dream Act/Open Borders, and all of the others, it is all the same on a different stage; the same old song and dance to the same old tune. It is not only the same tactics over and over again, but the same groups and individuals answering the call to take action on their free government cell phones. The same people – masked to hide their deceit and criminal behavior – spontaneously breaking out into mayhem, chaos, and, anarchy in the streets of our cities and all government supported.

It is never about what was done, but about what those anarchists and their demented leaders in our government want to accomplish. And what they want to accomplish is not for your benefit, but for theirs. They want to push their Socialist agenda down your throat no differently than they pushed Obama care in the same way, by deceit and behind-the-back government.

Over and over again these people who want to be your government keep using one crisis after another to continually cause mayhem while convincing you there is so much chaos around that you really need the Socialist Democrats in power. They want you to think that even though they are the creators of the chaos, it is they who are the only ones who can stop it. Were the Not My President rioters who illegally blocked streets and freeways, or set fires by throwing Molotov cocktails injuring police officers, destroying private and business properties, and defacing public buildings with graffiti day after day following the November 8th election, merely Soros rent-a-Dems? Could be! I can tell you for a fact that they were not Republicans.

These people are law breakers, supported by the Socialist Democrats. Have you ever noticed that the Socialist Democrats never take a stand against these rioters? Some of these people travel across state lines to riot and break federal law, but they don't care because as good socialists they have no concern for Rule of Law. They don't care about your protection or safety. They only care about doing what their Socialist leaders tell them to do, because they are, after all, only the Socialist leaders, the useful idiots. They are trained to do what they are told without regard for the consequences.

To this Conservative voice, it is past time to follow the money. These acts of criminal and destructive behavior have occurred far too often and need to be stopped. They are negative, destructive, and they don't solve problems. They do not change attitudes. These people are what I call the downward pull against our Democratic Republic. Everyone that believes in our democracy needs to wage an intense, lifelong battle against the constant downward pull of the moron fringe that works against our values and principles. They are like weeds in a garden, and if you relax and let down, those weeds will take over your garden. When that happens, you will have lost all that is of value to you and your life.

We need to use the legal system to find and stop the flow of funding to these anarchists. Stop the bussing companies from transporting these people to their riot locations; and find out, with an audit, who provides the funds for this transportation. That Shadow Group should be stopped. These providers need to be held accountable and responsible for supporting these criminal acts. Their financial records should be subpoenaed and charged with organized crime related offenses. It is futile to go after and prosecute the rioters because the funders will pay the fines and the rioters will be back to work with the next free cell call. These rioters don't have the money or the means to carry out these strategic activities. Stop their money flow and they are dead in the water.

Barack Obama, as we have already alluded to, along with George Soros tried their damnedest to bankrupt this country. Between the Marxist Communist mentality of Obama and the greed and financial evil of George Soros, they have done all they could to bring this country to its knees from within. Their war between capitalism and Marxist Socialist communism is not over. Karl Marx said, "The last Capitalist that we hang shall be the one that sold us the rope." We haven't gotten to that last piece of rope yet; but I do believe this shows that Karl Marx, Saul Alinsky, and those they mentored through their writings – such as Obama and Hillary Clinton – were dead serious about putting an end to capitalism in America and replacing it with Marxism.

Obama made a direct quote from the Communist Manifesto in one of his speeches. He said, "The inherent vice of capitalism is the unique distribution of wealth." How absurdly ignorant is that? To this Capitalist, the inherent vice of communism is the unique distribution of wealth in just the elitists. Karl Marx believed, Alinsky believed, Bill Ayres believes, Barack Obama believes, and Hillary Clinton believes that the wealth in America must be redistributed and thus are driven to passing laws that will legislate the poor into prosperity while legislating the wealthy out of prosperity. A fool's plan by fools.

The people have to be actors; we cannot rely on the current system of government to take the appropriate actions to save our constitution in order for this country to keep what we have. We must not be the last Capitalist to hang; we must instead make the Socialists 'feel the burn' that capitalism is here to stay. The ranks of the Socialist states will be dead and turned to dust, yet capitalism will remain and continue to flourish for all Americans who want to take advantage of what free enterprise has to offer.

I will never forget a quote from my economics professor at Oregon State College. I have no idea who he quoted, or if it was of his own thoughts, but this is what he said, "Success in America is nothing more than a few simple disciplines, practiced every day; while failure is simply a few errors in judgment, repeated every day." I understood it then and I understand it today. Success is the accumulative weight of our disciplines and our judgments that leads each of us to either find our fortune or experience our failure. Personally, I find it fascinating that most people plan their vacations with better care than they do their lives.

Most young people need to learn not to be sucked into philosophies that offer no future, and they need to take more responsibility for practicing their own simple disciplines for success. Learning the simple disciplines for success is not the easiest of skills, in fact, it is far more difficult than allowing yourself to simply be the mushroom in the garden of the Socialist Democrats allowing them to keep you in the dark and feed you BS. I can tell you for certain that hard work, honesty, forbearance, and tolerance will do more positive good for a man than leaning on the words of a false prophet.

America's constitution is the basis for our liberties, and this is the reason that the Socialist Democrats want to destroy it. Our constitution clearly defines the limits of government power, but Socialists do not want there to be limits to their control and power. Our constitution definitely defines the rights of each American citizen, but the Socialist Democrats are not interested in the citizens having rights at the expense of Socialist control.

Make no mistake about it; the destruction of America began when the elected representatives and government agencies (IRS, FBI, CIA, EPA) began to act illegally in defiance of the Constitution. When the Socialists, elected by the people, gained control of the Democratic Party and began the process of transforming America and weaponizing the agencies of government, marks the beginning of the destruction this country. When these people (Socialists) began to refuse to enforce existing, duly passed laws while imposing their own unconstitutional laws, the war had begun. Donald Trump is the legally elected president, yet – though he did nothing impeachable – these Socialists in the Democrat Party who make it up as they go along took it upon themselves to impeach. The vile action of this group was out to nullify the voice of the people. As Jerry Nadler said, "The people cannot be trusted in the election to get rid of this president." What this Socialist is saying is that you, the voters, cannot be trusted to carry out his agenda to get this president out of office. Just another example of the Socialist Democrats all superior belief that they have the answers and your judgment does not matter.

This is as clear as it gets with these radicals. What is important to them is themselves. You, as a citizen with your political views, have no credibility, no trust, and no value in the decision making process in this country.

Living in denial by erroneously believing that America's destruction is not happening, and is not possible, is the recipe for disaster. Always remember that the Socialist Democrats trust that we will not stop them, that we are too blind to what they are doing, that we are too apathetic, and that they are superior in thought and on the side of right, which is the side of Marxist Socialist communism. Understand this: "The great civilizations of our history that eventually crumbled, never gave thought that their civilization would not last forever. And always remember, that none of those great civilizations ever returned to the form of their greatness.

The Socialists rant that they are the champions of the middle class. But keep in mind that there are only two classes of people in socialism: The elitists and the poor. Only the wealthy and rich business leaders own property. The poor don't own property; the job of the poor is to produce and share. You don't become wealthy by producing for the government when they don't even trust you to share what you produce. They will take and share what you produce. There is no middle class in this system. Every single one of the Socialist Democrat Leaders is an elitist, the Hollywood and entertainment crowd are elitists. They will remain what they are because they will foot the bill for all of the Socialist projects. This is why Barack Obama worked so hard and secretly to bring them to Marxism.

Obama well knew that the 'Fantasywood' crowd didn't have much under their hat, and would not be able to tell the difference between a wealthy Nanny state and a fully bloomed Marxist state that owned all of the means of production, including them. You need a little more under your hat than just hair to understand the folly of Marxist Socialist communism. In my conservative way of thinking, I find it amazing that people like our Hollywood friends can justify a political process that is responsible for the deaths of millions to put themselves in power, yet go completely bananas if a sicko takes a gun and murders a group of people. Any support of an immoral system of government like Marxism, for any reason, is ignominious and shameful.

Have you ever noticed that the voice of the moderate Democrat is strangely silent these days? Can you even name a moderate Democrat in either the Senate, or the House of Representatives? No, you can't. That's because they have no voice today. To the Socialist Democrat, the moderate Democrat is the same as any Republican, or certainly a Conservative Republican; they don't want to hear from them. Moderates have no credibility in a Marxist Socialist controlled politic. They are silenced with the same intolerance that the radicals try to silence everyone else.

Have you noticed who else has been eliminated from this Socialist plan? You and me. We are certainly not in their elite, so we must be the workers of the poor. Can you imagine, we are of the poor class, but even dumbbell Maxine Watters is an elitist. Robert de Niro is an elitist. Good Lord, even dumber of the 'dumber and dumbest' is an elitist. Go figure! And by the way, how in holy hell did Maxine Watters afford a $3 million mansion on a $170,000 annual salary? Well, why not, the majority of the members of Congress are, in fact, millionaires.

So, here's Socialist Barack Obama as president in 2008 with a salary of $400,000 per year, has maybe a net worth of $1.3 million, but maybe not quite. So, fast forward to 2015, just a year before his second term as president ended in 2016 and his disclosures show a net worth of $2-$7 million. In 2018, just two years after his Presidency, Barack Obama's net worth jumped to $40 million. This is pretty good for a single income family over the past twelve years. In 2017 the Obama's bought a mansion in Washington D.C. for $8.1 million that was big enough to house their entire shadow government. But then, after just three years of building their equity, they bought the beach property at Martha's Vineyard in 2019 for $14.8. Now I have to tell you that this is doing well for an old couple, one of whom is on government pension and the other which has no pension and a houseful of shadow writers.

Hillary and Bill Clinton were amazing in their ability to accumulate wealth after leaving the White House. Bill, himself said they he was one of the lowest presidents in personal net worth on becoming president. Apparently, their finances were so bad that Hillary stole White House silverware, furniture, and antiques when they left. When this became apparent, she returned the booty, explaining that it was nothing more than a mix up. After they moved, they purchased a $2.85 million home not far from the White House, which was a pretty good purchase of a couple more than $1 million in legal debt from the Lewinsky affair, and a net worth of practically nothing. Hillary proclaimed upon leaving the White House that they were flat broke. But fortunately for them Bill Clinton established the Clinton Foundation in 1998 and just like that, over the next fifteen years through their foundation and a nicely conceived pay to play scheme, they were able to earn $230 million before taxes.

During this fifteen year period Bill Clinton made the bulk of their income, earning about 80% through speaking engagements, writing, and consulting. Hillary earned the rest in writing and speaking, plus her salary as Secretary of State. In my opinion, you can bet that their non-profit Clinton Foundation played a significant role in their financial recovery. There have been numerous cases cited concerning the foundation being involved in a pay-to-play scheme while Hillary was Secretary of State for Barack Obama.

This foundation has a net worth of about $109 million. Its investments returned just $2.9 million in 2015, however from donations it has raised over $2 billion over its life-time. Foreign governments found the foundation very attractive because of their access and influence with American policymakers. In other words, they were quite confident that a sizable donation would give them access in the State Department. For this reason, the foundation records show that they received large gifts of more than $25 million by seven different sources, and another nineteen entities worth $10-$25 million.

When any foundation has an insatiable appetite for donations, one has to question the possibility of unsavory motivation on the part of the donors. Many critics point to the fact that the multi-million dollar donations have slowed measurably since Hillary Clinton failed in her presidential run. They are quick to suggest that the pay-to-play is no longer inviting and gives the foreign countries little reason to keep their donations flowing.

These Socialist Democrats ooze with deceit in order to achieve their ends, and they seldom miss an opportunity to take advantage of the world they live in. Plato wrote a script at one time that I'd like to think applies to the deceitful manner in which the Socialist Democrats operate. It would seem that even Plato observed their mentality way back when.

He wrote, "There are three classes of men; lovers of wisdom, lovers of honor, and lovers of gain." Men (or politicians) who are lovers of wisdom are those who will spend their entire careers seeking knowledge, gaining productive experiences, and making sound and unbiased judgments. They are, in the field of politics, the handful that others will turn to for sound advice. Those who are the lovers of honor spend their careers conducting themselves in such a manner that they naturally receive high respect, praise, and great overwhelming esteem. They have a great adherence to what is right and always try to follow the path of right vs wrong. These are people gifted with great homage, reverence, and integrity.

Lovers of gain will spend their entire lives seeking to fulfill themselves with valuable and desirable personal wealth and power. They are not the people interested in wisdom and honor but are solely motivated by what brings wealth, notoriety, possessions, and power. They are full of statements with great moral content that have been used too often to be thoughtful in nature or supportive of others less fortunate but, in reality, they are only platitudes, and are meaningless, trite, and worse than even a bad cliché. These are the people of the Socialist Democrats who love to talk the talk, but seldom walk the walk. So, the question becomes when was the last time you saw Hillary Clinton display wisdom or honor? Or, for that matter, when in the past fifteen to twenty years have you seen any these qualities in a Socialist Democrat? Deceit does not live in the house with wisdom; deceit does not live side by side with the man of honor. Deceit is the way to gain by the Socialist Democrats.

It should not be that there is a lack of honorable men and women in our government. It should not be that there are few men and women in our government who lack the wisdom to lead by unbiased judgments. It should not be that our government is overloaded with men and women who are driven by their personal ambitions for gain and fame than they are for love of country. It should not be that in our government reverence is lost to the sin of hate. It should not be in our government that wealth motivates choices and decisions. It should not be that there are so few in our government that can offer sound, and sane advice. It should not be in our government that so few have a firm moral compass that recognizes their accountability to the morality of man's life. It should not be in our government that there are so few men and women who actually have the visionary power to understand the impact of their choices and decisions on our future. It should not be that our government is flowing with men and women who believe that Marxist Socialist communism is the way to the good life. It should not be that in our government so many men and women use the tactic of deceit to control the people where simple wisdom could do a better job.

And finally, at this point, what is wrong with a little truth? Why must those in our government be guided by desire, emotion, and their interpretation of what knowledge they have? Why not truth? It is too far-fetched to believe that truth is among the most honorable of all practices. Plato said, "The love of truth can arouse man to the creation of great ideas." With truth in our government, we can wipe out the idea of deceit in a day. Yet, falsehood is in our government more today than ever before, and the power of its evil nature somehow, even though all good men understand it, forces truth to sit and wait. It should not be that in our government the men and women rely on falsehood at the expense of truth. Plato also said, "Along with goodness, truth is the highest principle in life." Why should we not insist that our elected representatives, men and women in our government, adhere to the highest principle in life? A better question is, "Why do men and women run for offices in our government who do not adhere to the highest principle in life? Truth.

A WEB OF DECEIT

How is your government run these days?
Deceit is their game,
A congress that is run this way,
Could not stand without blame,
The men we elect to these offices,
We find to be dishonorable and insincere,
They seem to be lost, and oblivious,
In this unworthy atmosphere.

Behind the pageant we daily view,
Those thought to be gallant men, brave and true,
In the Senate and Lower House,
Men who are not true to you,
A fact that is concealed in deceit,
Lies there, hidden by those who would cheat,
These are men who we would least suspect,
Who manipulate and our values disconnect.

There are those favored 'shadow' groups,
In charge of this and that,
Who answer to know one at all,
Each one a Sociocrat,
Then there are those with special interest,
With their deep pockets lying in wait,
And those subtle foreign agencies,
Plotting, deceiving, and infiltrating.

In fourteen score and four years we proudly find,
Some have made America great again,
Yet still a very troubled land,
With a grim and uncertain fate,
For there are Socialists to be watched,
Lest we slip within their grip,
For they have one clear goal in mind,
A total Socialist Dictatorship.

Chapter 14
Bipartisanism Closed: Gone Fishing

When half of your legislators are Socialists and the other half are Capitalists you can be certain that bipartisan lawmaking is at a stand-still. There is little possibility that the GOP and the Socialist Democrats can consistently cooperate to reach agreements in passing laws of national importance. Political parties, by their very nature, are filled with strong point of views that border on bias and intolerance. But when the combatants are of polar opposites, as with the Capitalists vs Marxist Socialists, political and national progress will come to a screeching halt.

When half of your government feels that they do not have to listen to the arguments of the other voices of government, and the other half of the government sees no way to penetrate the views of the other party, all bipartisan legislation becomes stagnant and forever divided beyond repair. For about 232 years our lawmakers avoided the division, and with only rare instances could not conduct business with a mutual respect for the views of each other. Anytime a radicalized voice enters the equation, bipartisan government struggles to find a way to cooperate and be effective. If you have a radicalized set of views on either or both sides of the argument the issue becomes lost in mayhem, chaos, blame, and loss of accountability.

So, when legislators can no longer work constructively together, where does their focus go? It certainly is not directed at the people they govern; it would seem to me that all this misplaced energy is directed inward to themselves. More than anything else they become focused on the protection of their own ego. Far too often what

I see in Socialist Democrats is the spending of their efforts endlessly creating ways to protect their own image from damage. For some there is a striking out in revenge for what they perceived as damage to them. Unfortunately, while distracted, they neglect the laws – they neglect the people and they seem to believe that no harm will come from their neglect – or it must be the work of others to look after the business of making laws. At any rate, little gets accomplished and clearly, when this selfish attitude is entertained by all who are supposed to look after the government, you are witnessing the decay of the nation. And the people we are speaking of simply don't care because they are too busy protecting themselves and building their own power structure.

We know that in our legislators it is their desires that dictate what priorities they have. If the desire of one party is to create a government of socialism and the other party has the desire to maintain a solid base for capitalism there is a fundamental division between the two sides of government. We also know that the priorities they establish, the things that matter most to Socialists, will be quite different from the priorities of the other party who is committed to capitalism. One will prioritize government control and the other will prioritize freedom of the people while the division becomes wider and more helpless.

We also know that those priorities will shape the choices they make to see that their sacred desires are met. Legislators who are Socialist in nature will foster bills that help create big government so they can have a foundation for strong government control and that will minimize government accountability. The choices of the capitalist voice will try to create laws that provide greater opportunity for the common people, or middle class, to play a greater role in the free enterprise system, and the division becomes wider and more hapless.

Other choices that create the division between politicians and their unique desires are pro-life vs all abortion at any time and at government (taxpayer) expense. Keep in mind the government can't give anyone anything that they don't take from somebody else. Lower taxes to help the people in pocket vs raised taxes to pay for their Nanny projects, or sovereignty of our nation through protected borders vs open borders with no restrictions and no clearances. This is a major difference between the parties and one that becomes more divisive all the time. And it is unique because less than twenty years ago all the leaders of today's 2020 Socialist Democrat Party spoke out opposite of their policy on the borders today. Today they call for unlimited access to the borders, while at the turn of the century these same people were screaming for tougher border safety, including a border wall. It is amazing how the face and voice of the party has changed in such a short span of time.

The Socialist Democrats want to take away your guns and suppress your free speech. There are many today within the leadership of the party that would go so far as abolishing the first and second amendments to our Constitution that protects these freedoms. The GOP will have nothing to do with these acts, and, in fact, support strengthening both the first and second amendments.

Other extreme choices that are causing divisiveness between the parties are GOP, strengthening the military to ensure peace through strength, and supporting the protection of religious liberty as opposed to the left who calls for greater restrictions on Christians because they interfere with other religious groups. Whereas the Republicans are going all out under President Trump in education, calling for smaller classrooms, better teacher pay, and more money filtered into the classroom, the Socialists are not participating in educational improvements. They are more concerned, and all in, for reparations for slavery, and the removal of the Electoral College. And finally, the Socialist Democrats are spending millions on the defense of illegal aliens and creating city and state sanctuaries in defiance of Rule of Law.

These political differences are huge and each is, unto itself, a major split between the parties. Collectively they are the divisiveness that creates a toxic legislative process in America at all levels of government. When these policy differences occur in normal political settings they can often be met and dealt with in a cooperative bipartisan manner. But, as we have already noted, when you put the radicalized efforts of socialism into the mix the process becomes even more toxic, unbearable, and dysfunctional.

The actions of these choices that the Socialist Democrats take generally seem to throw even more fuel on the already blazing divisiveness. I have already spoken at length of the underhanded and behind-the-back tactics (actions) this party takes to meet their desires. It is only left to say that their actions are fully in line with the historical practices of Marxist Socialist Communist choices, priorities, and desires. Throughout the history of Joseph Stalin's take-over of the Soviet Union, and Mao's gaining of power in the Communist Republic of China, we have seen the deceit, underhanded, and behind-the-back – and I might add – murderous actions of Socialist communism.

The Socialist Democrat Party of the United States is, today, a clear-cut party of Socialists, with only a small voice from the moderate Democrats with none from the moderate Democrats of old. Today, between the House and the Senate, the Democrats hold 280 seats out of the total of 534. They hold 235 seats in the House and forty-five seats in the Senate. Of the total of 280 there are upwards of 100 plus that are, in fact, Socialists or one of several other Socialist or

Communist affiliations. None of these people are Democrats in any way, shape or form. These are people who have had long time involvement and close association with the Communist Party of America. There may be as many as twenty-two members of Congress today that have direct association with the Communist party, or are active with affiliates of the party. In the Democratic Socialist Party of America (DSPA), as many as twenty members of Congress have long term associations with the DSPA, or with other close affiliates. There are more, but these numbers represent those with the strongest ties and are the most active in the Socialist Democrat Party today.

The numbers of Socialist Communists in government are between ninety to over one hundred; they do not represent a majority of the party in either the House or the Senate. But considering their tactics to close down the voices of opposition, the moderate voices within their party are the voices of opposition to Socialists and Communists. It is a sad and dangerous case for all Americans. They don't want bipartisanship, they don't want cooperation, and they don't want other voices to be heard even within their party. This political minority of the Socialist Democrat Party has emotionally, mentally, and tactically taken over the Democrat Party and has no intentions of giving it back or sharing the wealth.

For the past thirty years the Democrat Party has been declining in numbers. Prior to that time, during the period of 1932-1994, the Democrat Party was strong, and for the clear majority of the election cycles they dominated either the Senate or the House, oftentimes both. That was a time when the Democrats could communicate a clear, strong, and powerful message to both their party and the citizens. They stood proudly for worker's rights, civil rights, abortion rights, and for social programs that promised to help the poor, as well as for equality in public schools. These policies were concise, consistent, and historically tested.

While these Democrats were clear in what they supported, they were also clear and strongly opposed to what was, in their mind, any infringement of individual's rights, the death penalty, and tax cuts that generally benefited the wealthy. These Democrats were Liberal and Progressive and working for the average Americans from the middle class to the poor.

From this early period forward (1980's-2000) the strength of the Democrat Party began to dwindle. Socialism and communism began to infiltrate the party and great changes lay just ahead. With more and more Socialist Communists in the party, with loud and undeniable voices, the message of the Democrats became less clearly defined. The party, by the 2000 election, was far more diverse than at any time prior in their history. Their views were beginning to develop a much wider range and it was becoming more difficult with each election cycle, after 2000, to narrow down their views to a clear understanding within the party as to just exactly who they were and what they stood for.

Once the movement began and they were under assault and being overrun by the more aggressive Socialists and Communists, it took little time for the moderate voice of the party to be silenced. They were not even Liberals anymore, nor were they Progressives. They had become, by the time of Obama, a party of social justice featuring such things as political correctness, big government (which was about to explode), and they stood for heavy taxation and spending to finance to huge and bizarre social welfare programs. The most obvious Socialist change was in the area of national debt. For centuries closely guarded, it was now becoming a road race destined to collide with an unsustainable level that could bankrupt the country.

The GOP could easily see what was happening, but mostly remained quiet as though they didn't want to rock this nasty boat. They could smell the blood but were clearly uncertain about how to work against it. The Cold War against the Soviet Union was only recently over and many were resting on their laurels – they didn't have to worry about communism anymore. Communism seems to be that ugly critter that just keeps getting beaten down but continues to raise its ugly head over and over again, never going away. The entire second half of the 20th century we fought against the ugliness of communism in the Korean War and again in the Vietnam War followed by that long and engaging Cold War. Yet, here they are again in all of the glory of their ugliness operating within the walls of our government.

The GOP called them a party of no real-world ideas who were living in the same fantasy world as their Hollywood friends. They gave them labels of Liberal Democrats, Hollywood kooks, and elitists. The GOP considered them to be fiscally exploitive and inept and were nothing more than do-gooders out to line their own pockets with the money of those who claimed they were in it to help. It is clear in the mind of this Conservative voice that the Socialist Democrats had no idea of who they were, or how to carry out a fiscally viable agenda. They have become today a party of 'mis-identity,' of dysfunctional desires, weak and nondescript priorities, making the same old bad choices carried out by the same old actions of behind-the-back and underhanded tactics.

Where have all the moderates gone? William Bennett, Secretary of Education from 1985-1988, wrote an article on this same subject in 2011. It was clearly recognizable to him what was happening within the Democrat Party back then. This was just two years into the Barack Obama presidency. Secretary Bennett pointed out three things that happened in the party that marked the end of the moderate voice. He said that three moderates, Joe Leiberman, Jim Webb, and Jane Harman all decided to retire at this time (2011). Three moderate voices out, and it is highly probable that those voices would not be coming back.

Secretary Bennett also pointed out that the House Blue Dog Democrats had drawn down from fifty-four members in the previous year to just twenty-five members by 2012. The Blue Dog Coalition (Caucus) was a strong fiscally conservative centrist part of the party, and this current trend clearly shows that their moderate value to the party was ending rapidly. As of the 116th Congress there are just twenty-five members remaining in the Blue Dog Caucus. There is a good probability that in the next Congress, after 2020 there will be fewer still. You can be assured that the Shadow Party groups are working overtime to find and back more candidates that can replace the remaining voices of the Blue Dogs.

The third point William Bennett cites that the end is coming was the information that the funding for the Democratic Leadership Council had dried up and would be closing their doors. This council was formed in 1985 and upon its foundation argued that the U.S. Democratic Party should shift away from the 'Left turn' it had taken in the late 1960s-1980s. One of their main purposes was to win back the White middle class voters by fostering ideas that more expressly addressed their concerns. Their decision to suspend operations in 2011 marks the conclusion of a long descent from its peak period of the Clinton era, with which they had very strong ties. It should be noted that the Liberal critics (Socialists) were already 'dancing on their grave.'

It was said at the time the closure was clear evidence that the Progressives (Socialists) of the party were winning the battle for control over the party policies. This demise of the DLC was seen by the Progressive Socialists as a rejection of all they despise of the moderate voice. A penchant towards compromise, which they openly reject, a lack of principle and a willingness on the part of the DLC to sell out the poor and the African-Americans voters who the Progressives see as the base of their party. Also, they were forcing out the old DLC views of pushing for a balanced budget, tough-on-crime policies, and welfare reform that were not in the plans of the progressive socialists.

It would be up to Obama to put the knock-out blow to the moderates in the party. With more moderates retiring, and others routinely being defeated at the polls by more aggressive, Progressive Socialists, it is no surprise that a clear pathway to the control of the Democratic Party by the Socialist mentality and agenda came as soundly as it has. Obama, trying his best to sound moderate but tactically Progressive, seemed to be trying to appease both elements of the party. But no one doubts the Socialist conviction that he pushed through his policies, executive orders, and regulations on the people and businesses.

So, the Blue Dogs have gone along with most of the other moderates and old school voices from earlier times. However, I think it is fair to say that their voices will be missed very much. This Conservative voice misses them even more than do the Socialists of the Democrat Party, because I miss the ability of the legislative process to debate, to cooperate, to compromise, and to arrive at peaceful and respectful laws that are bipartisan and constructive for the progress of this great country. The moderate value which allowed this to happen is silenced, perhaps forever, by a loud-mouthed, boisterous, and destructive voice that believes in none of the moderate ideas.

The Socialist Democrat Party has lost something else that will place more nails in the coffin of the Democrat Party and this is an ability to communicate their views in a rational, sound, and realistic manner. I would predict that if the Socialist Democrats do not learn how to talk with people rather than at people, and learn to play well with others, and even more importantly, if they do not learn to communicate their passion with tolerance and communicate fairness in that it is okay to disagree with the thoughts or opinions expressed by others. Equally, to understand that just because you disagree does not give you the right to deny others the right to express themselves. If they cannot learn these things they will be on the outside looking in. Without these things there is no voice of reason left in the party and there will never be a return to the Democratic principles and values of the party.

"Today you are king, tomorrow a pauper." People, groups, and parties with greater principles and character than that of Socialists have failed to hold their grip on the wealth and power that they fight so hard to achieve. More often than not their failure came from a much unexpected source. Booker T. Washington said, "I learned the lesson that great men cultivate love and that only little men cherish a spirit of hatred." Hatred is the emotion of a disturbed mind, and it is the focal point of the emotion of socialism. They not only hate capitalism, they hate everything about capitalism and everything that is surrounded by it including the people who live beneath its umbrella. That is the mentality of Lenin and Mao that led them to slaughter their own people. It is the mentality of Barack Obama that led him to the Oval Office just to transform it.

It always requires greater adjustments to remain at the top than was required to climb to the top. The restrictive mentality of hate does not allow one to make adjustments effectively. My personal belief is that Marxist Socialist communism has built within its very foundation the fatal flaw of hate that does not allow them to adjust to remain strong. Marxist Socialist communism is the culture of little men.

THE SOCIALIST DEMOCRATS HAVE LOST THEIR WAY

The Socialists have lost their way----
They silence the voice of reason, so it seems.
Their chance to glorify the people's place----
Is ending in a dirge of their own disgrace.
This nation that has been a paradise----
Is now corrupt, and the people will pay the price.

Just how great the sum, how vast the score----
God help us if these Socialists take us to civil war.
If this would be the road that they choose----
All life within this troubled country will lose.
And all the hopes and prayers that have been said----
Will die, and be buried with the dead.

Now the leaders of this country must decide----
Will it be peace, or will it be national suicide.
Now at the crossroads the combatants stand----
The future for us rests in these Socialists hands.
So, now at the mercy of these tyrant's whims----
We all stand balanced on a cauldron's rim.

Deep in our hearts, we feel the shame----
And we are certain to share the blame.
We have seen the havoc they have wrought----
Is our great promise all for naught?
Full our splendor would be, if we could turn the tide----
To stop the tyrants who we cannot abide.

Chapter 15
Bernie Sanders: Socialist Democrat

We cannot talk about the growth of socialism in our government in the year of the 2020 election without calling out Bernie Sanders and dealing with his impact on that growth. Senator Sanders is in his thirtieth year in Congress, having served sixteen years in the House of Representatives and is in his fourteenth year in the Senate. He is like a lone pup in a house full of barking dogs. As an Independent, though caucusing with the Democrats, he has managed to find a way to serve as a go-between for the two parties. As we consider the mess in congress, we may conclude that, as a middleman, he has largely failed to deliver.

It would appear that this self-described Socialist regularly gets involved with the discussion, but rarely completes any legislation with any significant impact. Always ready to discuss his pet issues of health care, taking on big banks and corporations, fighting for individual rights, and raising focus on his favorite Socialist issue such as income equality, it can be argued that for twenty-nine years it has been a failed effort. One thing is a fact, and that is for those twenty-nine years this wolf in sheep's clothing, representing the voice of socialism, has been hiding behind the mantle of Independent thinkers while masked as a Democrat. He is neither Independent, nor a Democrat.

It is well known in both the House and the Senate that nothing of significance he has sponsored or co-sponsored ever became law. In his sixteen years in the House the best that could be said is he was nicknamed the 'Amendment King.' He constantly held up bills to add an amendment of his pet socialist, or Vermont appeals, but never accomplished a sponsored bill of his own. Worse, he never was able to block any bill in which he disagreed with to stop it from becoming law.

In his youth Sanders was a ne'er-do-well Communist activist, who was usually unemployed, could not hold a job, or didn't want to work at all. While at the University of Chicago, he was an active member of the Young People's Socialist League. This group was the youth wing of the Socialist Party of the USA. At this same time he worked as an organizer for a communist front, The United Packinghouse Workers Union, which was under investigation by the House Committee on un-American activities.

Sanders began his long socialist career in the third-party, left wing politics in the Liberty Union Party (LUP). While a member of the LUP he made two futile attempts to win the governor's house in Vermont in 1972 and 1974; and to run for the US Senate seat in a special election in 1972 and again in 1974. He failed both times with meager vote counts. He ran again for governor in 1976 and failed, upon which the LUP dissolved and Bernie Sanders was a man without a party.

After joining a leftist civic-action group in 1981, Sanders won his first election as mayor of Burlington, Vermont, by just ten votes. Fate sometimes plays such funny tricks; but for just half of those votes Bernie Sanders may never have had an opportunity for a career in politics at the highest level in this country. After this point, Bernie was on his political path to socialism. In Burlington he set price controls and raised property taxes to pay for communal land trusts. Quickly the local people noted that the new mayor does not believe in free enterprise and early on the cat was out of the bag on this Socialist.

American voters should all be asking a simple question with regard to Bernie Sanders: "Is he a Communist?" And if this question is answered with a resounding yes!, then I think the next question should be: "Do you want a Communist in the Oval Office, along with all of his personal advisors and his picks for presidential positions swarming the White House?" First of all, this Conservative voice feels that the answer to the first question is, yes! This Conservative voice basically believes that Bernie Sanders is a Communist. He always has been, and if elected to the office of President of the U.S. could become the most ruthless president in our history.

The fact that Bernie Sanders has never done ruthless only means that he has, to this point, never had the opportunity. We are fully aware of what ruthless means in the universal history of socialism. So, Americans have to ask themselves, "What does Bernie Sanders really stand for? What would he do if he had the power?" And, perhaps more directly, "What would you do if Bernie was president and began passing executive orders that put into play the basic foundations of communism into our government, and by doing so took away your rights and freedoms."

Communism, remember, moves the bar of government control vs citizen freedoms as far-left as the bar can go. When that bar reaches total Communist control, it has also reached total absence of personal freedoms and liberties mean to you, "What will be your next step?" You have been losing one freedom after another, while the government has been taking more control over your life.

As an American born into, or one migrated into, the birthright of living under the 'Freedom for All' banner, how long does this go on before you say enough is enough, and prepare to strike back? The time has come! But, wait a minute, you have already lost your right to peacefully assemble and there is a strictly enforced curfew; you have lost your freedom of speech and are not allowed to speak out against your new government; your guns for your families protection are long gone, and there are few weapons left for you to form a militia which is no longer guaranteed to you and protected for you by your Constitution. There are only a few illegal weapons, but ammunition is practically non-existent.

All the right Communist moves have been made. Bernie owns all the means of production now. You make little money and what money there is, is controlled and dispersed by the government according to need. Now communism has us between a rock and a hard spot. We don't like what they have done, but there is little we can do to stop it. Life is just not the same as what our forefathers had promised. And somehow we just let it slip away from our grip – while sweet-talking Bernie, good ole Uncle Bernie, our savior, promising everything, but ending up taking everything – has hoodwinked the uninformed followers that voted for him.

So, what does Bernie do now? Now he has the power and the control. If the people are in an uprising against his Socialist Communist policies, speaking out against this Communist mess, what will Bernie do now that he has the power? Plato wrote a script that could shed some light on how Sanders might react to revolution. He wrote, "The measure of a great leader is by what greatness he does with his power; whereas the measure of a tyrant by what damage they do with the abuse of his power." You never really know what kind of a man you are placing your faith and confidence in until that man has had a taste of power and you have been a witness to his power. Is Bernie Sanders a great man (Communist); or is he a tyrant (Communist) who would do much damage to this country by abusing his power in the name of Communist principles at the expense of the principles of this constitutional Democratic Republic?

Will Bernie Sanders walk in the shoes of his Stalin-Linen mentors? Imprison the traitors; slaughter the dissenters; create concentration camps for the resistors? Which would it be if he turned out to be a tyrant? All of the above? He has never had the power to be confronted by these choices, but if his desire is to maintain his Communist control he might have to consider the alternatives.

There was a time before gaining their power that Lenin, Stalin, Mao, and Hitler all had to rely on narrative, convincing conversation, and sweet talk to gain the confidence of enough people to place them in power. If you are considering a vote for Bernie Sanders, a Communist, then you need to know who he is and what he stands for far better than you think you know. The future of a country under Socialist Communist control is far different than what you could ever imagine.

Always and foremost remember this: Liberals seldom tell the truth, not to you, or to anyone else. Progressives and Socialists never tell the truth, and seldom even recognize truth when confronted by it. Communists never tell the truth, never recognize the truth, and only want you to know what they want you to know.

Having said all this, it is time to take a closer look at the Socialist Communist ideas that Bernie Sanders brings forward in this next 2020 election. His government control conceptions are no less Socialist Communist-based today than they were in the 2016 primary race with Hillary Clinton for the Socialist Democrat nomination. Rest assured that he has had four years to clarify, redefine, and evaluate his platform this time around. There is far more support in Congress from a beehive of Socialists that will make it more difficult for the

DNC to cheat him from the nomination. Already, as I am writing, the primaries are down to just two survivors: Bernie Sanders, and Joe Biden. Clearly, the DNC is pulling out all stops by pushing Joe Biden down the throats of their base, but very likely they are creating a divide within their party that is beyond anything they have ever imagined. While Socialist Communists are terrific cheaters, they will not stand for being cheated out of the nomination for a second time.

During the 2020 campaign Sanders has been calling for a $15 per hour across-the-board minimum wage. Many of the other Socialist Democrat candidates (now long gone) were reinforcing his same song. He has been pushing companies to do as Amazon.com has done and raise their minimum wage to $15 per hour. Most businesses are fighting against this raise because they know that it would force them to reduce hours or cut jobs. They feel that an across-the-board raise of this nature does not fit with the concept that raises should be determined by the needs and availabilities of the society. What one area can afford in wages is not necessarily what another business can afford in an entirely different setting.

Being confronted by this pay raise issue, numerous businesses and large companies have moved to high technology that is replacing workers. In my mind, if Sanders were to be elected, how far would he go to install, by executive order, a new higher minimum wage?

In the realm of taxation Bernie Sanders stands for major increases. There is nothing different here, Democrats have been calling for tax increases since the beginning of their existence, and now that they are Socialist Democrats it is only a matter of degree and how high will they go. Sanders chastised the 2017 President Trump tax reduction in a sound rebuke by claiming it to be an unnecessary advantage to corporations and the ultra-wealthy. These are, of course, the very groups that Sanders wants to raise taxes on to pay for all of the insane welfare programs that he would be working for if elected president.

Just recently, when asked in an interview about his taxation policy he claimed, "Taxing the 1% may not be enough to help the poor; the middle class would have to be taxed as well." Another of his recent (2019) proposals on the campaign trail suggests that he would issue an estate tax starting at $3.5 million and up which, ironically, is just about his estate value. He could be expected to push for a 77% rate on the billionaire estates.

The banking industry has always been a sore point for Bernie Sanders, and it would be my guess that to nationalize the banks would be one of his first Communist take overs. He has been criticizing Wall Street for years and in October of 2019 he introduced a bill to cap the size of financial institutions, which would effectively break up the banks like J.P. Morgan Chase and Goldman Sachs. This bill did not pass, thank God for a Republican majority in the Senate. More recently he presented a plan to restrict stock purchases which would put conditions on share buybacks. It is noteworthy that this was co-sponsored by Chuck Schumer which demonstrates the depth of socialism in the party. This one failed as well.

It should be mentioned here that Bernie's efforts to gain control of the nation's money is not the first attack. Barack Obama tried, with all his power, to seize control over the free flow of the nation's money. He and Bernie are both well-schooled in Marxist Theory of gaining control of the country's finances. Obama made it abundantly clear that he wanted to convert stock that the U.S. government owns in the nation's banks from preferred stock, which was the current case, to common stock. This modification to the type of stock may seem insignificant and innocent at first, but could be a

Pandora's Box with severe and far-reaching consequences in the future. This is likely one of the single greatest communist policies that the U.S. government has adopted.

This policy literally means that the Federal Government will control all of the currency publicly traded by major banks and financial institutions in the country which are currently in the hands of individual shareholders. Obviously, the shareholder's rights were being trampled. This tactic of control of the nation's flow of money is the first keystone of communism. This policy in the hands of a Communist president would mark the end of the public control of the free flow of money.

We are all aware of the communist attitude toward education. It is their full intention to take control of what people read and listen to, and to take control of what the children learn in school. We have all seen, over the past eleven years, just how far the Socialist Communists will go to propagandize the entire educational process. We are all aware of the Marxist infiltration of the schools, from elementary to our universities to ensure that communism is seen only in a positive light and capitalism as an evil entity that has enslaved the people in poverty.

Bernie Sander's primary focus in education is all public colleges and universities should be tuition free. In 2017 he introduced a plan to make community college tuition free and to eliminate tuition at four-year universities for students from families with incomes of $125,000 or less. He also, along with many of his Socialist Democrats, pushed for student loan forgiveness.

Barack Obama had already launched legislation to remove private lenders from student loans, which in essence would allow all student loans to be provided by the Federal Government directly. This would, in effect, allow the Federal Government to choose in a totalitarian manner who receives the loans and who does not. Many educational institutions were up in arms over this legislation as it shifts admissions policy from the colleges and universities to the government.

Control over education, as in Obama's Pell Grant entitlements, is a universal principle of communism to ensure that the students are ideologically indoctrinated. Without question, any of Bernie Sander's legislation would give greater control over the educational process to the government.

Others may think that these laws by the government are harmless, but in this Conservative voice, I am clear that each step taken by the Communists encroaching in the educational system will serve the purpose of communism. The use of a propagandized base is for indoctrination, and that is not education. The strength of America's educational system has always been that it offers a well-rounded education free from indoctrination. The difference between education and indoctrination is that education opens the mind, while indoctrination closes the mind; propaganda is the tool of closing the mind. Education is a process-driven approach to engaging the knowledge and ideas of the world. Education involves the seeking of facts, and learning about what is the truth, and what is not. Indoctrination is aimed at influencing people to believe in facts, without being able to back up these newfound facts with anything but opinion. To follow the Obama policies in our schools with the policies of Bernie Sanders would serve only to minimize education and maximize indoctrination.

Bernie Sanders says that the Socialist movement in America stems from the expansion of welfare states through programs like the

New Deal, and the Great Society. He claims there are values in these programs and, they are the reason he calls himself a Democratic Socialist. The New Deal was an innovative collection of social and financial reforms designed to bring recovery from the Great Depression. The Great Society (1964-1965) was launched by Lyndon B. Johnson as the largest social and financial recovery since Franklin D. Roosevelt. Mostly domestic programs its stated goal, by President Johnson, was to totally eliminate poverty and racial injustice.

This Great Society plan featured new major spending programs that addressed issues in education, medical care, urban problems, rural poverty, and transportation. Sanders would, even back in the day, stand shoulder-to-shoulder with the ideas of these two democratic programs. It is from these Liberal ideas, passing through progressivism that we see how Bernie Sanders would feel that the work of the Democratic Party would not be finished until socialism becomes their mantra.

As a young communist, Sanders visited numerous communist countries, learned from them, admired their accomplishments, and built up his support of their policies. He visited the Soviet Union and returned as a stronger Communist, even after speaking with many of the working class who reportedly were not happy with how the Communist promise turned out while craving the return to much of the freedoms they had lost. He visited Nicaragua, under the dictatorship of Daniel Ortega, returned home and proclaimed, "I was impressed." The Nicaraguans later threw Ortega out because of his tyrannical leadership.

When Sanders visited Cuba, he was obviously enamored with Castro and could not speak more highly of his accomplishments. He said he was amazed in the improvements in the lives of the people, while again admitting that there were great deficiencies in the values of democracy. It is ironic that he heaped such praise on their free medical care, free education, and free housing, which are largely responsible for the economic failure of communism in Cuba today. It is largely as a result of all the free stuff that Cuba is suffering today from record levels of poverty. No one wants to relocate to Cuba, but Cubans are fleeing to the U.S. and other Central American countries by the thousands. Cuba stands today as a clear example of another Socialist Communist failure. At the rate that Bernie Sanders wants to implement the free stuff concept into the America, it would result in an unsustainable level of outward money flow by the end of his first four years in office.

The push for Socialist Communist reform by Bernie Sanders has not gone on deaf ears. There has been, as we have noted, much recruitment to his banter over the years. He is not alone in this movement. Freshman Representative in the House, Alexandria Ocasio-Cortez, has largely become the face and voice of this movement for the millennials today. She is a member of the Democratic Socialists of America (DSA) and follows a radically hard line to socialism that clearly complements Bernie Sanders. Popularly called AOC, she represents the 14th district in NYC in the House. This district represents the east side of the Bronx, and portions of north-central Queens of New York City.

This former bartender is responsible for introducing the Green New Deal which was, for several months, the talk of all of the environmentalists and Socialist Democrat presidential candidates. No one seemed concerned about how much this plan would cost the American public; they just jumped on the band wagon as they always do and started selling it as the cure-all snake oil for all that was wrong in the environment.

The Green New Deal was estimated to have a potential cost at $600,000 per household. The organization estimated the cost for eliminating carbon emissions from the transportation system at $1.3-2.7 trillion, guaranteeing a job to every American $6.8-44.6 trillion, and universal health care estimated close to $36 trillion. There is only one word that would describe the financial impact of this plan and that word is bankrupt. Though very popular as a talking point for those with no vision, it is financially unfeasible as a working plan. But it serves a purpose here. It is a classic example of how Socialist Democrats have no idea of what they are doing and have zero concern for the expense their ideas have on the taxpayers.

The major issues this young Hispanic Socialist Democrat has been pandering, besides the Green New Deal, are Medicare for All, a federal jobs guarantee, abolishment of the U.S. Immigration and Customs Enforcement (ICE), and calling for a new generation of Democrats. These ideas alone show how close she is to Bernie Sanders. To a large extent, I can see, much like Sanders, how she could flow right past socialism and settle her policies right at the feet of communism. She is that close to stepping over the line of full government control of everyone's lives. Clearly, just as she is a hero to the Socialists, she is a villain to the Conservative right.

Hillary Clinton is gone from the minds-eye of the Left, and AOC has risen to the top of the impact list. As such, she takes her hacks from the Right. She considered by much of the Right, including me, as not having a brain in her head. It is clear to this Conservative voice that she lacks visionary power to see into the future and understand the impact of her proposals. In my view, she is very much like a hot rod with the throttle smashed to the floor and pays no attention to the 'Curves Ahead' sign.

When you add to this mix the lives of the very complex Rashida Tlaib of the House of Representatives, a Jew-hating, Trump-hating, Constitution-hating, free enterprise-hating, anti-American, along with about forty others elected to the Socialist Democrat lunatic-fringe, you have a fringe that needs to be addressed. They are a radical group of inexperienced Socialists driving the party to complete and thorough political and social change. They are particularly dangerous because they advocate the worst kind of change. Like Obama who was out to completely transform this country, they are so adamant about how they want to change things for no other reason than to simply change it. Change for the sake of change is irresponsible and more times than not ends in destructive results. These people are extremists who know no middle ground and are interested in all change because in their mind any change is good.

These people of the Socialist Democrat Party are unafraid to laying bare what, in the political realm, is hidden and uncomfortable. They have no fear of attacking or upsetting the status quo or common sense concepts of any kind. The intensity of their radical Socialist Communist loyalty is what makes this movement within their party a danger. By nature, it carries within itself much destruction before any iota of constructive change can occur. Built within this fact is the understanding that what is must be destroyed before what will be is produced. Based on this concept, the Bernie Sanders, AOC, Tlaib, and all the rest of these radicals must agree that democracy and capitalism must be gutted before Marxist Socialist communism can be built.

Socialism is an idea with an anguishing history. It is a history of numbers and those numbers come in the form of a body count. One hundred million bodies in the 20th century is the number.

SOCIALISM PULLS THE STRINGS

Who manipulates to keep our people foiled?
Who keeps this country in hate embroiled?
What evil force, concealed, disguised,
How is this great country kept so hypnotized?
Is this the work of grim and evil men?
Who sets this stage again and again?

Is it for power and control that they vie?
Is it for 'this' that we shall live and die?
It is not war that is our toy for control,
But socialism who attack a part and destroy the whole.
Now, or never, we must decide and choose our fate,
Our peace of love, or their war of hate.

So sad this nation with socialism in our face,
Have we a feeling of dire disgrace?
Deep in our hearts, we feel the shame,
And we are certain to share the blame.
We have seen the havoc and hate they have wrought,
Is our great promise all for naught?

Chapter 16

Donald J. Trump Meets Rodan

Donald Trump was born in the borough of Queens, New York. His father was Fredrick Christ Trump, a successful developer whose parents were German immigrants. His mother, Mary Anne Macleod Trump, was a Scottish-born housewife. Donald grew up in Queens until the age of thirteen when he enrolled in the New York Military Academy, a private military boarding school. In 1964 he enrolled at Fordham University, and finally in 1966 he landed in Wharton School of the University of Pennsylvania where he received his bachelor's degree in economics.

Donald Trump is a confirmed Presbyterian of the First Presbyterian Church in Jamaica, Queens, NY. His family regularly attended church there until in the 1970's when his parents joined the Marble Collegiate Church in Manhattan. The pastor at Marble was Norman Vincent Peale, who was a famous American minister and author known for his work in popularizing the concept of positive thinking. He ministered to the Trump family and mentored Donald and his siblings until his death in 1993.

As we have noted on the clear influence of Reverend Jerimiah Wright on President Barack Obama, it is fair to say that Norman Vincent Peale probably had a large influence on President Donald J. Trump. Some notable quotes by Reverend Peale that have no doubt had significant effect on President Trump are, "Believe in yourself! Have faith in your abilities! Without reasonable confidence in your own powers you cannot be successful or happy."

Another quotation of Reverend Peale is, "The trouble with most of us is that we would rather be ruined by praise than saved by criticism." And a third quote that is attributed to Norman Vincent Peale is, "Change your thoughts and you change your world." I think it is fair to say that President Trump learned a lot about both his religion and his life through his association with Reverend Peale. While campaigning for the presidency, candidate Trump made reference to his book, *The Art of the Deal*, and said it was his second favorite book and, "Nothing beats the Bible."

In 1971, at the age of twenty-five, Donald Trump took charge of the family's real-estate business and renamed it the Trump Organization. By 1982 he was listed in the Forbes list of wealthiest individuals as having a share of his family's estimated $200 million net worth. After dropping off the list between 1990 and 1995 the Trump Organization gradually rebounded, and in the 2019 billionaires ranking his estimated net worth was $3.1 billion. Ranked 715th in the world and 259th in the U.S. makes him one of the wealthiest politicians in American history. It is noteworthy that during the three years since President Trump announced his presidential run in 2015, Forbes estimated his net worth declined 31% and that his ranking fell 138 spots. It is also interesting that the president has refused to be paid for his services as president of the U.S., and has instead donated his quarterly pay-check to various groups and organizations. As we know, the Trump Organization has vast, world-wide holdings, ranging from elite hotels to his personal Mar-a-Lago golfing estate in Palm Beach, Florida and gambling casinos in Atlantic City. His branding hotels are found in at least seven different countries. He is not actively involved in the on-going management of his family holdings.

Donald Trump's political allegiances and points of view have never been cast in stone. Ideologically, he leaned toward the policy of the Republican Party at first, registering with the GOP in 1987. He left the GOP in 1999 and joined the Reform Party of Ross Perot. He dropped out of the party after the 2000 presidential campaign, disavowing several of its members including Pat Buchanan and David Duke who was a former member of the Ku Klux Klan (KKK). He then joined the Democratic Party in 2001. Completing the full cycle of political parties, he left the Democrats and rejoined the Republican Party in 2009. When Barack Obama entered the scene for the Democrats, Donald Trump was very outspoken about his socialist leanings and his lack of transparency. He strongly attacked Obama about his birth certificate and became a leader in the group that came to be called the 'Birthers.' Trump felt that Obama had no proof of citizenship and was, therefore, ineligible to run for president.

In the beginning of his political career (1987), Trump advocated for peace in Central America, accelerated nuclear disarmament talks with the Soviet Union and called for a reduction of the federal budget deficit by forcing American allies to pay their fair share for military defenses.

While with the Reform Party in 2000, Donald Trump filed an exploratory committee to seek the nomination of the party in the presidential race. Political polls at the time showed Donald Trump matching up against George W. Bush of the GOP, and likely Al Gore of the Democratic Party. The early polls showed him with just 7% support and in February 2000 he dropped out of the race. Early on there were several high-profile candidates for the party, but with Donald Trump dropping out it left a clear pathway for Pat Buchanan to represent the party.

In 2012, now a Republican, he thought about another run, but after several speaking engagements in 2011, he decided once again not to run. So, it would not be until 16 June 2015, that Donald Trump would announce his candidacy for President of the United States.

At this time, he made a speech at the Trump Tower in Manhattan, and we first get a taste of the political views from a Republican leaning. The things he discussed included illegal immigration, offshoring of American jobs, the U.S. national debt, and Islamic terrorism, which all remained large priorities during his campaign. It was at this time that he announced his campaign slogan, 'Make America Great Again.' He told his audience that his wealth would make him immune to pressure from campaign donors, and he declared that he would be funding his own campaign, which he largely did.

Ironically, candidate Trump was not initially taken seriously by the pundits who had little reason for their negative take on him, other than that he was a Republican. However, in spite of their analysis he quickly rose to the top of the opinion polls. On 'Super Tuesday' Donald Trump received the most votes, and he remained the front-runner throughout the primaries. By March he was positioned to win the Republican nomination. After an avalanche of support from Indiana in May the only two other candidates remaining, Ted Cruz and John Kasich, both suspended their campaigns and the RNC named Donald Trump the presumptive Republican nominee.

After receiving the GOP nomination, candidate Trump began focusing on Hillary Clinton, the Democrat nominee. Hillary surged early on with the deep and biased support of mainstream media led by CNN, MSN3C, and ABC news networks and established a significant lead over Trump in the national polls. But in July, Clinton's lead began to narrow following the FBI's announcement that they would reopen its investigation into her ongoing email controversy. Even before this FBI action, many Americans had already begun to have serious doubts about the moral and ethical compass of Hillary Clinton. In spite of the news networks hiding her activities as corrupt and deceitful, the word was out among middle America and with them, her tactics would not fly.

It wasn't long before Trump and Clinton came face to face in their first presidential debate. They battled through three debates in New York, Missouri, and Las Vegas, Nevada. I believe there were two very important take-aways from the debates that demonstrate who the Democrats are. One is Donna Brazille (DNC) hand feeding, prior to one of the debates, the questions to be asked by the news network moderators, and secondly, Donald Trump choosing not to answer the question whether of he would accept the results of the election regardless of the outcome.

After repeatedly denying that she leaked debate questions to Hillary before the debate, Donna Brazille finally admitted that she had, in fact, sent her the questions. This behavior on the part of Donna, Hillary, and the entire DNC is verification of all of the charges I have been making about the deceitful, behind-the-back tactics of the entire Socialist Democrat Party. It goes to the heart of their priorities that, "Why play on a level playing field when you can cheat and put the field in your advantage for the only thing that is important - Victory!"

Donna Brazille is just as despicable as Hillary Clinton. When caught red-handed she had two statements that show the level of her character and principles, "It was a mistake that I will never regret." Wow! She not only doesn't care that she was caught in the unethical or immoral act of being a cheat, but doesn't care that everyone knows her to be a cheat. What credibility does a person with this mentality have? This Conservative voice believes that it would be little to none.

Then she denies all responsibility for her ethical failure by saying, "It was my job to make sure that Hillary looked as good as she could in the debates." Well, let me suggest what she looks like. What you both look like is a couple of cheats. One cannot keep doing what everyone believes to be wrong and simply write it off as part of the job and not recognize your responsibility in the results.

This story line reminds me of another story that involved evil but the party involved simply wrote it off. Franz Stang, commandant of the Sobibór and Treblinka death camps in WWII was found guilty of war crimes against mankind for his involvement in the deaths of 900,000 Jews. His comment upon his death sentence was, "My conscience is clear; I was just following orders." At some point in the minds of moral cripples there must be a better understanding of the values between right and wrong, and good and bad. If you are a party to the part that simply cannot distinguish between right and wrong, and good and evil, you are the problem.

The second irony that came from the debates between Trump and Hillary Clinton was in the question posed as to whether he would accept the results of the election. As we know, what he what he said in Las Vegas was this, "I might not accept the results of next month's election if I felt it was rigged against me." Hillary blasted this statement as horrifying. Of course, the media became unhinged, and said it was tantamount to the destruction of American Democracy. They went after Donald Trump like 'ugly on ape' all over its body. And once again the Socialist Democrats joined in with their favorite tune, 'the sky is falling; the sky is falling.' In their greatest moment they wanted to know how he could so undermine democracy.

One month later, the election of 2016 was over, Hillary had lost miserably, the Socialist Democrats were irate, confused, and had very soiled diapers. They could not, for the next four years, accept the results of the election that had chosen Donald Trump over the Socialist Democrat mentality, and the corruption and underhanded, behind-the-back tactics of Hillary Clinton.

These two messages of the Socialist Democrats send a clear signal to the American people that number one in their priority list is certainly their party, and not America. Donald Trump sent us all a message that America comes first. I'm not going to say that the Socialist Democrats do not want America to succeed, but they do not want it to be number one in its present form. Believing that America must change before it can be an honorable country is only verification for them believing that America is not the greatest nation on this planet. How can they even prioritize what is most important for this country, when they have no understanding of what this country means to the world. What is most important must never be at the mercy of what is least important; party must never be most important, and country must never be least important.

So, what are the things that are most important to Donald Trump as he winds his way through the campaign to become President of the United States? Here are the things that he considered as uppermost importance to make this country great again. He called for renegotiating the U.S.–China relations and free trade agreements such as NAFTA and the Trans-Pacific Partnership, a strong enforcement of immigration laws, and the building of a new wall along the U.S.–Mexico border. He called for developing energy independence, opposing climate change regulations such as the clean Power Plan and the Paris Agreement, modernizing and creating better services for our veterans, investing in infrastructure, simplifying the tax code, reducing taxes for all economic classes, and imposing tariffs on imports by companies that offshore jobs.

One of his most significant parts of his platform was calling for a largely non-intervention foreign policy, while increasing military spending to reinforce its strength. He pushed for extreme vetting, or banning, of immigrants from Muslim majority countries to control domestic terrorism. He spent a lot of time speaking about the failures of NATO and called it obsolete.

By many, on both sides of the isle, Trump is considered to be a Populist. A Populist is a person, or politician, who tries to appeal to the ordinary masses who feel that their concerns are disregarded, or not taken seriously, by the established elite groups in government. In the short of it they are people who stand against the elite. Their flowing to Donald Trump can be attributed largely by his motto, "Drain the Swamp." In the minds of the Populists, the swamp is the elite who have neglected them for decades, except for election time. Many of these people saw in Donald Trump an opportunity to get back in the game and have their long-silenced voice back in the Oval Office.

Many of Trumps views cross party lines, which is probably the result of his having been involved, over his early years, with both political parties. He follows, for example, the Republican line by calling for deregulation and lower taxation, while leaning for the democratic agenda of infrastructure investment. Infrastructure has a long history with the Democrats. Being a builder and developer, it is very easy to see why President Trump would throw his support behind the development of our infrastructure.

In my mind Donald Trump is less a Populist than a Conservative to middle ground Republican who follows his instincts to serve the greater need. He has the uncanny ability to see what is most important for the country and provide the energy to bring about positive solutions. I love that he has better visionary power than most any president you can name, to see into the seeable future and understand the impact of his decisions. Making the right choices is what being president is all about. During both the 2016 and the 2020 elections we have seen far too many candidates who significantly lack of visionary power, and we have witnessed a myriad of poor choices in their careers.

Even in the GOP, early on in the election campaign, Trump was not seen to be a true Conservative. Most saw him as leaning more to the middle (moderate) than anywhere close to a pure Conservative. In December of 2015, Senator Lindsey Graham sarcastically said, "You want to know how to make America great again? Tell Donald Trump to go to hell." Graham further chided that President Trump "…doesn't represent my party. He doesn't represent the values that men and women who wear the uniform are fighting for." With respect to Trump not following the views of the GOP, Ted Cruz felt much the same. Both were extremely outspoken critics of the president in the beginning, but it is fair to say that these two leaders in the party, along with most all of the party, now support who Donald Trump is and what he is trying to do. They still do not believe that he is Conservative enough, but then no one is 100% conservative, and he is clearly representative of the Republican views. Any way you carve it up many Americans, especially Republicans, are dead tired of being trampled by the elitist mentality of the Socialist Democrats and had rallied to candidate Trump to help make him the 45th American President.

So, just where Donald Trump lies along the political spectrum is still up in the air, but I have to believe that the one who knows best is probably President Trump himself. In the New Hampshire debate he was asked to reply to criticisms that he is not conservative enough. Candidate Trump replied, "Well, I think I am, and to me, I view the word conservative as a derivative of the word conserve. We want to conserve our money. We want to conserve our wealth. We want to conserve our country." It was certainly not a typical political definition of conservative, but it clearly gives one an understanding of what it means to Donald Trump, and how he would go about the job of conserving the resources of the county, for better usage by and for the people. I, for one, can understand it and I can live with it. When I see how, as president, he has utilized his understanding of conservativism to bring about the great accomplishments in our economy in such a short period of time I think maybe he is right.

Many Conservatives complain that they cannot support President Trump because he has no record as a conservative. I think it's pretty clear that he had no record of anything when he became president because he came from the private sector, not the government sector. As an entrepreneur from the private sector, he is an economist who has likely applied his view of conserving to his building and developing empire. With a good understanding of economics, I think you can bring to the White House no better credentials, and I think it is about time someone did. When I look at our last four presidents, I think we may well have been better off in the last three decades had someone had better credentials in economics.

When you consider the major issues that separate the Conservatives and the Socialist Democrats, remember that the Socialists believe in government controlled power whereas the Conservatives favor state, and locally controlled power. There is no question that Donald Trump believes that the distributed power should be maintained in the separate states, each with its own power. In the issues of education and the environment, he believes that the states must have the say in maintaining, improving, and controlling them at the states own local level. With regard to immigration and the law, Conservatives tend to support the Rule of Law and to oppose lawlessness, but Socialists tend to favor the side of many issues that are not in the best interests in support of Rule of Law and, in fact, encourage lawlessness thus creating a huge division among people. Donald Trump has promised to support the law and those whose job it is to enforce the law. There is not much that is more conservative than this.

Even in the Muslim immigration issue, the battle lines are wide apart. Remember that Islam is the only major religion that still believes in conquering the world by force, and while the Socialist Democrats were admitting them by the thousands, with little to no vetting, President Trump has pledged to control or ban their admittance until a strong vetting program can be effective. For this stance he earned the Socialist slander of being a racist. It seems clear that on virtually every issue separating the Conservatives and the Socialist Democrats Donald Trump is on the side of the Conservative GOP.

At any rate, 8 2016 was one of the most memorable nights in our electoral history. Donald Trump won the Electoral College with 304 votes to Hillary Clinton's 227. He received nearly 2.9 million fewer popular votes. Of the 3,141 counties in the U.S. Trump won 3,084 while Hillary Clinton won only fifty-seven. It was only by a total vote count in California for 3.4 million in favor of Hillary Clinton that gave her the popular vote. Take that Socialist controlled state out of the mix and Donald Trump would have had a clear sweep of the popular, electoral, and county vote for this presidential election.

As it was, President Trump's victory could be summarized in two words: Politically stunning. This was an upset incomparable to any in our history. All of the polls were consistently projecting Hillary Clinton as the leader and probable winner. While President Trump's support had been grossly underestimated, that of Hillary Clinton was severely overestimated. The national polls were poorly done and the pollsters clearly overstated Hillary's support among well-educated and non-White voters. At the same time those polls underestimated Trumps support among the White working-class. In the end it doesn't matter what effect those polls had on the outcome of the election because Hillary Clinton and her Socialist Democrats refused to accept the results and she came up with about a dozen nondescript reasons for blaming others for her loss.

With all said and done Donald J. Trump owned the White House and both chambers of Congress. President Trump had won thirty states and Hillary just twenty. The middle of the country spoke loud and clear; Hillary could blame her loss on whatever and whoever, but the fact remained. The hard-working middle America had had enough of her and her ilk.

The Socialist Democrats wasted no time in organizing protests against President Trump. The protests were occurring in the U.S. and in Europe against his entry into the 2016 presidential campaign. They protested everything they could think of from his rhetoric speaking to simply his electoral victory, his inauguration, alleged sexual misconduct, and even various presidential actions. The most notable of these protests was his family separation policy involving illegal immigrants at the U.S.–Mexico border. These protests were a reaction to the Trump administration policy of separating children from their parents or guardians who crossed the U.S. border, either illegally or to request asylum, and jailing the adults and locating the minors at separate facilities under the care of the Department of Health and Human Services. This was another case of Soros funded Shadow Groups providing the funds and organization for a group called Families Belong Together.

President Trump had started a zero tolerance policy in May of 2018 under which any person crossing the U.S. border may be charged with a federal misdemeanor. Attorney General, Jeff Sessions, announced, during remarks made on May 7 in Scottsdale, Arizona, "If you are smuggling a child then we will prosecute you, and that child will be separated from you as required by law." The minor children would then be held at a detention center. Sessions also announced that the U.S. would no longer accept asylum applications for migrants who are victims of domestic abuse or gang violence. This was a strong and viable approach to dealing with the ambush at our southern borders, but once again the Socialist Democrats who wanted those borders open for all to enter, became unhinged and created their own hate filled narratives to enrage their ill-informed followers.

Some of the many protests took the form of walk-outs, business closures, and petitions, as well as rallies along with the marches. Most of the protests were peaceful; however some actionable conduct such as vandalism, business destruction, and assaults against Trump supporters did occur. There were some groups that were considerably more violent than others and among these group's arrests were made. The largest and most boisterous organized protest against President Trump occurred on 21 January 2017, on the day after his inauguration address. This was the Women's March and it was obviously well planned, in advance, orchestrated by one of the George Soros Shadow Groups with the strong backing and support of the Socialist Democrats. This march, collectively, was the largest single-day protest in our history.

The goal of these collective marches was to send a bold message to our new administration on their first day of office, and to the world that women's rights are human rights. A noble concept and approach but I seriously doubt that President Trump would see women's rights any other way. All through the campaign the Socialist Democrats had tried to raise a question mark on his attitude toward women by raising issues of what they called scandalous behavior. Obviously, these marches were an attempt to continue with this narrative. In my opinion, the march was simply a platform for the leaders of the women's rights movement to sound off and be heard about unity in their diverse range of issues. It was their attempt to bring about unity in the hope of creating social change. Unfortunately, many could not contain themselves and resorted to verbal and slanderous attacks on the president and his administration.

Tensions had risen during the campaigns that were interpreted by some as anti-women, or otherwise offensive. For these people, in actuality, it was a part of a political correctness exercise that had been fostered by Barack Obama, as a tool to gain control of a crisis that would help the cause of the Socialist Democrats. These protests and verbal assaults were designed to do nothing more than undermine the presidency of Donald Trump. Like a bunch of little children who didn't get their way, this is their way of throwing a temper tantrum to convince someone that they should be in control of the government. But, why would you put little children in charge of something as important as running a country?

The next huge example of immaturity on the part of the Socialist Democrats was 'the obstruction issue.' Obstruction is like saying if I don't get to play I'm taking my baseball and going home. Immediately the Socialists came out with the idea that since they didn't win the election they will simply obstruct everything President Trump tries to pass. No legislation with the Donald Trump stamp on it will be passed. Staff replacement personnel, urgently needed to move the government forward for the people, were held in limbo for months, and as we all saw on national television judicial appointments were threated in a three-ring-circus like commandants from a WWII Nazi extermination camp. This was a pitiful, ugly, and hostile display by the Socialist Democrats of their total lack of integrity.

You have to go back a long way in our history to find an example where a single party of the government exploited congressional rules to systematically obstruct a president from staffing his administration or refusing to pass presidential supported legislation for no other reason than they hate the president. And treating our prestigious Judicial and Supreme Court judges as criminals without ever witnessing a crime, or having any proof a crime occurred is beyond the pale of being dignified and is clearly outside the standards of decency. This level of obstruction is unfair to the president's administration and more importantly, to the American people. If it is not stopped and prevented from future occurrence, we can guarantee that this type of incorrigible behavior will create a precedence that would befall every future president regardless of the party. If it continues, I can say, "Welcome to the third-world rule by tyranny."

The mentality of these Socialist Democrats is no different from that of the 1865 Southern Democrats who were responsible for the assassination of President Lincoln. In April of 1865 America ended its Civil War against the South and the Southern Democrats. Only a matter of a few days after the end of this conflict President Lincoln was assassinated at the Ford Theatre. Those involved with this horrendous act were supporters of the South and hated Abraham Lincoln. These Democrats were attempting to remove a president through any means necessary. What they were doing was seditious and treasonous.

The Civil War had started in 1861 when the Southern State Democrats seceded from the Union and started their own country. These Democrats would not recognize the Republican president of the United States. They tried to obstruct, ridicule, slander, and undermine everything he tried to do. After four years of noncompliance and the deaths of more than 620,000 soldiers, the War ended, and President Lincoln issued the Emancipation Proclamation that effectively freed the slaves. This was the final straw that broke the camel's back for the Southern Democrats. The Proclamation did not sit well with those left to pick up the pieces of the shattered Southern States. In their final act of violence against this president and this country, they murdered President Lincoln. Make no mistake about it, this was a coup designed to take out the President of the United States. It was based on hate that is a hate no different than the hate of today's Socialist Democrats.

The Socialist Democrats and their deep state and corrupt media clearly connived a plan to remove President Trump through the made-up crimes that Trump colluded with Russia to win the 2016 election. This tyrannical investigation began even before President Trump was elected and made no stops after his inauguration. They orchestrated a special investigation carried out by Robert Mueller even though a crime had not been committed. This was an investigation searching for a crime. They gave Mueller authority to look at anything, no particular crime, just dig up some dirt so we can impeach this president. The team Mueller put together was all Trump haters, and former Hillary Clinton allies. It is not strange that the media never addressed any of this activity, because the media was a part of the attempted coup.

Mueller took a back seat during the investigation and turned the process over to his Hillary Clinton allies to gather the material. He simply allowed his soldiers in arms in the deep state Department of Justice (DOJ) and FBI to leak abusive and dishonest material to their pawns in the media and let it all fall where it would. It seems odd that the Mueller investigation was assembled to investigate the Russian collusion issue, given the okay to go where you must go, but only investigated Trump and his team. Later information proves that others associated with Hillary Clinton were much more involved with collusion that anyone on the Trump team.

In the beginning it appeared that this whole process of the coup was merely an attempt to harass and remove the president while covering up deep state crimes. In the end, that proved to be true. When all this backfired in their face and even the best investigators the Socialist Democrats could come up with, given a wide-open throttle to go after the president, failed to find evidence of anything there was a clear result. Americans were very angry with Mueller, the media, and the deep state, and worst of all, the absolute hoodlums of the Socialist Democrat Party in Congress. When finally the sham was over the American people were unified in their conclusion of, "Wow! If the government can do this to a sitting president of the U.S. then what chance do we have, as common people, against this tyrannical gang of Socialists."

There was no collusion. It was all about an obstruction trap. Attorney General Barr reported on the conclusion of the investigation that, "There was no collusion; no obstruction." You can take one thing to the bank, and it just might make you a 1%er. If a gang of thieves working this Mueller report had found anything remotely close to a crime, they would have reported it and hung their hat on the post.

One word summarizes their investigation: "Nothing!" Maybe two words: "Absolutely nothing!"

You would think that this would be the end of their travesty, but some people simply do not know when their time is over. If you bring a horse to water, even the horse can tell not to drink from a cesspool. How many times must these Socialists fail before they realize they have failed? You at least have to believe that the Socialist Democrats are a very motivated group. The hate runs deep, and since they have no soul, they don't understand what they are doing is wrong. They clearly remind me of a quote that my college baseball coach at Oregon State College, Paul Valenti, told me. "Motivation alone is not enough. If you have an idiot and you motivate him, now you have a motivated idiot." I never quite understood why he told me that; in practice I would go after anything he hit, but today, watching the Socialist Democrats I think I understand.

When the Socialist Democrats saw the writing on the wall that the Mueller report was not only a failure for their cause, but it sunk another of their battleships, they turned to a phone call that President Trump had with the President of the Ukraine to renew their attempt to impeach him. The deep state in the White House was spying on the president and others were listening in on the president's call. They attempted to change the transcript of the call but fortunately the president had already secured the official transcript so that it could not be edited. Curses, foiled again.

Finally, the House of Representatives filed for impeachment under the deranged leadership of Nancy Pelosi, and the driving of the radical Socialist Democrats. Another bad idea followed by a parade of inept, counter-productive witnesses carefully coached by Adam Schiff and Jerry Nader. They brought in the complaint of a whistle blower who had not even been privy to the call but was reporting what they had been told, supposedly, by second and third sources. They brought in leakers and deep state spies, including a former Ambassador to the Ukraine – a young undercover CIA agent who had been spying in the White House – and at least one U.S. Representative overseeing a sham committee in the House that leaked out their plan. My goodness, the best of the Laurel and Hardy films couldn't have been more hilarious. These people are tyrants and seditious traitors. They must think that they are right but they are blinded by hate. But then, so was John Wilkes Booth, a seditious traitor blinded by hate.

These Socialist Democrats are very lucky indeed. In 1865 John Wilkes Booth along with several hundred people were rounded up by the government after the assassination of President Lincoln, most all released for lack of evidence, but other than several killed trying to escape. Four were hanged for their role related to the murder of President Lincoln. Why are today's Socialist Democrats lucky? Because they won't be hanged or shot trying to escape; they are just as much seditious traitors as those who were hanged, but today they will simply go down in history as traitors to the country. The Benedict Arnold's of today's Socialist Democrat revolution; may they be so lucky as Benedict Arnold and live the life as a traitor and then die of gout.

If this Socialist Democrat mentality is to be stopped then it can happen only in concert with the ending of the emotion of hate as the motivating factor of your actions. As long as there is hate there will be obstruction. Hate, at this level in government, goes beyond the reasonable understanding of the question of why. Hate is an emotion that goes well beyond the scope of dislike. It is not like disliking string beans with your dinner. It literally means that the Socialist Democrats would be happy to see harm come to a person, like President Trump, or going so far as to do anything to eliminate the person, including violence. This is insane. This is insanity at its absolute lowest level of humanity. Where is the soundness of mind that a sane person must have? Where is the good judgment that a sane person is required to possess in his everyday life regardless of whether it is in the comforts of his home, or the rigors of his work place? Where is the display of sound sense that all sane people must demonstrate as they interrelate with people and environment? This is government by the insane.

These same insane people incite others to act the same way. It is as though they are forming a club of hate and the only way into the club is to develop the same form of hate for President Trump that is as unhinged as that of the leaders of the club. And they teach these new members to be just as resistant and intolerant to Trump and his followers and opposed to any cooperation with them.

How can this level of hate develop in such a short period? It has only been four years since Donald trump entered the political arena. Four years back he was probably one of the most sought after people to know in the entire country. Most all people liked him including those who worked for him whether Black, Brown, or White; whether they were leaders of industry or government, or simply the common man whose path crossed with Donald Trump. No one called him names; no one tried to humiliate him or drag his family down into the dirt. He was revered enough in Hollywood to have his handprint in the Hollywood Walk of Fame. Legislators constantly came to him for support of their political causes for money, as well as his personal support. Now many of those who wanted his support in the Socialist Democrat Party are the very ones who find, just four years later, that Donald Trump is a man of evil.

No one can ever report that Donald Trump was called a racist, a homophobe, an Islamophobe, a Hitler, an evil man, or even just a bad guy. These are the slanderous name calling of the Socialist Democrats who are just not smart enough to figure out how to be successful without being hateful. They have developed, what is today called, the Trump derangement syndrome, which refers to their negative, destructive, criticizing reactions to anything that President Trump does. It refers to their irrational and hate-filled behavior that has little to do with anything involving his actual positions, or actions. It has far more to do with who they are.

Most probably this hate comes from fear, and in all likelihood it is the fear of Donald Trump himself. He has never demonstrated any signs of tyrannical designs, he has never committed heinous atrocities of any kind, he has no resemblance to behaviors that follow Nazi ideals as espoused by Adolph Hitler, Stalin, Mao, or even Idi Amin. Yet out of their personally concocted minds, he is an evil villain filled with vile and self-righteous beliefs and policies. Good heavens, the Republican beliefs and policies are evil and vile? If this is the case, we can expect that all Conservative Republicans would be treated the same as President Trump.

Certainly President Trump carries different beliefs than the Socialist Democrats, but so has every Republican president in the history of this country, and none of them, with the exception of the Southern State Democrats of the Civil War era, were obstructive, hateful, and so completely self-serving in their own interests as to throw a road block at the sitting president to shut down his ability to lead the country. President Trump's differences of political views are certainly not a crime. This should be simple disagreements, and they should not merit the growth of hate for anyone.

Make no mistake about it, this is full blown, deep-seated hate and it applies equally at the president and his followers as well. To call the president a racist based solely on their intolerant hate is no different than calling his followers a basket of deplorables, and verbally hoping that they all die by being infected with the coronavirus. In my opinion this serves as the real reason that the Socialist Democrats are so hateful. They are totally incensed that their candidate lost the 2016 election to those who have a different set of views and values, and they are frightened out of their skull that the president will completely derail their Socialist agenda. As a result, they have taken the position of intolerance, and as such, in their demented mind, there is no room for agreement or discussion.

So, do the Socialists really hate President Trump this bad? You bet your bippy they do, and they hate you with the same evil veracity. It is way more than just bad sportsmanship, and you can count on the fact that as long as President Trump occupies the Oval Office they will hate him, and you, probably even worse tomorrow than they do today. They have totally lost control of their hate and it spreads with greater intensity and evil each and every day. Since the Socialist Democrats own the media (CNN, MSNBC) they carefully choreograph the stories they want you to see and hear, pass their propaganda on to the news network of mainstream media, and from there to the people to build on the level of hate that rules the narratives of the Socialist Democrats.

The vast majority of the public will not accept their underhanded tactics, but they will reach their useful idiots who will continue to carry the flag of this evil, hate that the Socialist Democrats own. This is the direction that their hate takes; their followers hate because they are told to hate, not because they have come to their conclusions on their own. This is what they hear the CNN and MSNBC anchors saying, and they have little to no other information. So, they take what they hear and run with it like a basket full of misinformation. The Socialist Democrats send the talking points to their Socialist dominated news networks and they send their stories out full of the propaganda they want you to know so they can feel assured that they have created another useful idiot.

THE ELECTION MIRACLE

When the time to vote approached we were pleased to take our turn
'The Donald' was hopeful for our country, but great was our concern,
We prayed that integrity would prevail, and only right will flourish,
If we elect 'The Donald' to office, the greatest good he will nourish,
With judgements born of great wisdom, every problem he'll pursue,
While keeping us all informed, our enemies he will subdue.

All this we know is true, yet each opponent in turn,
Takes the position his rival had much to learn
To give the Socialists our precious vote would indeed be a mistake
The issues that they so glibly state would bring havoc in their wake,
Their platform at its shaky best, no doubt the opening for treason,
So, for the good of man and country, these clowns must be beaten.

Now comes the election day, and our hopes and dreams lay in question,
Certainly 'The Donald' will answer our prayers, and give no concession,
We watch the results, we follow the score,
We see the signs and with joy in our hearts it goes against what we deplore,
Yes, 'The Donald,' who just a short time before, was uncertain of the nod,
Has now come through, a leader, ordained by God?

Chapter 17

My Name Is Hate: I Am Ugly to the Bone

For those hoping or looking for relief of the tension between political parties over the past eleven years to ease in the election year of 2020, don't kill yourself holding your breath. None of the emotions of anger, disappointment, and hate have narrowed, or reached their peak. The Republicans of 2020 are still full throttle disappointment and anger that the Democrat Party has allowed themselves to lose control to the Socialists. The democrats are all in with their hatred of President Trump, as demonstrated by their behavior in trying to impeach him and are already promising more of the same.

The tension brought by the release of the Mueller report; hate tweets, name-calling, and the impeachment trial are only the tip of the iceberg that produce a higher level of hate with each questionable action. There was a time, not long past, that easily half of my friends, associates, and family were either Democrats or Independents, and we spoke freely, enjoyed each other's company and were each tolerant of the others' political, social, and religious views. I wasn't angry about their Democratic stance, and I'm certain they didn't hate me for my views, which have not changed since Donald Trump became president.

Today I have no friends that are Democrats, no associates, and only one family member who is a Democrat with whom I feel comfortable engaging in any conversation or friendly activity. And it is not just me; it is literally the same for those Democrats who use to share a good time with me, as well. I dropped some and some of them dropped me.

It is an odd thing about meaningful relationships, that when diversity overpowers friendly, the only thing remaining is to go your separate ways. It sometimes amazes me how those blinded by their own bigotry find their own friendliness so superficial. My good friend's wife had a friend from their high school days. They knew that she was extremely progressive and 100% abhors President Trump. They don't engage each other, but on occasion they run into them around town. When they did, his wife and this lady hugged and exchanged pleasantries each time. They'd talk for a few minutes, my friend does the same with her husband, and away they go.

The other day this lady put a post on Facebook that was a long, long narrative so full of hate, name calling, and criticisms of both the president and all of his followers that it was difficult to finish reading without becoming extremely angry. "Everyone that supported President Trump was worse than a basket of deplorables, were somehow subhuman and clearly not responsible enough to live in this country. We should all go elsewhere, or just die." Needless to say, my friend's wife was very upset, felt betrayed, and their friendship compromised as though she had been stabbed in the back. She said, "She is talking about me! She doesn't know I'm a Republican, but she is talking about me."

He could see the pain on her face and hear it in her voice. Her eyes narrowed as with someone suffering the effect of a devastating migraine. The corners of her mouth tightened as she tried to understand the disappointment of this personal attack from a friend. They had only been back in her hometown four years, and the two knew little of each other, but this lady was the first that his wife had reacquainted with since her return. The agony of these insults is, indeed, a blow to her memories and expectations of this lady.

She asked him, "How will I handle this? What will I do the next time we come together? I don't know if I can genuinely hug her with a feeling of sincerity or speak with an honest smile on my face."

Now it was making him angry because this lady had caused a needless pain for his wife. It was hard to answer her in a way that she could shed the pain, but hopefully they could search their heart for some understanding that would minimize the pain. I know, from my own perspective, that there were times when I thought about today's Socialists and questioned, "What is wrong with those people? How can they have these Socialist ideas and want to force them on this entire country?" If I leave it right there, then there is a huge difference between my thinking process and this lady's outright assault on all of Trump followers.

If you have read this far into this book you are well aware that I have collectivized in my writings no less than the words of this lady on Facebook. To collectivize is to consolidate individual thoughts, opinions, and behaviors into one group or category. That means that if you don't like someone like President Trump, or in my case socialism, because of what they say or do, then everyone who acts the same way must be bad people just like Trump, or Socialists. You know nothing about these people beyond this single example, yet you collectivize them as all being alike, just like a bin full of pieces of coal. Clearly, when we do this we hurt people's image of you and even more likely you hurt their feelings. If you are foolish enough to use collectivization you may not really care about your own image, or the feelings of others, because your own motivation is to strike out in your anger.

This lady not only does not care, she is, like so many others, totally oblivious that she may be causing pain at all. In fact, let's go one step further. She may even gain pleasure from inflicting this pain. Remember, we have already stated that we are the target of their hate. Perhaps they want us to know that their hate is real, and they don't care if we feel the pain of their hate for President Trump, because we deserve it too.

Not caring is the real reason why so much of this political hate is thrown out there. Those who hate to this magnitude are just too blinded by the hate to even understand the impact of their hate. It does not matter which side of the isle you are on, hate is hate and it is simply ugly. The saddest thing about all of this hate is that it is so dehumanizing. This is what hate mongers do. Through their attacks haters deprive people of the human qualities of their personalities and their dignity. They aim to degrade you. They do not understand the simple fact that if you treat people with respect, you get respect back. They are cruel people to the core.

This lady is politically polarized. Partisan polarization has been around a long, long time, but the difference is that now the division is driven more than at any time before by hatred of the other side – and their views and actions – rather than devotion to their own cause. Nonpartisan politics is a thing of the past. This could not be clearer than the impeachment trial of President Trump; before the trial even started the lawmakers were already lining up for or against the president strictly along party lines. Here's another rub: This, before any evidence had been presented, or witnesses heard.

Clearly, America's political divisions are not limited to just issues, but largely they are about sides. Partisanship in politics in legislation in the judicial system, one or two generations back, people took seriously to the ballot boxes. Today not so much; it is handled in the news media, the schools, and the communities. This nonpartisan trend did not start with President Trump, but it has very much accelerated during his term in office. But, that's only three years. It did not start with Barack Obama either, but there was a huge acceleration during his eight years in office. It has been a couple of generations coming from past presidents such as George W. Bush and on past the others, to even John F. Kennedy. With each passing president the division and nonpartisanship in government has grown larger.

So, hate, division, and nonpartisan government is fully bloomed in our constitutional Democratic Republic, and we Americans, with our love-hate partisan relationships will feel the pain as the division pulls us apart. There is no question that both parties are in full accord that the other party is not only taking this country in the wrong direction, but far worse are so misguided that they are a danger to this nation. To this, this Conservative voice would have to agree. As the intensity grows in the early months of the 2020 election, expect the divide, the partisanship, and even the hate to accelerate far into the election cycle and beyond the election.

Can we do anything about this worsening problem? If we could, it would have to start with the hate. Can we rid a nation of its hate that strikes out at its own people? It appears to be almost as devastating as the coronavirus and just keeps multiplying and multiplying. But what we know beyond all else is that hate is not inborn, it is learned. Every single person in this country, who hates Black Americans, or socialism, or White Americans, learned to do so. Every single person in this country that hates the Dodgers, or the Diamondbacks, learned to do so; and every single person in this country who hates America, or socialism, learned to do so. So, perhaps we should think about this: Not one person in this country was born with hate in their heart for Donald Trump. You learned it. We must, in this country, find a way back to unity and the only way that will happen again is through unlearning our hate.

Perhaps this is a good time for each of us to ask ourselves, "Who taught me to hate?" Who is it that you respected so much that you bought their hate and made it your own? Everyone knows the destructive force of hate, there comes a time in each of us that if you don't get rid of that hate, it will take you down.

Born with hate you are not; but born with compassion you are. Compassion literally means to suffer together. It can be defined as the feeling that arises when you are confronted with another person's suffering and that person feels motivated to help relieve the suffering. Compassion motivates people to go out of their way to help people with physical, mental, or emotional pains. It is the opposite of hate, which motivates one to cause mental or emotional pain, and even sometimes physical pain in others. You cannot truly be a compassionate person while your heart is motivated by hate.

Destroy the hate with an abundance of compassion. Someone once said that everyone has hate in their heart about one thing or another. Hatred is one of our deepest secrets. We don't like to live with it, but we don't want to admit it because most all people see hatred as repulsive, and those who bare it as repulsive as well, even though they have it buried somewhere in their own soul. So that's a lot of hate to dump and replace with compassion just so you can clean up a little division and nonpartisanship. But Lord, wouldn't it be great, even in politics to have to wake up in the morning, look at the paper, and say: "Hmmm, the Dodgers won last night, they beat my Diamondbacks; darn, we'll get then tonight." Or, read about President Trump and the fact that the unemployment rate went down again, and simply say: "Wow! This country is smoking. It must be true that even a broken clock is right twice a day. Good to see all these American's working and bringing pay checks home." That would create a whole lot less pain.

Each one of us has to break our own cycle of hate. But the fact is the key to overcoming hate is in education. It has to be at home, in our schools, and in our communities. Those are the places where if your look hard you will find the person that made you a hater. Sometimes we hook up with the wrong people in our schools that have distorted or demented ideas that they are eager to share with students who are gullible, or ill-informed. Sometimes that distortion is all about hate. Sometimes their practices in the classroom are propaganda forced on you by repeating it until you believe it. The adults in the communities and the schools must get these 'Judas goats' out. These people are all about indoctrination which is about force feeding their ideas; while education is about giving students the opportunity to discover through exploration. Get the haters out of our schools so they cannot be mentors for hate to your children.

Don't think for a second that hate doesn't come from the home, or the youth organizations, or churches in the community. It does indeed. There are false prophets for hate in all of your favorite haunts. Parents can be, and often are, haters without even being aware that they are passing hate right into the next generation through their own children. Certainly, it is important that children respect the values, principles, and opinions of their parents, but it is unhealthy to close their minds through your own bigotry.

It is far more profitable for children to be allowed to make their mistakes, correct their mistakes, and plan ways not to make the same bad choices over again. Your children are the most susceptible to hate than at any time in their lives; don't make them start off with your hate and then years later have to find a way to kick it out to find compassion.

The community is loaded with people who would take advantage of a young person's inexperience of mind and soul. I can attest to the good side of the community who mentored my physical, mental, and emotional well-being. In church, youth clubs, and athletics I was so fortunate to be mentored by great and caring people with strong personal values, principles and, to the person who would not allow me to step over the line, while encouraging me to make my own mind and way. It is easy for me to conclude that, at this level, I was not confronted by haters that forced themselves on my life. I made mistakes, I corrected them, and I made my choices based on my standards. Hate was not a part of it.

So, this is where the eradication of hate begins. Teaching young people that compassion for others that allows people to be moved by suffering, and to want to find ways to alleviate and prevent suffering that they see in others, is far better than filling their hearts with hate that will make their lives, at the very least, uncomfortable. There is nothing that heals like compassion. There is nothing that destroys hate like compassion. Perhaps Dr. Booker T. Washington, who I have quoted before, puts hate in its place through a strong resolve; "I shall allow no man to belittle my soul by making me hate him."

For some reason the Socialist actually believe that the election of Donald Trump created all of this hate that grows throughout this country; that it was his election that divided the nation among groups, and that it must have been Donald Trump himself that put this country on a collision course with our ultimate destruction. They have long been 'the sky is falling' party of haters, and as we have implied the hate we see has been building for a very long time. President

Trump didn't create it; but his election did reveal the truth about just how badly the divisiveness and hatred had begun to destroy God's greatest gift to the world.

We were finding out, as a result of this election, just how badly we hated ourselves to death. It is not just that they hate America's freedoms, values, and liberties, but the fact is they want nothing less than this country to become extinct. They want the land, the beautiful buildings, the amazing coast-to-coast infrastructure, and all the technology that is America, all created by the best that man could offer. All of this created by the capitalism and free enterprise, that they don't want to keep.

These socialist democrats feel that the only thing good about this country is what lies between the land and the technology, and everything else is oppressive and is the result of racist, bigoted forefathers. They hate our constitution, so it must go, which by the way, was a document like no other in the world, created to protect the minority from the tyranny of the majority. They hate capitalism, so it must be replaced with socialism. Free enterprise is nasty and must be ended with all enterprise controlled by the state. The short sightedness, of these people is astounding. Their inability to see consequences is like two little kids playing in an open field and one stumbles over an object. It is a bomb, an unexploded relic from WWII lying in the dirt for decades. Well, let's pick it up and take it home. There is a good chance this is not going to end well. And if you put your betting money on socialism, there's a good chance the bomb will explode. Oh, I'm sorry, I apologize, if you are a Socialist, you don't have betting money.

To hell with those who built this country; to hell with those who protected and sacrificed their blood and lives for this country; to hell with those who came before your parents or their parents, who paved the way for the growth of this great nation bathed in a freedom that billions over the ages never knew. Well, to hell with you! You just want our land and buildings so you can turn it over to the hate and tyranny of socialism. Sorry Bubba, it ain't gonna happen.

Socialist Democrats hate so much that they even hate White people. Good Lord, 90% of the socialist democrats are White people. They must hold some kind of a free pass that I will never understand. Since when does simply being White merit being spit on collectively? Probably about the same as when Conservative Republicans merit being chased, beaten, slandered, name-called, and run out of restaurants simply because collectively they are Conservative Republicans. Socialist Democrats are convinced that this country would be a much better place if all White people would just either die or leave.

Of course, Barack Obama and Michelle would second that idea whole-heartedly, and Oprah said as much when she said, "There will be hate-racism in America until the last old White man dies." What an ignorant statement of pure collectivization. I should say, "There will be crime and murder in America until the last old Black man dies, or is imprisoned." I would say that, but it would be an equally ignorant statement, so I won't.

I remember a quote from my college days by Dr. William Glasser, "Would it surprise you to know that an alcoholic really hates alcohol but they hate life more?" Socialist Democrats remind me of an alcoholic. They are lost in this bottle of hate, they can't live without it, they will manufacture ways to fulfill themselves by crying out hate absurdities whenever they need a fix; they are out of control of their emotions so badly that all they can feel is to hate. They can't get out of it because they really don't know what they hate the most, or the least. It could be Trump, or the Constitution, or White men, or capitalism, or racism, or homophobia, Islamophobia, illegal alienophobia, or even just their mother-in-lawophobia. They just simply hate so much they cannot escape from the entrapment of their bottle. In my humble opinion, they hate so much that they have lost their way and probably just hate themselves like every other hateophobic.

Just as a side note, when was the last time you saw a Socialist Democrat with a big ole smile on their face, like they were having a good time. I mean besides the impeachment trial. Right, me either. Even during that impeachment trial poor Nadler slept though most of it; Schiff was awake but didn't really know it, and Nancy was in deep haplessness. She was so stressed: "How stressed was she?" Wait for it, wait for it. "She was so stressed that even her facial lines had lines on them." Sadly, it is virtually impossible to hate as much as these people and still be healthy of mind, body, or soul.

These Socialist Democrats are a left wing party whose sole existence is to despise, attack, and destroy all that is good within America. They are a hate group unto themselves that want nothing more fervently than to demonize this nation, our law abiding and morally upright citizens, our unborn children, constitutional Conservatives, our legal gun owners, job producing businesses in oil, gas, and ore production, our rural and small town America, the ranching and farming of the middle and western America, our small business owners, our police, military and our veterans, and above all they want to demonize God, the Bible, and Christianity. And they demonize with their hate every single day.

From the moment Barack Obama came to the Oval Office they have found it important to not uplift, inspire, and unify but rather to berate with hate, lecture, and divide Americans. To them radical Black lives matter, gay and lesbian lives matter, radical Islamic lives matter, illegal aliens lives matter, convicted criminal's lives matter. But, in the meanwhile, the lives of ordinary law abiding, responsible working Americans do not matter, the lives of Christians, foreign or domestic do not matter, the lives of American military services men and women do not matter, and the lives of our veterans do not matter, nor do the lives of our thin blue line of the peace officers in our police and sheriff's departments around this country. They have shown these groups little, but disdain.

This is what the Socialist Democrat Party has become in the half century since the assassination of President John F. Kennedy. The party has become a well-organized, full throttle, take no prisoners, hell bent for leather, no apology needed or given, full-fledged hate group. They do not care who gets in their way of fulfilling their destiny; they will be eliminated by whatever means necessary.

'Don't Tread on Me' means nothing to them, 'In God we Trust' means nothing to them, 'Freedom and Unity,' means nothing to them, 'United we stand Divided we Fall' means nothing to them, 'With God All Things are Possible' means nothing to them, 'Live Free or Die' means nothing to them, 'E Pluribus Unum' meaning out of many means nothing to them, the Marine Corps motto, 'Semper Fidelis' meaning always faithful means nothing to them, the US. Army motto, 'This we'll Defend' means nothing to them, the U.S. Navy motto 'Non Sibi Sed Patriae' meaning not self but country means nothing to them, the U.S. Coast Guard motto, 'Semper Paratus' meaning always ready means nothing to them, the U.S. Air Force motto, 'Aim High—Fly—Fight—Win' means nothing to them, and the Delaware state motto, 'Liberty and Independence' means nothing but words to the Socialist Democrat.

Unfortunately, what does matter to the socialist democrats are the mottos of socialism, "From each according to his ability, to each according to his needs," and the motto of communism, "Workers of the World Unite." What these two mottos mean is that your government does not think you are good enough, or capable enough to lift yourself up, so we, the government will take care of you. Again by Dr. William Glasser, "It is almost impossible for anyone, even the most ineffective among us, to choose misery after becoming aware that it is a choice."

Through the power of hate, we could be witnessing the destruction of a great nation, and that hate is owned by the Socialists along with those who wave their flag for transforming America into a Socialist nation. Our schools and universities – overwhelmed by Marxist doctrine – are teaching disrespect if not hatred of White people and heterosexual males; a constant barrage of anti-male propaganda designed to put maleness in its place. The impact of such demeaning on young White males can be devastating and cause frustrating results. Much is done to demoralize them, but little to help them. Suicide of young males has escalated and reached a peak in 2017. From the Socialist point of view, it all comes from the same basket. If you destroy one part of the society, you can destroy the whole. Always at the core of their assault is hate.

It is pathetic that during President Trump's entire term he has had to spend his energy resisting the orchestrated attacks designed to remove him from office because of hate. Their outrageous activities have had a counter effect that was very unexpected for the Socialist Democrats. Their attacks have thoroughly destroyed the image of the Democratic Party; they have become the Socialist Democrat Party, the party of hate and chaos. Recovery will be slow.

IMAGINE THIS

Hate has made this nation a brutal place,
And leaves us a great mountain to climb,
It's man against man, their patience grows thin,
Their enmity the curse, and the crime.
Just imagine how grand this nation would be,
If Love, and Peace, and Harmony,
Replaced the hate that we know,
How great our souls would grow.
If this country took the way of ardor,
And in the place of mindless rancor,
They laid the plans for brotherhood,
Determined that the common good,
Would be the course we must pursue,
Just imagine what that would mean to you,
To you, and the millions unborn,
If you could wake upon the morn,
And know the disgust of hate was past,
That tenderness had returned at last,
This blessed change could come about,
Just imagine if Americans all made it Paramount,
To make your leaders understand,
By urgent and popular demand,
For the hate to be banished, disrespect must cease,
Just image that all would know the beauty of love and peace.
Unfortunately, it would seem,
At best, this image is but a dream,
For America as our history shows,
The way of tranquility, she rarely goes,
So, America, 'til Love can dominate our scene,
This country will wait ... 'neath our own made Guillotine.
There is nothing to imagine in a place laid bare from hate,
But much to discover when we come back to debate.

Chapter 18

Donald J. Trump:

The 45th President of the United States

This is the final chapter of this book and it is dedicated to Donald J. Trump, his first-term Presidency, his work, and his accomplishments. It will emphasize more about the man and his job than the stumbling blocks placed in his way during his first three years in the Oval Office. It will deal more with what he did to accomplish his vision for America and the promises he made to America as the 45th President of the United States.

But, before this chapter begins, I would like to tell one last story concerning my personal feelings regarding the election of this president. I am a proud American; I believe in this country with all my heart, and I feel so blessed to have been born an American. Sometimes we overlook the significance of that birthright and take it for granted. Being an American is to belong to a rather prestigious club. There are billions of people on this earth, and I am just one of a selected 330 million Americans, and I will stand by this country with the resolve of Patrick Henry and the ferociousness of General George S. Patton.

I am a life-long Democrat turned Conservative Republican because I could see the break of the Democratic Party with morality, ethics, and a divisive mentality that placed party ahead of family, religion, and country. I was a John F. Kennedy Democrat who stood by him and his administration in the same manner that I stand by Donald Trump today. When William F. Clinton made a mockery of the People's House, I left the party for all of the above reasons. He and Hillary Clinton were a sham on government and only interested in fulfilling their own destiny. Each Democratic president prior to Clinton gave me less and less reason to maintain my pride in the party, so it was time for change. From the time I left the party until today it has only gotten worse. As of now that party is gone, and in its place the Socialist Party of America.

Like all good Americans I was reading and watching all that I could about the people involved in the 2016 presidential election. I knew well who Hillary Clinton was, what she really stands for, and what I could expect from her if she was to become president. I was more interested in the myriad of Republican candidates who stepped up to challenge her and the Socialist Democrats for the White House. I knew our situation in America, and it was dire. I knew that if we did not win this election, we were beyond the crossroads between democracy and socialism. Barack Obama had brought us to the cauldron's rim. From this point forward America could go either way, from the trash heap of long dead democracy to the dying breed of modern-day socialism. Either of which would mark the destruction of our way of life.

I knew well what kind of a man needed to come forward from the mass of seventeen hopefuls, and I knew what qualities I needed to see in whoever won my vote. The Socialist Democrats are who they are. They are organized, with a ground game that is unmatched by the Republicans. They are bullies, devious, corrupt to the core, underhanded, and in many respects just plain evil. You cannot be just an average man or woman off the streets and defeat their ilk. You have to have played in the sewer right along with the rats; you have to have come face to face with evil, corruption, and behind-the-back trickery. You don't have to be that way, but you have to know all about it.

Here is who I was looking for to step up and slap these people in the face and say, "There's a new sheriff in town, and your line of crap isn't going to bode well in this town anymore." My candidate must have the personal strength of Godzilla himself. This will not be a job for a weakling; our president must be the one who can kick sand in the face of the weakling Democrats. I am not just speaking of physical strength here, or we would go out and grab up Arnold Schwarzenegger. I am speaking of the kind of strength that is mental, emotional, and all wrapped up in resolve. My president must have the resolve of the same Patrick Henry and the never say die determination of General George S. Patton.

The first criterion I must have in my president is that of a visionary. I have spoken of this numerous times throughout this book because the possession of vision or the lack of it is so important in politics. If you look at all at our greatest president's, one of the first things you could see was that of visionary power. We saw it in George Washington, Thomas Jefferson, Teddy Roosevelt, and Abraham Lincoln, and yes even in Franklin D. Roosevelt who had vast vision that more than helped guide us through WWII. This is the kind of leadership that can see into the seeable future. Like seldom in our history we need that leadership in the White House right now. We live in especially unsettling times, and like the great bald eagle, my president needs to have the foresight to see ahead in the distance and take preemptive measures to avert disaster. Far too many of our presidents have been decision and choice makers that led the nation into problems that bordered on disaster, because they did not possess the ability of foresight. Whichever one of the seventeen that survives the primaries must have vision beyond all of the others.

I will give you a little hint here, at the time of the first debate, which candidates I had my eye on and was hoping met the criteria I was seeking for my president. On my short list of seven finalists were Jeb Bush, Ted Cruz, Marco Rubio, Donald Trump, Scott Walker, Mike Huckabee, and Chris Christie. As the primaries and debates continued, I eliminated those who seemed not to meet my hopes. In these seven I saw some amount of vision in each, to varying degrees, but in all of these I also saw much of my second category which is a deep reverence for God.

As with vision, all of our great presidents had a strong feeling for God. It is imperative that the person seeking this office have strong moral values that recognize their accountability to God. The gigantic responsibilities of a president regarding social issues which affect the spiritual life and culture of a country are overwhelming. Whoever this person is must know what affects the heart of God, and you must be able to trace it through their words and deeds. With the frailties of man as they are, this is a tough onion to peel in politics. He does not have to be a Bible scholar, but I would like my president to have a clear relationship with his God.

Also, I would like my president to possess good character judgment and discretion. Character does matter – especially in the office of the presidency – the most prestigious office in the land and probably the world. Moral excellence should be the standard, not the exception. We have seen far too many examples of failed moral compasses in the Oval Office and it is not the place to be a hypocrite and espouse moral high ground while practicing lack of morals. Again, because of the nature of the beast of politics, it is another tough onion to peel.

In my conservative way of thinking, the man or woman who occupies the White House should embody the people's ideals. He should be able to empathize with the common folk, as well as with the affluent. We are a cross of all socioeconomic levels and you cannot relate with just one or two of these groups. A president cannot magnify himself above the people at any level. Along this line he must have good command of language, communicate well, and be able to think outside of the box. He should be well versed on important issues and not evade questions or engage in pandering simply to gain votes, as so many politicians do.

There is a serious shortage of saints in America, so do not expect to find all of these criteria at the highest level in each candidate. Hopefully the candidate I want will have some of each of these qualities to boost him above some of the others who appear not to be as strong. By the time we were approaching the end of the primaries and Trump blew out Indiana, Kasich and Cruz dropped out leaving Candidate Trump to stand alone and things were about over. I had two of the final three in my view, and I was wavering back and forth between Donald Trump and Ted Cruz. I like experience, but I was so darned tired of political experience that I was leaning towards Trump at the end. I liked Ted Cruz, but maybe it was time for fresh, nonpolitical change. Donald Trump had many of the qualities I wanted, and he had a little something in each one of the categories I listed as important. Besides, remember when I was talking about strength? My first remark about Donald Trump during the debates was, "Wow, he is like a bulldog." He showed no fear and if he went for you, it was your jugular that you needed to protect. And, in my mind, he is the best counter puncher since Muhammad Ali. If you try to set him up (which is exactly what the Socialist Democrats try to do), you are in deep kaka. That is exactly what knocked Jeb Bush out of the ring.

So, when the primaries were over, we had our candidate and I was quite happy. I was certain that he could take care of Hillary Clinton because she brought more baggage to the podium than anyone since her husband Bill. She was made to order for a jugular attack, and I knew Trump could handle anything she had to throw at him, but remember that Socialist Democrats steal signs and throw spitballs.

Now, this is the story I promised you. When November 8th finally arrived, I was more than ready to get my vote counted. I felt confident, but because of all that was at stake for America, I was very nervous and intense. I watched the progress of reporting the results, state by state, all evening long. There was joy, and disappointment; there was anger, and there was complacency. As we worked our way past the early evening, I became concerned that, too often, the expected results were not happening. I thought Donald Trump was in trouble and there was a good chance that Hillary was going to win. About 10:00 PM, with disappointment and disgust, I decided to go to bed. Oddly, I slept well, but at about 3:00 AM my wife threw on the lights in the bedroom, shook me awake and yelled, "He won, he won, he won." I jumped out of bed and went straight to the TV to see the results for myself. "My God, it is an election miracle. My God, thank you God, thank you, thank you, thank you."

My first thought after all those thank yous was, "By the miracle of God, this country has been saved from Marxist Socialist communism." At exactly that moment Fox News put on a clip that showed Bill Clinton dancing into a room, with arms stretched high screaming, "We won, we won, we won." But that was the exact moment that Hillary and Chelsea had just received the news that she had lost. In an instant the joy of victory became the agony of defeat. The smile that wrapped his face turned to whatever lays just below forlorn. He seemingly melted into the floor, and Hillary, in disbelief, was covered with agony that can only be described as a hopelessness that goes with the knowledge you did not succeed. Their realization was my realization. The Clintons were done. They were toast and Donald J. Trump was going to the White House.

I could not have been more excited, appreciative, and thankful. We had clearly dodged the silver bullet, and America was going to have a chance to redeem ourselves and place this country back on the road to a strong representative democracy. Someone once said – I believe it was Plato – "Democracy is a charming form of government, full of variety and disorder; and dispensing a sort of equality to equals and unequal's alike." Well, rather than scrapping this planet's last hope for a charming democracy, we now have the opportunity to show the world just how charming this democracy can be.

On January20, 2017 a huge crowd assembled at the west front of the United States Capital Building in Washington D.C. It was estimated to be a crowd of 300,000-600,000 very active Americans. There were an estimated 30.6 million watching the event on television. The address itself was short, just sixteen minutes, and was the shortest since the address by Jimmy Carter. It was short, sweet, and to the point. At 12:00 PM the President took the Oath of Office and in just a few moments he was ready to deliver his inaugural address to the people of America.

The custom of delivering an inauguration address was started with our very first inauguration – George Washington – on April 30, 1789. After taking his oath of office on the balcony of Federal Hall in New York City, President Washington proceeded to the Senate Chamber where he read a speech before the members of Congress and other dignitaries. Every president since George Washington has delivered an inaugural address. Most of these presidents used their inaugural address to present their vision of America, and to set forth their goals for the nation during their term in office. President Donald

J. Trump was no exception. Though it was short in length, it clearly identified his view for this country and what his hopes and vision was for the American people over the next four years.

The following is the complete transcript of President Trump's inaugural address.

Chief Justice Roberts, President Carter, President Clinton, President Bush, President Obama, fellow Americans, and people of the world: Thank you.

We, the citizens of America, are now joined in a great national effort to rebuild our country and to restore its promise for all of our people.

Together, we will determine the course of America and the world for years to come.

We will face challenges. We will confront hardships. But we will get the job done.

Every four years, we gather on these steps to carry out the orderly and peaceful transfer of power, and we are grateful to President Obama and First Lady Michelle Obama for their gracious aid throughout this transition. They have been magnificent.

Today's ceremony, however, has very special meaning. Because today we are not merely transferring power from one administration to another, or from one party to another, but we are transferring power from Washington, D.C. and giving it back to you, the American People.

For too long, a small group in our nation's Capital has reaped the rewards of government while the people have borne the cost.

Washington flourished but the people did not share in its wealth. Politicians prospered but the jobs left, and the factories closed.

The establishment protected itself, but not the citizens of our country.

Their victories have not been your victories; their triumphs have not been your triumphs; and while they celebrated in our nation's capital, there was little to celebrate for struggling families all across our land.

That all changes starting right here, and right now, because this moment is your moment: It belongs to you. It belongs to everyone gathered here today and everyone watching all across America.

This is your day. This is your celebration. And this, the United States of America, is your country.

What truly matters is not which party controls our government, but whether our government is controlled by the people.

January 20th 2017 will be remembered as the day the people became the rulers of this nation again.

The forgotten men and women of our country will be forgotten no longer. Everyone is listening to you now.

You came by the tens of millions to become part of a historic movement the likes of which the world has never seen before.

At the center of this movement is a crucial conviction: that a nation exists to serve its citizens.

Americans want great schools for their children, safe neighborhoods for their families, and good jobs for themselves.

These ae the just and reasonable demands of a righteous public.

But for too many of our citizens, a different reality exists: Mothers and children trapped in poverty in our inner cities; rusted-out factories scattered like tombstones across the landscape of our nation; an education system flushed with cash, but which leaves our young and beautiful students deprived of knowledge; and the crime and gangs and drugs that have stolen too many lives and robbed our country of so much unrealized potential. This American carnage stops right here and stops right now.

We are one nation, and their pain is our pain. Their dreams are our dreams; and their success will be our success. We share one heart, one home, and one glorious destiny.

The oath of office I take today is an oath of allegiance to all Americans. For many decades, we've enriched foreign industry at the expense of American industry; subsidized the armies of other countries while allowing for the very sad depletion of our military; we've defended other nation's borders while refusing to defend our own; and spent trillions of dollars overseas while America's infrastructure has fallen into disrepair and decay.

We've made other countries rich while the wealth, strength, and confidence of our country has disappeared over the horizon.

One by one, the factories shuttered and left our shores, with not even a thought about the millions upon millions of American workers left behind. The wealth of our middle class has been ripped from their homes and then redistributed across the entire world.

But that is the past and we are looking only at the future. From this day forward, a new vision will govern our land. From this moment on, it's going to be America First.

Every decision on trade, on taxes, on immigration, on foreign affairs, will be made to benefit American workers and American families.

We must protect our borders from the ravages of other countries making your products, stealing our companies, and destroying our jobs. Protection will lead to great prosperity and strength.

I will fight for you with every breath in by body, and I will never, ever let you down. America will start winning again, winning like never before.

We will bring back our jobs. We will bring back our borders. We will bring back our wealth. And we will bring back our dreams.

We will build new roads, and highways, and bridges, and airports, and tunnels, and railways all across our wonderful nation.

We will get our people off of welfare and back to work; rebuilding our country with American hands and American labor.

We will follow two simple rules: Buy American and hire American.

We will seek friendship and goodwill with the nations of the world, but we do so with the understanding that it is the right of all nations to put their own interests first.

We do not seek to impose our way of life on anyone, but rather to let it shine as an example for everyone to follow.

We will reinforce old alliances and form new ones, and unite the civilized world against radical Islamic terrorism, which we will eradicate completely from the face of the earth.

At the bedrock of our politics will be a total allegiance to the United States of America, and through our loyalty to our country, we will rediscover our loyalty to each other.

When you open your heart to patriotism there is no room for prejudice. The Bible tells us, "How good and pleasant it is when God's people live together in unity."

We must speak our minds openly, debate our disagreements honestly, but always pursue solidarity.

When America is united, America is totally unstoppable.

There should be no fear, we are protected, and we will always be protected.

We will be protected by the great men and women of our military and law enforcement and, most importantly, we are protected by God.

Finally, we must think big and dream even bigger.

In America, we understand that a nation is only living as long as it is striving.

We will no longer accept politicians who are all talk and no action, constantly complaining but never doing anything about it.

The time for empty talk is over. Now arrives the hour of action.

Do not let anyone tell you it cannot be done. No challenge can match the heart and fight and spirit of America.

We will not fail. Our country will thrive and prosper again.

We stand at the birth of a new millennium, ready to unlock the mysteries of space, to free the Earth from the miseries of disease, and to harness the energies, industries and technologies of tomorrow.

A new national pride will stir our souls, lift our sights, and heal our divisions.

It is time to remember that old wisdom our soldiers will never forget: that whether we are Black or Brown or White, we all bleed the same red blood of patriots, we all enjoy the same glorious freedoms, and we all salute the same great American flag.

And whether a child is born in the urban sprawl of Detroit or the windswept plains of Nebraska, they look up at the same night sky, they fill their heart with the same dreams, and they are infused with the breath of life by the same almighty Creator.

So, to all Americans, in every city near and far, small and large, from mountain to mountain, and from ocean to ocean, hear these words:

You will never be ignored again.

Your voice, your hopes, and your dreams will define our American destiny. And your courage and goodness and love will forever guide us along the way.

Together, we will make America strong again.

We will make wealthy again.

We will make America proud again.

We will make America safe again.

And yes, together, we will make America great again. Thank you. God bless you. And God bless America.

Obviously, there has been much said about the president's address, both good and critical. But that has always been the case throughout history, and it is simply the pattern of the two-party system. The Democrats seldom like what the Republicans say and visa-versa. It is particularly true in the presidential addresses because they always speak of a new direction that implies the old direction was wrong and was now going to be corrected. They always speak of new goals and out with the old goals. And they are always committing the people to a whole new set of dreams, pushing the old dreams aside as just so much of a waste of your time. And, of course, there are always the new promises that are clearly more in tune with what the American people want, need, and value than those old promises of the other guys, who just did not have a clear idea of what this country truly values and needs. So, I wouldn't place much stock in the criticisms of the Socialist Democrats, or their long arm of verification from the media. Nothing is more clearly biased than the criticism of a new president's address. It should be remembered that each president faces the particular challenges of his time and puts his own rhetorical stamp on their address.

The times of the Cold War were unique and a particular challenge to John F. Kennedy as well, and I thought his was one of the great inaugural address' of all time. Everything in the speech was about the particular problems that America was going through and how he was setting goals, making promises, and reaching out to the people. I could be biased because I was a Democrat at the time, and I was abashed at the criticisms of that nasty ole GOP. Clearly, they were unfair to the president and well beyond just being biased. I can remember thinking, "What is wrong with those people? Are they just ignorant?"

President Trump wasted no time in getting started with government business. As soon as he was inaugurated, during his first week in office, he signed six executive orders that all had to do with his campaign promises. The first was signed just hours after he was sworn into office. This was the EO 13765, titled Executive Order Minimizing the Economic Burden of the Patient Protection and Affordable Care Act, pending appeal. The order gave no details about what aspects of the law it was targeting. But its broad language gave federal agencies the latitude to change, delay, or waive provisions of the law that they considered too costly for insurers, drug makers, doctors, patients, or states. This suggests that the executive order could have wide ranging impact and would allow for the dismantling of the law even before Congress made a move to repeal Obama Care.

The second executive order that President Trump attacked was the Trans-Pacific Partnership, (TPP) which was Barack Obama's centerpiece for a strategic relationship with Asia. Before he withdrew the U.S. from the TPP it was set to become the world's largest free trade deal that would cover 40% of the global economy. It has long been clear to Donald Trump that free trade works negatively economically against the U.S. and he wanted nothing to do with it for America. He was convinced that trade agreements like the TPP would likely accelerate U.S. decline in manufacturing, increased lower wages, and steep increases in inequality. President Trump had campaigned diligently to remove the U.S. from any and all free trade agreements and he quickly made it clear that he would honor his promise to his followers.

Thirdly, the president signed a Presidential Memorandum directing the reinstatement of the Mexico City policy. Known as the Global Gag Rule, when activated this policy banned using U.S. foreign aid for abortion-related activities. The policy had been rescinded in 2009 by Barack Obama to allow these funds to be used to propagate such abortion activities, but now President Trump was putting it back in play for his pro-life Republicans. The nongovernmental entities targeted by this rule had to certify that they would not promote abortion as a method of family planning. Standing with the Republican pro-lifers was one of President Trump's major promises throughout the campaign and he did not let them down.

The Keystone XL and the Dakota Access Pipeline construction project had been held hostage by President Obama for his entire eight years in office. He had ample opportunity and support for passing these measures through, but he did not. He found one excuse after another not to go forward with the plans and it was clear that they were being held back for solely political reasons. Obviously, this was a payback to his deep pocket support by friendly Democrat donors and his allies in the environmentalist movement. Donald Trump signed the executive order for the Keystone XL to get Canadian crude oil flowing through our American pipeline to our largest refineries in the southeast corner of Texas, near Port Arthur, on the coast of the

Gulf of Mexico. This would enable the U.S. to stockpile huge amounts of crude and refine it for public use. It has always been the idea of President Trump that America has the resources and should become independent in the oil industry; the Keystone Pipeline along with the Dakota Access Pipeline should accomplish that goal.

At the same time as the Keystone XL, the Dakota Access Pipeline was signed into law. This pipeline would move crude oil from the Bakken Formation, which has vast amounts of light crude oil located in Montana and North Dakota. The crude is moved through a 1,172 mile-long underground oil pipeline to an oil terminal in Patoka, Illinois and then to Nederland, Texas and their vast refineries. This pipeline is the most environmentally sensitive way to transport crude oil in America. Both of these projects were met with a great deal of protests but have thus far proven to be very effective. This pipeline is certainly more effective and safer than earlier hauling by railroad.

Probably the most rewarding of President Trump's early executive orders was the signing of the one that started the planning and design process to construct the wall along the U.S. border with Mexico. No other issue was talked about more by candidate Trump and supported more diligently by his followers. To both sides, this was a passionate topic. The Socialist Democrats leadership who had over the past eight to ten years been entirely in favor of a border wall, now took the stand that a wall was not the answer to improve border issues with illegal crossings. Throughout the campaign and the first three years of his office this issue was a battle of words every day.

President Trump put it all on the table and the Socialists used every trick in their playbook to try to stop the wall from being built. They withdrew all funding, challenged the constitutionality of the wall and of the other sources of funding that Trump came up with. It is still a significant issue, but the Supreme Court sided with President Trump in his efforts to re-channel funds from the Pentagon and the wall is being built at a steady rate. In area's along the border where the wall has been completed reports show that there has been significant slowing of illegal immigrants crossing into the U.S.

In my mind, it was a 'red letter day' when in January 2017, President Trump nominated Neil Gorsuch to the U.S. Supreme Court. He was nominated to fill the seat of Justice Antonin Scalia, who held the seat until his death in 2016. By April of 2017 Justice Gorsuch was confirmed, and the honor of constitutionality took a major step forward in our government. This new red letter day was a huge event. One of my most important priorities in the GOP winning the Presidency was for exactly this reason. America could not afford a Democrat in the Oval Office and have them nominate another Progressive or Socialist Democrat to the Supreme Court. Later, when President Trump's nomination of Brett Kavanaugh was confirmed on 6 October 2018 another strict supporter of the Constitution was added to the Supreme Court. The GOP, and much of America, could not have been more satisfied. Both of these Trump nominations were outstanding judicial judges from the lower courts and will make a huge impact on America for decades.

We have been witness to the tactics of judges appointed by Obama, and earlier democratic presidents, and the biased Progressive-Socialist decisions that they hand down. Through their intolerance and hatred of President Trump they have been a constant stumbling block to the work of the president. Their incapable ability to deal with our constitution as it is, but rather interpret it so that it fits their personal agendas is a hallmark of their disdain for the president. It has been a nightmare with the Socialist Democrat leadership constantly turning to these judges to halt the progress on building the wall and many other plans that President Trump was working on for America. Just as the Socialist Democrats in the House are obstructionists so are the Socialist Democrat leaning judges of the appeals courts.

Along with his early executive orders President Trump took aim at our taxes and trade practices. Economic expansion coming out of the recession left a lot to be desired. From 2009-2015 the economy was just limping along with a remarkably slow rate of growth. Taxes had been raised, there was a myriad of regulations imposed on both businesses and individuals, domestic spending was out of control along with the national debt that was about to double the previous administration. Domestic spending was soaring and the money being spent on entitlements was outrageous as more and more people left the work force and entered various welfare programs.

Clearly, much had to be done and President Trump was clear in his mind what that was. In December of his first year he signed the Tax Cuts and Jobs Act of 2017, which cut the corporate tax rate to 21%, lowered personal tax brackets, increased child tax credit, doubled the estate tax exemption to $11.2 million, and limited state and local deductions to $10,000. This tax bill would be a good start but was likely not yet enough for the individual taxpayers. The Socialist Democrats screamed that it was too top heavy for the wealthy and didn't provide enough for the middle class. Pretty much the same old tune and the same old lyrics. President Trump wanted the corporations and industry to get a break in the right places, because his two forked goal was to entice industry to come back home and for them to create American jobs. For Donald Trump everything was about jobs for the creation of a strong economy, whereas the Socialist Democrats want to push for welfare entitlements.

President Trump has long been a cynic in regard to multilateral trade deals, and largely believed that they fostered unfair trade practices. He much more favored bilateral trade deals, because they would allow one party, who may not be satisfied with the fairness of the ongoing activity by the other party, to pull out at will. If America was to remain in a trade deal, he must recognize that the deal provided either neutral or positive balance of trade for America. Any trade deal that had, over time, provided a negative trade balance was ready for the chopping block.

As far back as the 1980's Donald Trump had criticized unfair trade deficits. He severely attacked The North Atlantic Free Trade Agreement (NAFTA) during the 2015 campaign. This agreement is noted to carry an extremely negative balance for the U.S. and candidate Trump was advocating to redo its provisions to create a better trade balance. This he did when he became president, and at present this fair trade agreement between the U.S., Mexico, and Canada carries what will prove to be a much more balanced approach for all members.

In early March of 2018, the president announced his intention to impose a 25% tariff on steel and a 10% tariff on aluminum imports. He was unafraid of trade wars and only a week later signed an order to impose the tariffs. He then launched into a trade war with China with sharply increased tariffs on 818 categories, with a value of some $50 million on Chinese goods imported into the U.S. President Trump had not been happy with the unfair trade practices of China for a long time before he became president.

He confronted China over a myriad of economic abuses that had gone back decades while previous presidents simply buried their heads in the sand because of their fear of creating a trade war.

President Trump was quite obviously a president of a different cut. At one point he said, "Trade wars are not so bad, they are easy to win." He accused China of everything from currency manipulation, to export subsidies, and economic espionage. Since the war started, the negotiations on these tariffs have been ongoing, and you can take it to the bank that President Trump will not back off. He will stand firm until he sees a fair balance between China and the workers of the U.S.

Two significant results of the negotiations are: In 2018 President Trump backed a reform giving U.S. regulators greater power to review foreign actions by China and others, and he blocked several attempted sales of U.S. technology companies to Chinese firms. He also ramped up restrictions on major Chinese technology firms operating in the U.S., including telecommunications giant, 'Huawei,' concerned that such firms could be manipulated by Beijing.

The president's argument is that China is playing the World Trade Organization (WHO) by taking advantage of special rules designed for developing countries, and as far as he is concerned, "The U.S. will leave the WHO if necessary." Trade and tariff disputes are always a tough matter, but not many U.S. presidents have the nerve (cohones) to take on the task. In today's world of horrific dysfunction, Donald Trump alone is unafraid to take on any, and all, comers if in the end America will become stronger and greater. In his short three years, he has taken on every tough opponent that all others who preceded him left untouched.

President Trump reminds me of an up and coming pugilist who wants to be champion in the worst kind of way. He stands in the middle of the ring with any opponent throwing haymakers in one exchange after another until the other guy is so tired that he just does not see the left hook coming out of nowhere. If the opponent starts throwing some good shots, Trump will resort to counterpunching and deflect everything that comes his way until his combatant just has nothing left in the tank. He will win and then take on another tough opponent, not a nobody; he will fight only the best because that is how you get to fight for the championship. You don't become a champion by beating the weak ones; you beat the toughest.

President Trump knows the insufferable regulations that have been imposed on Americans were having a devastating impact on the economy and jobs. He favored policies that would roll back and dismantle earlier government regulations. Over his first three years he has signed fifteen Congressional Review Acts to review earlier regulations that allow Congress to repeal executive regulations considered by the present administration as ill-conceived or inappropriate. President Trump is only the second president to sign any such resolutions after the first CRA resolution was passed in 2001. During his first six weeks in office, he delayed, suspended, or reversed ninety of these federal regulations. The vast majority of these were issued by Barack Obama. Ultimately, fourteen of these resolutions, repealing Obama administration rules, were passed and signed into law. Eliminating these regulations took a great deal of pressure off of businesses and many individual working groups that were shackled by these rules.

Though Donald Trump was in step with most of the GOP platform in 2016 he did have concerns about abortion. He favored modifying opposition to abortion by allowing for exceptions in cases of rape, incest, and circumstances that could endanger the health of the mother. He is clearly a strong pro-life Republican but felt that these aspects needed special consideration. He was committed to appointing pro-life justices, and did, from the Supreme Court down to the lower courts appoint strong constitutional pro-life judges. He professes to support traditional marriage but considers the nationwide legality of same-sex marriage a settled issue.

He supports the constitutional interpretation of the Second Amendment and claims he is opposed to gun control in general. He stands steadfastly with the premise of the Second Amendment that citizens have the clear right to ownership of guns and that right is protected by the Second Amendment. He does, however, oppose legalizing recreational marijuana but supports legalizing medical marijuana. He also favors capital punishment.

As we have noted, the immigration issue has been a hot bed for the president from the moment he took office. His proposed policies have been a bitter and contentious debate not only during the campaign but throughout his first three years. Beyond just building the border wall between Mexico and the U.S. he openly and repeatedly vowed that Mexico would be paying for it. He pledged massive deportation of illegal immigrants residing in the United States, and severely criticized birthright citizenship for creating anchor babies. He clarified that deportation would focus on criminals, visa overstays, and security threats. He would target habitual and violent criminals such as the gang MS-13. During his first three years numerous raids have been carried out against the MS-13, rounding them up and deporting or jailing them.

The travel ban question became a can of worms that raised the temperatures of Americans across the U.S. It was another issue that widely divided between the Trump supporters and the followers of the Socialist Democrats. Following the November 2015 Paris attacks, candidate Trump opened the controversy by proposing to ban Muslim foreigners from entering the United States until a stronger vetting system could be implemented. Obviously, he was interested in closing down American access by radical Muslims, mostly from countries that had open hostility toward the U.S. Immediately the Socialist Democrats started name calling and the media jumped in to overstate the entire issue. Later he restated his proposal to apply to countries with a proven history of terrorism.

Just short of two years later, after becoming president, he signed on 27 January 2017 executive order 13769, which suspended admission of refugees for 120 days and denied entry to citizens of Iraq, Iran, Libya, Somalia, Sudan, Syria, and Yemen for ninety days. And the travel ban war was on. The order was imposed without warning and took effect immediately. Since there was no time to prepare to carry out the order, there was much confusion and chaos. To make matters worse Sally Yates, the acting Attorney General, directed Justice Department lawyers not to defend the order, which she considered unenforceable and unconstitutional; President Trump wasted no time in firing her. There were now multiple legal challenges filed as Obama lower appeals court judges blocked its implementation throughout the country. A month later, President Trump revised the order, but again federal Obama judges from three Liberal states blocked the order. It was becoming a deep political battle. Finally, on 26 June 2017, the Supreme Court ruled that the ban could be enforced on visitors who lack a credible claim of a bona fide relationship with a person or entity in the United States.

Three months later, on 24 September the temporary order was replaced by Presidential Proclamation 9645, which permanently restricted travel from the originally targeted countries except for Iraq and Sudan, and further banned travelers from North Korea and Chad along with certain Venezuelan officials. After lower courts partially blocked the new restrictions, the Supreme Court allowed the September version to go into full effect on December 4, and later upheld the travel ban in June 2019. From start to finish there was much criticism and numerous challenges, but in the end the ban was supported by the weight of the Supreme Court and became law.

Most Americans were in support of the ban for no other reason that vetting needed to be done, and the present process was badly and sadly lacking. America is a melting pot and Americans are good with that, but it all comes down to the single word vetting. America, nor any other country should be forced to take in immigrants who are incapable of supporting themselves in a reasonable amount of time, or are a detriment to the laws, values, and principles of the country who is their host. No country should be forced to take in unvetted people who are not interested in becoming a part of that country and willing to support its constitution and legal system. This is basically what President Trump was all about as well, but the critics were so closed-minded that their intolerance of him overruled reality.

American's, both Republican and Democrat, believe in immigration, as we are and always have been a country ready and prepared to accept those from foreign lands who were eager to find the freedom that our forefathers sought. Our Statue of Liberty is the symbol of the willingness of Americans to open our borders and cities to newcomers. Imprinted on a plaque attached to our Lady of Liberty is the phrase 'Give me your tired, your poor, your huddled masses yearning to breathe free.' This quote comes from a sonnet, from Emma Lazarus called *New Colossus*. Her sonnet is printed in full below.

NEW COLOSSUS
(The Statue of Liberty Poem)

Not like the brazen giant of Greek fame,
With conquering limbs astride from land to land,
Here at our sea-washed, sunset gates shall stand

A mighty woman with a torch, whose flame
Is the imprisoned lightning, and her name
Mother of Exiles. From her beaconed-hand
Glows world-wide welcome, her mild
eyes command
The air-bridged harbor that twin cities frame.
"Keep, ancient lands, your storied pomp!" cries she
With silent lips. "Give me your tired your poor,
Your huddled masses yearning to breathe free,
The wretched refuse of your teeming shore.
Send these, the homeless, tempest-tossed to me.
I lift my lamp beside the golden door!"

Yes! Without a doubt, immigrants are still welcomed to this land. America has more immigrants than any other country in the world. Today, more than 44 million people living in the U.S. were born in another country. About one-fifth of the world's migrants in 2017 came to America. We have the most diverse population in the world, with just about every country in the world represented among U.S. immigrants. Today 77% of all immigrants in America are lawful immigrants – naturalized, lawful, permanent, and temporary – and the remaining 25% are unauthorized, or illegal immigrants. That total is in excess of 10.5 million. The only immigrants in this country who are in question are those who came here in defiance of our laws and have no intentions in becoming Americans. I agree with President Trump that those people should not be here; they should all be vetted, and if found to have been self-sufficient and productive law-abiding citizens they should have the opportunity to become Americans. Those who when vetted are found to not be self-sufficient, non-productive, or criminal should be sent back to their own countries.

By some, President Trump has been described as a noninterventionist, or an American nationalist. These people say that he believes in a foreign policy that holds that countries should not be involved in the affairs of foreign nations, while maintaining diplomatic and trade relationships. Given the clear opportunity, I believe he would maintain that stance. He has repeatedly said that he supports an America First foreign policy, and encourages that others do the same. His preference would be for America to look more inward and arrange its resources around domestic needs.

President Trump does not like wars, says we have been embroiled in the Middle East for far too long, and it is useless to hang on spending money uselessly and staying where we are clearly not wanted. We have lost too many good soldiers in what is a nonproductive war that under current conditions cannot be won. In December of 2018 he declared a victory over ISIS and ordered the withdrawal of all troops from Syria. General Mattis disagreed with this move and resigned the next day, saying that this move amounted to an abandonment of Kurd allies. Apparently, against his better judgment, President Trump backed off on the removal of all troops from Syria when on 6 January 2019 national security advisor John Bolton announced that America would remain in Syria. They would remain until ISIS was eradicated and Turkey would guarantee that it would not strike our Kurdish allies.

When, in October 2019 Turkey planned to carry out a military offensive in northern Syria, President Trump pulled troops out of that area in order to avoid interference with the operation. His action was severely criticized by both parties of Congress who argued that his move betrayed the American allied Kurds, and it would largely benefit ISIS, Turkey, Russia, Iran, and Bashar al-Assad's Syrian regime. Trump defended his move, citing the high cost of supporting the Kurds, and the lack of support from the Kurds in past U.S. wars. Eventually the move was condemned by an overwhelming vote in the

House. It was a very strong bipartisan vote of 354 to 60 that supported the complaint that the move undermined the fight against ISIS and was in all practical purposes an abandonment of U.S. allies.

Trump's other hot button was Iran; he described the leadership as being a 'rogue regime,' but insisted that he did not seek a regime change in Iran. During the campaign he repeatedly and severely criticized the Joint Comprehensive Plan of Action (JCPOA or Iran Nuclear Deal) that had been negotiated with the United States, Iran, and five other world powers in 2015. He called the plan terrible saying the Obama administration had negotiated it from desperation.

In January of 2017 Iran carried out ballistic missile tests, considered to be in violation of the nuclear deal, and President Trump imposed sanctions on twenty-five Iranian individuals and entities a month later. Trump tried to build support for the sanctions among European officials encouraging them against doing business with Iran. In August he signed into law the Countering America's Adversaries Through Sanctions Act (CAATSA) that grouped together sanctions against Iran Russia, and North Korea. Finally, on 18 May 2018 he announced that the United States unilateral departure from the JCPOA, or the Iran Nuclear Deal. Dealing with Iran during President Trump's first term has been more than a handful in spite of the constant sanctions they continually harass, and cause chaos, and mayhem in and around the Persian Gulf and the Gulf of Oman.

Recently, videos caught Iran red-handed removing an unexploded mine from the side of an oil tanker damaged in an attack in the Gulf of Oman. The United States also released images of a Japanese tanker apparently showing the unexploded mine before it was removed. Several other cases of similar attempts at damaging non-ally ships in the Gulf have likewise been identified. After several of these events U.S. Secretary of State Mike Pompeo said at a news conference, "It is the assessment of the U.S. that the Islamic Republic of Iran is responsible for these attacks." Of course, the Iranian President Hassan Rouhani denied any Iranian involvement and then like good Liberals, pointed the fickle finger of fate at the U.S. accusing them of being a serious threat to the stability in the Middle East.

Constant tit for tat between the two powers reached a climax when President Trump authorized the killing of Iranian General Soleimani. On 3 January 2019 Trump authorized the U.S. drone strike that killed Soleimani in Baghdad. Officials said that Soleimani was planning imminent attacks on Americans and this coupled with the fact that the U.S. held him responsible for hundreds of other American deaths decided it was time to take him out. The assassination had previously been requested by both Mike Pompeo and national security adviser John Bolton for earlier attacks on Americans, but President Trump declined stating he'd only take that step if Iran crossed his red line: Killing Americans. Finally, the opportunity came when and he gave the order to go.

The killing of Soleimani certainly ratcheted up tensions one more time between Iran and the U.S. and the Iranians meekly carried out a retaliatory missile attack on U.S. and coalition forces. But it was a futile show of non-force. Critics say that previous administrations opted against killing Soleimani over concerns it would endanger for Americans and civilians by creating greater unrest. These people forget that previous administrations had no problem when Bin Laden was taken out. It is clear that Soleimani had a lot of American blood on his hands and he had been held as responsible for other rocket attacks prior to his death that did kill a U.S. civilian contractor and wounded several other Americans. Let me assure you that, the picture painted of him being a 'saint,' by the media, was just so much baloney from the mainstream.

The Socialist Democrats made themselves look like fools by defending Soleimani simply because they would never support anything President Trump did no matter how much good it was for the country and the safety of Americans. Kellyanne Conway remarked, "I'm a little tired of the hero worshipping by the Democrats over whoever the president has taken out." The Socialist Democrats are so far out in left field that if President Trump recommended that Charlie Mansor be executed for his crimes they would be totally aghast and overwhelmingly shocked at such a barbaric attack on a model American.

All presidents do great things and all presidents make mistakes that I'm certain they would like a do-over button. Everyone has a different set of criteria they use to determine the success or failure of a president. In my conservative mind, if a presidential candidate announces his promises to the people, campaigns rigidly on those promises, and then wins the election for those who supported those promises, becomes the president and successfully brings those promises to reality of law, that is a great president. He is the first president in my recollection that has actually tried to keep every promise he made. He is not there yet, but what a remarkable attempt in just the first three years of his first term of office. Should he be reelected I would not be surprised in the least that he would complete his entire list. Even if he missed getting just one, it would still be remarkable.

I remember one of his early speeches where he promised to drain the swamp and I thought oooh, I'm not so sure he even realizes how deep that one goes. But above all the other promises, this one is likely the one that would, by the people, be the most appreciated.

America has no love relationship with Congress. We are equally disappointed with both sides. We have such sadness that our own party fails to stand strong against the absurdly dysfunctional Socialist Democrats. When we need to be our strongest, we shrivel up and let those mindless souls pistol whip us out of reality. When they do that, and the people start calling for term limits I feel like crying out, "Take ours first." But generally, common sense returns, and I understand that no matter how our Republicans in Congress fail, at their worst they are still a mountain higher than the Socialist Democrats. If Donald Trump would fall short of being one of the great presidents of all time, or since WWII, or whenever, it would be because he happened to have his presidency at the same time that socialism was weaseling its way into our legislative process. In fact, I would have to feel that those conditions are a plus for a great president. If you can actually function effectively in a democracy, under the weight of socialism, you must be a great president. I can think of very few from our past that even had to carry the load of performing for the people while fighting off the savagery, hostility, hate, intolerance, bigotry, defiance of half of your own people, and that half were Marxist Socialist Communists.

To this I say, thank you Mr. President. I admire your grit, your resolve, your steadfast love of our country and your willingness to place yourself in this situation for the sake of your people. I am so admiring of your family and their willingness to withstand the abuse, criticism, and slander; what tremendous strength you all possess. I am late in my life, but I cannot tell you how much I have learned about being an American. Watching you and your family deal with the constant barrage of the ugly and disrespectful side of this country has been an amazing experience. I can only suggest that there are few American Patriots in this country who could stand against an onslaught so wicked, vile, and evil. I often borrow a quote that says, "I will allow no man to belittle my soul, by making me hate them." I can say that the Socialist Democrats clearly tested my soul, by the tactics of hate deep into their very bones that they used to disrespect you and your family and the office of the Presidency. We often hear that our ancestors of the WWII era were the greatest generation. I believe this to be true, and I believe you and your family are a throwback to those times. They were collectively a people of patriots, who had great love of country and fully prepared to put it all on the line to protect their home. They were patriots in battle, patriots at home, and patriots in business and industry. The resolve of the greatest generation is unmatched by any other generation in our history, with the possible exception of our original patriots in arms. Your resolve and that of your family has been an extension of that of the greatest Generation.

FREEDOM NOT SLAVERY

Freedom when taken for granted
Is a treasure easily lost,
And we who have lived 'neath its blessings,
Have not forgotten the bloodshed it cost.
Two centuries ago we were full oppressed,
By a nation 'cross the sea,
And only the strength of brave stalwart men,
Broke the chains that set us free.

Now some have become delusioned,
For them a country that's lost its goals,
The fire of faith that burned brightly,
Is now dimming and turning to coals.
Will our children be free or live in slavery,
Only time alone will tell,
But this we must know and not forget,
Life without freedom is hell.

THE PORTRAIT OF A NATION

I didn't know the price we would pay
When we let gloom dictate our way
But life made sure I saw the light
I didn't understand it quite;
But then the realization grew
That life is largely a point of view.
A nation is not a deed of fate
A nation is something we create,
For thoughts are thing as we've been taught
And then this glimpse of truth I caught.
Upon the portrait of a nation

Gloom leaves a smudge,
Somehow the portrait seems to say,
"What right have you with sullen brush
To mar this painting, beauty crush?"
So now, on canvas stretched by dawn
The outline of this nation I have drawn.
I'll try to paint with colors clear
With hues of patience, love and cheer.
And when the final touch is made
And in the past this nation is laid,
Hung in the gallery of time,
A work of art may hang sublime.

THE SAGE

Love and Hate dwell side by side,
Within your thoughts they both abide.
Love or Hate are not a place,
Strangers are they to time and space.
Love and Hate each man creates,
By thoughts and deeds he formulates.
Love your higher nature knows
While Hate is lower nature woes.
And day by day, right where you dwell,
Love is there, and so is Hate.
As each country begins to sway
One nation appears to lead the way.

Bibliography

Abrams, Allison; "The Psychology of Hate," verified by Psychology Today, (March 9, 20017)

Argetsinger, Amy; "Why does everyone call Donald Trump 'The Donald?'" The Washington Post (September 1, 2015)

Badow, Doug; "Is Bernie Sanders Still a Communist at Heart?" American Spectator, ed. R. Emmitt Tyrrell, (November 22, 2019)

Bai, Matt; "Notion Building," New York Times Magazine, (October 2, 2003)

Beckel, Michael & Dave Levinthal; ed. In chief, "Wealthy Supporters fuel Obama Nonprofit," The Center For Public Integrity, (January 21, 2014)

Bennett, William J; "Where have all the Moderate Democrats Gone?" contributor to CNN, a Washington Fellow of Claremont Institute.

Birnbaum, Jeffrey H; "The New Soft Money," Fortune, (October 27, 2003)

Blumfeld, Laura; "Soros's Deep Pockets vs Bush," The Washington Post, (November 11, 2003)

Bryce, Tim; "Manufactured Hate," Bryce on Politics, (February 9, 2017)

Burton, D; "Comparing Free Enterprise and Socialism," The Heritage Foundation, (April 30, 2019)

Clarke, David, Sheriff; "The Democrats' Hatred of President Trump Itself is Appalling," official website, http://twitter.com/SheriffClarke (January 10, 2020)

Coleman, John; Take Ownership of your Actions by taking Responsibility," The Harvard Review, (August 30, 2012)

Crowley, Michael; "Shadow Warriors," New York Times, (August 12, 2004)

Curl, Joseph; "The Democrats and their Socialism Problems," Washington Times, (July 31, 2018)

Diamond, Jeremy & Sarah Murray; "Trump wrote inauguration Speech Himself," CNN, (January 20, 2017)

DiLaura, Gary; "Barack Obama is George Soros's Puppet on a String," Artvoice (AV), (October 28, 2018)

Fischer, Don; "Basically Bernie Sanders Is a Communist," The American Spectator, (June 18, 2019)

Ganim, Sara & Chris Welch; "Unmasking the Leftist Antifa movement," CNN-contributors, (May 3, 2019)

Giartelli, Anna; "Socialist candidates the future of our Party," says DNC Chairman—Tom Perez. Washington Examiner, (July 3, 2018)

Gill, Kathy; "Political Career of Barack Obama, Time-line," ThoughtCo. (updated) (October 23, 2019)

Gimein, Mark; "George Soros is Mad as Hell," Fortune, (October 27, 2003)

Harrington, Elizabeth; "The Hate Trump Agenda by the Democrats
    has gone too far," The Hill, opinion Contributor, (August 6,
    2019)

Hartiwanger, John; "Here's the difference between a Socialist and a
    Democratic Socialist," The Business Insider, (February 11,
    2020)

Hendrickson, Mark; "President Obama's Marxist-Leninist
    Economics," (July 26, 2012)

Hoft, Joe; "Four were Hanged in 1865 Democrat Coup Involving
    Lincolns Assassination," @gatewaypundit, twitter, (December
    2, 2019)

Horowitz, David & Poe Richard; "The Shadow Party" (2006) pp 131-
    136; 175-176; 122; and pp 196-198.

Jones, Susan; "Record 94,708,000 Americans not in the Labor Force; as
    Participation Rate drops," CNSNews.com (June 3, 2016)

Kaufman, Robert; "The Disaster of the Obama Presidency," (July 16,
    2014)

Klein, Aaron; "Sanders 1 or 69 Democrat Socialists in Congress,
    WorldNetDaily (WND), Wikipedia, (July 31, 2015)

LaRoche, Lyndon; "Hillary Clinton's Benghazi Revelations mean
    Obama must be impeached," Executive Intelligence Review
    (EIR), editorial, (June 17, 2014)

Laudon, Trevor; "2019 List of Socialists and Communists in
    Congress," The Federal Observer, printed in 'Perspective.'
    (October 8, 2019)

Levine, Andrew; "Democratic (Party) Socialism," Counterpunch, (March 29, 2019)

Limbaugh, Rush; "Democratic Party has Become the Largest Hate Group in the Country," RealClearPolitics, posted by Ian Schwartz, (June 20, 2017)

Logas, Rich; "Democrats: America's Original Hate Group," American Thinker, (May 20, 2019)

Mackinnon, Douglas; "Socialism is Back, and it's taking over the Democratic Party," Washington Examiner, (July 2, 2018)

Makos, Adam; "A Higher Call," NYT Best seller, Published by Dutton Caliber.

Markovsky, Alex; "Time to rebrand the Democratic Party as Socialists." American Thinker, (February 19, 2018)

Milligan, Susan; "States of Hate," U.S. News, (January 3, 2020)

Montano, Johnathan; "Is Donald Trump a Conservative?" History News Network, (December 22, 2019)

Ngo, Andy; "Liberals Cheer as Antifa violence escalates," New York Post, (July 17, 2019)

Pierce, Gary; "Inside Politics," The Washington Times, (March 3, 2003)

Puisseger, Leon; "When did the Democratic Party become Socialist?" The Freedom Outpost, (August 18, 2015)

Richman, Howard & Raymond Richman; "Is Trump a True Conservative?" American Thinker, (February 8, 2016)

Roberts, Paul Craig; "As the Democratic Party Hates Trump deplorables, how can it represent White People?" The Institute of Political Economy, (February 3, 2020)

Root, Wayne Allen; "Obama's Plan hatched at Columbia University," Human Events Powerful Conservative Voices, (April 14, 2013)

Shapiro, Ben; "Is Donald Trump Conservative?" Breitbart, (January 24, 2016)

Shuler, Pete; "Where have all the Democrats Gone?" City Beat, (July 9, 2003)

Simonson, Joseph; "Bernie Sanders in 1972: I don't mind people calling me a Communist." Washington Examiner, (February 4, 2020)

Sirota, David; "What's the difference between a Liberal and a Progressive?" The Huffington Post, (October 19, 2005)

Soros, George; "Bush's Inflated Sense of Supremacy," Financial Times, (March 13, 2007)

Sowell, Thomas; "Is Personal Responsibility Obsolete?" Pt.2, The Creators Syndicate, (June 7, 2016)

Sperry, Paul; "Don't be fooled by Bernie Sanders---Communist," New York Post, (January 16. 2016)

Summitt, Dale; "The Democratic Party is America's most Powerful Hate Group,' ipatriot.com (September 21, 2016)

Vaugh, Russ; "Why the Democrats are so crazy to impeach," American Thinker, (December 16, 2019)

Waldman, Paul; "Republican's say Obama has been historically
    Divisive," The Week, (January 19, 2016)

Wall, Noah; "The Democratic Party is in a Socialist Spiral,"
    Washington Examiner, (February 20, 2019)

West, Diana; "Welcome to Obamaland---Unopposed Invasion on our
    Nation's Borders," The Verde Independent, commentary.

Williams, Katie Bo; "Antifa Activists say Violence is Necessary," The
    Hill, (September 14, 2017)

Williamson, Kevin D; "The Democrats are the Socialist Party Again,"
    National Review, (June 20, 2019)

Wisdom, Manley; "The Mark of a Great President," (2011)

York, Byron; "The Soros Agenda: Free Speech for Billionaires only,"
    Wall Street Journal, (January 2004)

York, Byron; "The Vast Left Wing Conspiracy," (2005), pp 8; 62; and
    pp 86-87.

"Shadow Party" (SP), Discover the Networks (February 10, 2020)

"America Coming Together," Discover the Networks, (February 19,
    2020)

About the Author

Jerry Macke was born in Dayton, Washington, in 1938, and spent most of his youth in a small Alaskan fishing village called Sitka. That little town had a great history and a multicultural family. It was composed of descendants of early Russian migrants, native Tlingit Indians, and transplanted Scandinavian fishermen, along with many White Americans  seeking new lives from the lower forty-eight states. He was always intrigued by its rich history and spent a great deal of time learning about this small town's beginnings.

With this background, he developed a never-ending appetite to learn about all history. In 1957 he graduated from Sitka High School, and then left to attend college at Oregon State College (now University) in Corvallis, OR. He studied history, psychology, and physical education, his three greatest passions.

After his education was interrupted in 1959 by a tour in the U.S. Army, he returned to his studies at Northern Arizona University (NAU) in Flagstaff, AZ. He earned his bachelor's degree in 1962, and he and his wife moved to Lompoc, CA to begin a teaching career. After a year of teaching, he and his wife moved back to Arizona so he could complete his master's degree studies. Combining studies from Cal Poly in San Luis Obispo and the University of California in Santa Barbara, he received his master's degree in social sciences and psychology from NAU. He spent his entire career teaching psychology, history, and coaching baseball and basketball in Lompoc, CA at Cabrillo High School.

After forty-two years in the classroom he and his wife Do' returned to Arizona, and he finally found time to begin writing. His first book was a family history, *Nichols and Mickles: They All Came Together,* written about the Nichols and Mickle family ancestry in honor of his wife. His passion for politics was fueled by a rising discontent throughout the country, and he began writing about it from the early 2000's forward. His own dissatisfaction with the prevailing social and political situation in America, and with the explosion of socialism in the Democratic Party in the early years of the century, was the spearhead that motivated him to write this book: *A Patriot, The Conservative Voice.*

www.ingramcontent.com/pod-product-compliance
Lightning Source LLC
Chambersburg PA
CBHW070650250726
48662CB00001B/50

I0766247

GUIDED MEDITATION

Introduction

If you choose to use these scripts to facilitate a guided meditation journey for others, please preface the trip for them through reminding them that no longer all people "sees" matters for the duration of a guided meditation. This is very important, because our purpose is for them to go a bit closer to their personal soul during the journey, now not to supply them one more cause to consider they've failed.

In the years that I've been using these guided meditations, many human beings have shared experiences with me where they weren't capable to see anything, but they did hear something. Or they felt the environment with imaginary kinesthetic touch. Or they just had a deep sense of internal understanding about something all through the internal journey. All of this is perfectly okay! And as soon as in a while, any person doesn't see, hear, sense or think about anything. That's flawlessly okay as well. Certain internal journeys simply don't "fit" with some people. And sometimes, a guided meditation desires to be listened to and experienced more than once in order to sufficiently loosen up and open up a person's internal world.

Also, at the cease of facilitating one of these Inner Journeys, please allow participants ample time to manner their experience. You might favor to supply them various minutes to write in their journals, or you may prefer to invite small group voluntary sharing. It also may help to make yourself available afterwards for a personal conversation about their journey within the meditation. It's surely essential that every man or woman have a way to specific and combine the guided meditation experience. For some people, this capacity verbal sharing with others; for others, this potential time to absorb it quietly and in solitude, into their very own reality.

Each of these Magical Inner Journeys was given to me as a direct present from Spirit. I hope that you revel in experiencing them and facilitating them as a whole lot as I have.

And A Word About Inner Voices Our internal voices are additionally regarded as our internal parts, or persona aspects. I in my view like referring to mine as a Committee. I sincerely think of a huge convention desk in an office building, and everybody sitting around it are individual parts of ME that have something to say about what I do and who I am. You may want to also suppose of it as your inner family, and image them sitting round a huge dining room table. And of course, every family member has something to say, an opinion to give.

CHAPTER 1
Relax by focusing the mind:
A Therapy

Use these guided meditation to calm the mind and relax the physique the use of methods such as respiration awareness, counting, and different convenient guided meditation techniques.

Feeling relaxed and assured can assist you examine an instrument or other new skill extra easily. This meditation aims to help increase self-belief and motivation when studying to play an instrument.

Remember that you are getting to know the talent of focusing the mind, and you will get higher at this with practice. Don't try to make something happen; simply allow and observe. It is flawlessly normal for your thinking to wander. That is why audio can be useful - listening to the meditation script helps to carry your attention lower back to the exercising at hand.

Whenever your thought wanders, simply carry it again to the meditation exercise. Be variety to yourself! Remember that when your thinking wanders, it potential that you have a normal, active, wondering brain. It does NOT imply that you are doing something wrong.

 Daily meditation practice is ideal, and this will be the high-quality way to ride all the benefits of meditation and the leisure response. Start small. If meditation is difficult, just meditate for a couple of minutes. Work up to longer meditation sessions. Most human beings locate that 10 to 20 minutes of meditation is a long time.

VISUALIZATION

 Visualization can be referred to as a motivational technique which can help you obtain personal goals. If you really favor something to come to fruition, then you have to put your inventive mind to work. See the result in the front of you, play the sport you are going to play in your mind, or watch your self-accepting your degree at college. The solely restrict is your own mind. Visualization is additionally a beneficial intellectual talent which allows you to photo an photograph or scenario not straight away in the front of your eyes.

Visualizing Your Goals

**1. Visualize the activity, event, or end result
desired.** Close your eyes and photograph a intention
that you have in mind. Let's say you prefer to
envision that you get a promoting at work. Imagine
your manufacturer new workplace with your name in
gold-emblazoned letters on the door. Imagine the
black, swivel chair in the back of your huge
mahogany desk. Imagine the Renoir copy between
your diplomas.

 Once you cover the large stuff, get smaller. Get down
to the dirt in the corners and the residue of the coffee
in your mug. The way the mild hits the carpeting as it
peeks thru the slats in the blinds.

**2. Visualize with optimistic, high quality
thoughts.** Nothing is going to enhance when you
experience lousy about yourself and your
probabilities in life. So, rather of thinking, "I'm
horrible at basketball; there's no way I'll improve,"
think something like, "I'm now not amazing now, but

I'll be a good deal higher in 6 months." Then visualize your self-sinking some 3-point shots or dunking on the competition.

 Visualization is type of like hypnosis: if you don't assume it'll work, it won't. Be aware that thinking positively is the first step to making sure this visualization is absolutely effective. It's the first step to making these needs a part of real life.
 Remember that lifestyles is just as a great deal about the trip you take to attain your desires as it is about the vacation spot you have in mind. Visualization can make the manner of accomplishing your purpose greater enjoyable with the aid of maintaining you focused and motivated, making it a high quality addition to your life.

3. Always try moving your visualization into the real world. And after you have spent a moment, or a few days, visualizing your goal, make adjustments in your lifestyles to convey the aim about. Right earlier than you function the activity, task, or tournament that will acquire an effect or an effect toward your goal, center of attention truly on the photo of the action you are about to make. Even if it's something intangible like "make greater money" and it's relevant to your everyday life, it can be used before starting to work or every commercial enterprise possibility.

For example, if you are making an attempt to hit a baseball, picture hitting it surely in your mind, stroke with the aid of stroke, at the right peak and the proper speed. Watch the ball being hit by means of your bat, flying through the air and touchdown anywhere it is supposed to land. Visualize the trip with all of your senses: hear the coming near ball, hear and sense the impact, and odor the grass.

4. Think about a chain of activities wanted to reap your goal. Big changes in your lifestyles take time and focus, and comprise a wide variety of small steps. If you're visualizing reaching a unique aim or end-point, think about how you would get there. So, if you choose to be president, think about aspects of your political career: walking your campaign, attending fundraisers, delivering a speech.

How would your new self take care of these situations?

5. Visualize the character qualities needed to get you where you choose to be. It's now not enough to want to be the vice-president of the corporation you work for. You want to suppose about the qualities that will help you in getting there. Visualize not solely the vice-presidency but also the abilities of open communication, persuasiveness, sharing, listening, discussing, deflecting criticism with skill and respect, etc.

Imagine your self-acting in the way that you're visualizing. So, if you recognise that a vice-president needs to have self-belief in their work performance, visualize your self-performing with confidence round the office.

6. Use affirmative phrases to inspire yourself. Pictures are great, however words work well, too. If you see a healthier, more fit you, lounging round in the department at your office, say to yourself, "I have the physique I dream of. I am getting more healthy and it feels good." If you want to improve at sport, think "I can see the ball and hit it with force".

You can repeat this type of phrase to your self as many instances as you need. Just make positive you accept as true with it!

7. Visualize whilst you're focused, calm and comfortable. Visualization only works if you are calm, cool, and inclined to supply yourself time to center of attention in peace, free from on the spot worries. Visualization is a approach very shut to meditation, solely it is more active and vivid. In visualization you are prompted to suppose actively about the possibilities, but as with meditation, you ought to go away aside something extraneous to your goals and goals and only focal point on them.

If you can, make yourself at ease when you visualize. Not having distractions will make this process easier and more effective. It'll assist you suppose greater relaxed, too, when less is going on around you.

8. Imagine your self-overcoming setbacks. Obstacles are a everyday phase of life, and no one reaches success besides first encountering failure. Know that you will make mistakes, however have in mind that you can overcome them. How you leap back after a setback is more necessary than the fact that you made a mistake in the first place.

 Ask yourself daily, "What can I do nowadays to make myself higher tomorrow?"

 A extremely good useful resource for studying how to overcome setbacks is the book Mindset

Refining Your Technique

1. Give visualizing some time to sense regular and produce results. At the very beginning, this visualization component may sense pretty frou-frou, if you will. It'll sense weird and it'll sense foreign. You have to push past that! It does go away. At the beginning it's herbal to feel uncomfortable being fed on with the aid of this dream world, however it's simply a phase. Be conscious that whenever if it doesn't feel a little funny, you're possibly no longer doing it right.

And this is only remedied by practice, that's all. There's no other key than time. As with anything, there's a getting to know curve. It'll only appear steep if you don't commit. Let yourself go and it'll go away! You're the only impediment to your visualization success.

Over time, visualization can set off your talent in the same way that certainly doing the exercise can. Your brain may not even be capable to tell the difference! Tke for example, if you are afraid to sing in the front of a crowd, you can think about your self doing it. This tricks your Genius into thinking that you've finished it, helping you in getting up and sing in front of a public when you have the opportunity.

2. Focus on long-term goals. Anybody who needs exchange in a single day will be disappointed. Instead, design to make attention of your hopes and desires long term. Always visualize where you will be in 5, 10 and 15 years and the varieties of consequences you want. How will your situation be distinctive and how will you be different? Allow yourself to imagine what that lifestyles will be like.

And for example, it's helpful to visualize going to bed in the past or taking a jog at night. But visualizing can additionally help you attain more large goals. For example, visualize what sort of father or mother you favor to be, the legacy you'll go away your children, and the variety of character you'll be when they're developing up.

Visualize what you favor to achieve as a human being and what legacies you will leave your buddies and community.

3. Always try creating a vision board to remind you of the life you want. However, this will help you visualize your goals on a ordinary basis. To make a imaginative and prescient board, put up a collection of photos and words that represent your future goals. That way, you can appear at them each and every day to remain influenced as you pursue the lifestyles you want.

And for example, if your goal is to open a restaurant, you may want to encompass pics of eating places you prefer to mannequin yours after, as properly as dishes you will serve. You would possibly also encompass snap shots of human beings happily enjoying a meal.

4. Think in the affirmative about your goals. When it comes to visualization or simply fantastic thinking, you want to assume affirmatively about what you desire to achieve. Meanwhile, zeroing in on "not being poor" isn't exactly helpful. So as an alternative of now not wanting some thing or not being something or not having something, center of attention on what you do want, what you are, or what you have. For example, consider statements like: "I desire economic security," or "I have the guts to move throughout the country."

Think actively and in the existing tense, too. If you are visualizing your self not smoking anymore, don't recite the mantra, "I will strive to quit." Think along the strains of, "Cigarettes are disgusting. I don't prefer them.

5. Always be realistic about the goals you visualize. Like if you're a boxer and you're trying to visualize your next suit and you really dominating, it's now not going to do you any desirable picturing yourself as Muhammad Ali. You'll simply stop up in the ring not living up to the standards you set for yourself. Be aware that you'll end up frustrated and exhausted with yourself.

Instead, think about your swings like the nice swings you've ever had. So, imagine your opponent as that bag in the gym that you pummel on a daily basis. Imagine your train shouting reward as you provide the great performance of your career.

These things should happen. And there's no reason why they won't.

6. Visualize from your own first-person perspective. This will help your visualizations experience more, tangible, real and achievable.

Nugget: Do not picture your future successes and goals as a movie—your visualizations need to be from your own perspective. In your visualizations, you are no longer the audience. Reming yourself that this is your stage and your time to shine.

For example, if you're visualizing your future profession as a doctor, don't think of it from the viewpoint of a affected person you're treating or a colleague across the room. So, instead, visualize yourself treating a patient: imagine the stethoscope in your hands, etc.

This is what it capacity to wholly visualize. It is a reality as if viewed via your very own eyes. You're no longer having some kind of out of physique experience; it's the future

Some sort of Visualization Techniques to Justify Your Desired Outcomes: A Step-by-Step Approach

Visualization techniques have been used by way of profitable people to visualize their preferred effects for ages. The exercise has even given some excessive achievers what seems like super-powers, supporting them create their dream lives via undertaking one intention or challenge at a time with hyper focus and complete confidence.

In fact, we all have this notable power, but most of us have by no means been taught to use it effectively. Some elite athletes use it the same way the super-rich use it. Peak performers in any field use it. That strength is referred to as visualization.

The each day practice of visualizing your goals as already whole can rapidly speed up your achievement of those dreams, goals, and ambitions.

Using visualization techniques to focus on your desires and desires yields 4 very essential benefits.

1.) It prompts your creative subconscious which will begin producing creative ideas to acquire your goal.

2.) It programs your Genius to more effectively become aware of and understand the sources you will want to gain your dreams and aspirations.

3.) It also activates the law of attraction, thereby drawing into your lifestyles the people, resources, and occasions you will need to achieve your goals.

4.) It builds your interior motivation to take the imperative movements to reap your dreams.

Visualization is absolutely pretty simple. You take a seat in a relaxed position, shut your eyes and imagine — in detail — what you would be doing if the dream you have have been already realized. Imagine being interior of yourself, searching out via your eyes at the best result.

Visualize with the 'Mental Rehearsal' Technique

For athletes, visualization technique is called "mental rehearsal," and they have been using these exercises since the Sixties when we learned about it from the Russians.

So, all you need do is set aside a few minutes a day. The fine instances are when you first wake up, after meditation or prayer, and right earlier than you go to bed. Remember, these are the times you are most relaxed.

Go through the following three steps:

STEP 1. Imagine sitting in a film theater, the lights dim, and then the movie commences. It is a movie of you performing perfectly anything it is that you prefer to do better. See as plenty element as you can create, inclusive of your clothing, the expression on your face, small body movements, the surroundings and any different people that might be around. You could add in any sounds you would be hearing — traffic, music, other human beings talking, cheering. And finally, recreate in your physique any feelings you assume you would be experiencing as you have interaction in this activity or any other related one.

STEP 2. You could as well get out of your chair, walk up to the screen, open a door in the display and enter into the movie. Now experience the complete factor once more from inside of yourself, looking out thru your eyes. This is referred to as an "embodied image" instead than a "distant image." It will deepen the affect of the experience. Also, see everything in vivid detail the same way you hear the sounds with the feel the feelings you would feel at any point you feel like.

STEP 3: So, finally, walk back out of the screen that is still showing the photograph of you performing very well, return to your place in the theater, reach out and seize the display and cut back it down to the dimension of a cracker. Then, carry this miniature screen up to your mouth, chunk it up and swallow it. Imagine that every tiny piece — just like a hologram — consists of the full picture of you performing well. Imagine all these little screens journeying down into your belly and out thru the bloodstream into each telephone of your body. Then think about that every telephone of your body is lit up with a movie of you performing perfectly. It's like one of those appliance keep windows the place 50 televisions are all tuned to the identical channels.

After this process — it ought to take much less than 5 minutes — open your eyes and go about your normal day. If you make this phase of your daily routine, you will be amazed at how a good deal improvement you will see in your life.

Create Goal Pictures

Another effective visualization method is to create a picture or picture of your self with your goal, as if it have been already completed. If one of your desires is to very own a new car, take your camera down to your neighborhood auto dealer and have a image taken of yourself sitting in the back of the wheel of your dream car. If your goal is to go to Paris, discover a photo or poster of the Eiffel Tower and cut out a photo of yourself and location it into the picture.

Do create a Visual Picture and an Affirmation for Each Goal

We recommend that you locate or create a photo of each aspect of your dream life. Create a picture or a visible illustration for every aim you have — financial, career, recreation, new capabilities and abilities, matters you want to purchase, and so on.

Index Cards

We exercise a similar discipline each and every day. Remember, we each have a list of about 30-40 dreams we are presently working on. We write every purpose on a 3×5 index card and preserve these playing cards near our bed. Each morning and every night we go thru the stack of cards, one at a time, examine the card, close our eyes, see the completion of that intention in its best favored state for nearly 15 seconds, then open our eyes and repeat the manner with the next card.

Use Affirmations to Support Your Visualization

An affirmation is a declaration that conjures up not only a picture, however the journey of already having what you want. Here's an example of an affirmation:

Repeating an affirmation quite a few instances a day continues you focused on your goal, strengthens your motivation, and programs your unconscious by sending an order to your crew to do some thing it takes to make that purpose happen.

Expect Results

Through writing down your goals, the use of the power of visualization and repeating your day by day affirmations, you can achieve gorgeous results.

Visualization and affirmations permit you to change your beliefs, assumptions, and opinions about the most vital man or woman in your existence — YOU! And they allow you to harness the 18 billion talent neurons in your brain and get them working in a singular and purposeful direction.

Your unconscious will come to be engaged in a technique that transforms you forever. The method is invisible and doesn't take a long time. It just occurs over time, as long as you put in the time to visualize and affirm, exercise your techniques, encompass your self with superb people, examine uplifting books and listen to audio programs that flood your thought with positive, life-affirming messages.

An Approach: How to Spend the Some Important Minutes of Your Day

Harness the Subconscious Mind with Visualization Techniques

Visualization – seeing the intention as already entire in your mind's eye – is a core technique used via the world's most profitable people. Visualization is advantageous due to the fact it harnesses the energy of our subconscious mind.

When we visualize desires as complete, it creates a warfare in our subconscious thinking between what we are visualizing right now and what we currently own. Our minds are hard-wired to get to the bottom of such conflicts by means of working to create a cutting-edge reality that fits the one we have envisioned.

Visualization activates the creative powers of the unconscious mind, motivating it to work more difficult at creating solutions. You'll also be aware new levels of motivation and locate your self doing matters that commonly you would avoid, however that will take you nearer to success.

The 0.33 way visualization boosts success is through programming the Reticular Activating System, which serves as a filter for the information that is streaming into our brain all the time.

The RAS thinks in pictures, not words. Daily visualization feeds the RAS the pics it wishes to begin filtering data differently. And as a result, your RAS will start to pay interest to something that would possibly assist you gain your dreams – information that it in any other case may ignore.

Live in the Moment

Although a day by day practice of visualization is vital, we don't need to spend all day thinking about our desires for this approach to work. And in fact, spending too much time in visualization can rob you of some thing quintessential – living in the moment.

Daily rituals help to set up the right stability between wondering about the future and dwelling in the moment. Start by way of choosing a time in the course of which you'll evaluate your dreams and visualize the process along success. And ideally, it would be nice to do this twice a day – first factor in the morning and then right before you go to bed. So, the process typically takes about 10 minutes or less.

And in the event that you meditate, guided or not, do your visualizations immediately after your meditation. The deepened kingdom reached at some point of meditation heightens the have an effect on of visualization.

For biggest effect, study your dreams or affirmations out loud. After every one, shut your eyes and create the visual photograph of the done goal in your mind.

And to multiply the effects, add sound, smells, and tastes. Most importantly, add the feelings and bodily sensations you would be feeling if you had already accomplished your goal.

This is a powerful visualization technique.

Research has revealed that photos or scenes that are accompanied by means of excessive emotion will stay locked in our memory forever. The greater passion, exhilaration and strength we muster in the course of visualization, the more powerful the outcomes will be.

Be Present Instantly

An handy way to right away grow to be present is to center of attention on your bodily sensations. It's impossible to center of attention on our our bodies and be in the past or the future at the same time. Here are some examples. Focus on your left foot right now. What are you feeling? Pay interest to the sensation for a minute. Then be aware what you're feeling in your right foot, and spend a few moments actually feeling the sensation. If you had been capable to pay interest to your feet, congratulations. You were clearly present.

And if you find your mind thinking about the future at some point of the day, you can use one of the extra fundamental visualization techniques. Just let go of any fears or issues that arise. Shift your ideas to what you desire the future to seem to be like when you get there. Then convey your attention returned to the moment.

A famous sentence says "Today is a gift—that's why it's called the present." Use visualization techniques to obtain your goals, however make investments the majority of your time playing the gift of today.

Repeat your affirmations every morning and night time for a month and they will end up an computerized section of your thinking… woven into the very material of your being.

Weoften hear that visualization can assist us gain greater stages of success. Many of those who are distinctly successful in their fields — such as Oprah,

Tiger Woods, and Jim Carey, amongst others — have brazenly stated that visualization has been a valuable device in their profession progress.

Yet, most of us don't use it.

So, as I studied hypnosis and NLP, I got here to understand the functioning of the thinking better, and to apprehend why and how visualization truly works. I grew to be satisfied of its benefits and determined to make it part of my morning routine.

This book is about the "how" and the "why". It will be nice to share four reasons with you, backed by way of science, about why visualization can accelerate your course to success.

I've additionally delivered a method for visualizing more correctly at the give up of the book.

So, right here we go…

1. Overcoming Fear and Building Self-Confidence

Several studies have proven that the intelligence doesn't differentiate between a real memory and an imagined (visualized) one.

This means that when you imagine some thing vividly and with emotion, your talent chemistry modifications as although the ride was real, and your idea data it as a actual memory.

Because of this attribute of the mind, we can use visualization to overcome concern and construct self-confidence, via "making the unknown known".

Trick Your Brain by using And Making the Unknown Known

Fear and anxiety come from a bad anticipation of possible future events, of something you don't know yet. If you can imagine a future event, your thinking will file it as a actual memory; the scenario will come to be something known, something you've "already experienced".

Not only will the emotions of insecurity be reduced, however you'll sense assured in your ability to go thru the scenario because you will have efficiently carried out it earlier than (although solely in your memory).

2. Developing New Skills Faster

Studies have demonstrated that mental practice can be as high-quality to improve skills as actual practice. You can improve and make stronger real abilities with the aid of visualizing your self practicing them. When our brain visualize an action, the same regions of the Genius are inspired as when we operate it and the identical neural connections are built.

This explains why visualization is a fundamental part of all world-class athletes' training: it works!

3. Programing Your Inner GPS

Visualization communicates what to focal point on to the mind. It's necessary that we tell our minds what to center of attention on because the object of our focal point determines our perception of reality.

There's a biological explanation at the back of this phenomenon, known as the reticular activating system.

What's the RAS?

The reticular activating system (RAS) is a system of neurons located in the intelligence that feature make certain our brain doesn't have to deal with greater facts than it can handle.

It determines what sensory records we discover from our surroundings and what will stay unnoticed.

The RAS is a filter; out of all the data coming to our senses from the environment, it selects what will be seen and given attention to with the aid of the mindful mind. Without our RAS, our brain would be filled with useless data.

What Does the RAS Notice?

The RAS filters what it believes isn't important. It prioritizes the whole lot that issues our survival and protection as properly as the matters that fit the present day content of our minds: beliefs, thoughts, emotions, etc.

Basically, your RAS continuously looks for facts in your environment that matches and reinforces your ideas and beliefs.

How to Program Your RAS

Your RAS is like an internal GPS. If you want your GPS to work well for you — at noticing possibilities that will take you nearer to your objectives — you must application it accordingly. And the pleasant way to program it is by means of visualizing your goals.

4. Overriding Limiting Beliefs

Visualization beneath deep relaxation is additionally referred as self-hypnosis. When you relax deeply, your brainwaves cross from Beta (12 to 30 Hz) to Alpha (8 to 12 Hz), and every now and then even Theta (4 to eight Hz).

Alpha and Theta frequencies are suggestible states in which it becomes possible to reprogram patterns and beliefs at an unconscious level.

If you visualize yourself conducting some thing you agree with you can't do whilst at these ranges of the mind — and do it various times (repetition is important!) — you'll commence to override the old, limiting beliefs that averted you from succeeding with a new belief: your ability to obtain it.

To attain a extra suggestible state, you must relax your body and mind.
You can start with a body-scan rest — enjoyable every phase of your body, one by using one, from head to toe — prior to visualizing your objective. Focusing on your respiratory will also help you relax, as properly as counting down from twenty to zero.

Application: How to Visualize More Effectively

There are key standards to make your intellectual simulation perfect.

Close your eyes and establish an intention: mentally say what you prefer to gain (your goal) in an affirmation.

Imagine the scenario or future tournament you would like to work on. Make the scene as actual as you can, like a simulation, the use of your five senses. The greater vividly you can imagine the scene, the higher it will be recorded in your thinking as a "memory". Always incorporate sturdy fantastic emotions. This is key; except a sturdy emotion, the tournament visualized won't seem enough actual to be recorded as a memory.

Repeat the technique often. Try to visualize day by day until you be aware perfect modifications in your behavior, skills, confidence, etc.

How to Reduce Anxiety Symptoms

If you have been identified with panic disorder, then you have likely experienced regular emotions of concern and anxiety. Research has proven that the usage of leisure techniques can help limit anxiousness and enhance your rest response. By enhancing your leisure skills, you are can decrease your flight-or-fight response that is regularly brought on during times of increased anxiety and panic attacks.

Some common rest methods encompass respiration exercises, modern muscle relaxation, yoga, and meditation. These methods are fairly handy to research and can be practiced on a daily foundation to help with getting thru panic attacks.

What Is Visualization?

Visualization is any other powerful method that can assist you unwind and relieve stress. Visualization includes the use of mental imagery to gain a more at ease kingdom of mind. Similar to daydreaming, visualization is executed through the use of your imagination.

There are a number of motives why visualization can help you cope with panic disorder, panic attacks, and agoraphobia. Consider how your thoughts wander when you sense panic or anxiety. When experiencing a panic attack, your thought may additionally focus on the worry, the worst things that can manifest and different cognitive distortions that only add to your feel of fearfulness.

Visualization works to increase your capacity to relaxation and relax by means of focusing your thinking on more calming and serene images. Before starting any of these visualization exercises, make sure your environment is set up for your comfort. To better relax, remove any distractions, such as phones, pets or television. Try to find a quiet location the place you will most in all likelihood be undisturbed. Remove any heavy earrings or limiting clothing, such as tight belts or scarves. Get equipped to loosen up by using either sitting or lying down in a role that feels most comfortable to you.

To begin, it can be beneficial to slow your respiration down with a deep-breathing technique. Close your eyes and try to let go of any tension you may additionally be feeling for the duration of your body. To loosen up your body and mind even further, it may additionally be really useful to strive a progressive muscle rest workout earlier than you start your visualization. Try to set aside about 5 to 15 minutes to visualize.

Once this leisure feels complete, imagine that you get up and slowly stroll away from the beach. Remember that this beautiful place is right here for you on every occasion you want to come back. Take your time and open your eyes, slowly.

Use Your Creativity

If the seashore scene doesn't actually in shape you, strive coming up with your own visualization. Think of a area or scenario that you locate to be very relaxing, such as mendacity down in a large discipline of flora and grass, or playing a relaxing view of a mountain or forest. When viewing your scene, think about whatever you are experiencing from all of your senses. Notice what you hear, smell, style and how your body feels. When you experience equipped to go away your rest scene, take your time and regularly return your thinking to the present.

To get higher at visualization, attempt practicing at least countless instances a day. Relaxation strategies have a tendency to be extra beneficial if you first begin training when you are not having an high anxiety status. Through everyday practice, you will extra easily be able to use visualization when you definitely need that, such as when you feel the symptoms of panic and anxiety.

Becoming a Person Who Can Visualize Results: How-To Approach

So you have a dream, however you have no concept how to get there? Don't worry. You're no longer alone. Many humans are in the same boat. They know what they want, however on occasion they don't even believe it's possible. So what happens? They both don't try, or, if they do, they supply up before they reap their goal. If you're one of these people, below are 7 things you can do to visualize your effects and make them happen:

1. Focus on what you can do now.

Let's say you have no cash in financial savings due to the fact you are literally residing paycheck-to-paycheck. How is it viable to ever imagine having a few thousand greenbacks in financial savings when all you see is cash going out the door? You may additionally no longer assume it is. But you don't have to begin big. Reach in your purse or pocket and snatch that spare change. Put it in a jar. Make a habit of doing this. If you do it lengthy enough, be sure that it will add up. After this, then move up and put a dollar in the jar–then five. And if you get a tax refund, stick some of it in savings. I suppose you see the point. Just do something. Any little action towards your intention makes a distinction in supporting you get there.

2. Break down your intention into small steps.

Maybe you favor to start your very own business. And you may be high-quality at seeing the stop result. And you get excited about it, but then you recognize that your large vision is at least 10 years off. Then you get overwhelmed, frustrated, and you persuade your self that you can't do it. Think in terms of infant steps. Start through building a website. Educate your self on how to attract clients. And slowly, you will make your way toward your stop result. Remember, it's not a race. No one is judging you for how speedy you get there.

3. Turn your steps into a chronological plan.

Once you have the small steps damaged down, prioritize them. Maybe you favor to lose 50 pounds. You have already finished the first step via disposing of one specific meals from your weight loss plan that will reduce out a lot of calories. Then you listed out the other ingredients you can dispose of and calories you can count. So, for step three, put them on your calendar. And for example: "by June 1st, I will have eradicated these three ingredients from my diet. By July 1st, will be consuming 1,700 energy a day. And you get the point. Write your goals on a calendar and follow it.

4. Pretend that it has already happened.

With any of the three eventualities above, you can act like your aim is already accomplished. Get your bank assertion out and write in the quantity of money you want to see in your savings account. Hang it up somewhere. Talk to your self about how splendid it is to have $2,000 in your savings. Or faux that the commercial enterprise you just started is a smashing success. Clients are breaking down your doors. Or see yourself feeling splendid after losing all that weight. Trick your thought into believing it has already happened.

5. Figure out what proof you want that you have carried out your goal.

It is so effortless to get frustrated and supply up. But if you do, you'll by no means get where you prefer to be. How a lot money do you want in your financial savings to feel like you are surely making progress? How many purchasers or website visitors do you need to feel like your enterprise is on its way to success? So how many pounds do you need to lose to get excited and feel like you don't prefer to supply up? It's up to you. But you want to determine it out so you don't quit.

6. Visualize it.

If you are visible person, shut your eyes, and see it done. Do this in the morning earlier than you get out bed, and when you go to sleep at night. Or meditate on it at your convenience. The key is to do this each day. The extra you can do it, the better. However, not only does it get you into the dependancy of focusing on the quit result, it actually does trick your unconscious mind into thinking it is reality. If you're no longer a visible person, write down affirmations and repeat them each day. However you pick out to do it, the key is consistency. Keep doing it.

7. Talk about it to everyone.

Telling different people about your goals makes them real. And it represents a commitment. If you inform your friends, "I'm beginning a business," then they will preserve asking you how it's going. Or if you desire to lose that weight, your pals and household will most possibly assist you. The extra you speak about it, the greater you get caught up and excited about the give up result. It will go from delusion to reality.

Remember, each person gets discouraged at some factor when they try to gain a goal. It's normal. But the distinction between the humans who be triumphant and the people who don't is dedication and consistency.

What is Mindfulness Meditation?

Mindfulness meditation is a intellectual education practice that involves focusing your idea on your experiences (like your very own emotions, thoughts, and sensations) in the existing moment.

Mindfulness meditation can contain breathing practice, intellectual imagery, cognizance of physique and mind, and muscle and physique relaxation.

How to Do It:

Be aware that one of the original standardized programs for mindfulness meditation is the Mindfulness-Based Stress Reduction (MBSR) program, developed by means of Jon Kabat-Zinn, PhD (who used to be a pupil of the Buddhist monk and scholar Thich Nhat Hanh). MBSR focuses on attention and interest to the present. While others are simplified, secular mindfulness meditation interventions have been increasingly included into clinical settings to treat stress, pain, insomnia, and different fitness situations.

Learning mindfulness mediation is simple, but a teacher or software can assist you as you begin (particularly if you're doing it for fitness goals). Some people do it for up to10 minutes, but even a few minutes every day can make a difference. Here is a fundamental method for you to get started:

1. Find a quiet place. Sit in a chair or just stay the floor with your head and neck straight however now not stiff.

2. Try to put apart all thoughts of the previous and the future and be in the present.

3. Pay close attention to your breath, focusing on the sensation of air transferring in and out of your body as you breathe. Feel your belly upward jab and fall, and the air enter your nostrils and leave your mouth. Pay attention to the way every breath adjustments and is different.

4. Watch each and every idea come and go, whether or not it be a worrying one or fear, anxiety or hope. If thoughts come up in your subconscious, do not suppress them but genuinely word them, continue to be quiet and let your breathing be your anchor.

5. If you get carried away in your thoughts, study the place your idea went off to, without judging, and surely return to your breathing. Remember now not to be tough on your self if this happens.

6. As the time comes to a close, take a seat for a minute or two, becoming aware of the place you are. Wake up gradually.

Mindfulness Into Your Life:

There's no law that says you must be in a quiet room to practice mindfulness. Mindfulness mediation is one technique, but each day existence gives masses of opportunities to practice.3

Here are Kate Hanley's pointers on cultivating mindfulness in your each day routine:

Doing the dishes. Have you ever seen how no one is trying to get your interest whilst you're doing the dishes? The aggregate of by myself time and physical activity makes cleaning up after dinner a notable time to attempt a little mindfulness.

Savor the feeling of the heat water on your hands, the appear of bubbles, the sounds of the pans. Zen trainer Thich Nhat Hanh calls this exercising "washing the dishes for the purpose of washing the dishes", not to get them done so you can do something else.

When you supply yourself over to the experience, you get the intellectual refreshment of a mind-body exercise and a easy kitchen. It's multi-tasking at its best!

Brushing your teeth. You can not go a day besides brushing your teeth, making this each day mission the perfect chance to practice meditation. Notice your feet, the brush in your hand, your arm transferring up and down. Einstein stated he did his quality thinking whilst he was once shaving--I'd argue that what he used to be virtually doing in those moments was once working towards mindfulness!

Driving. It's easy to area out while driving, maybe thinking about the dinner or what you have to do at work. Use your powers of mindfulness to hold your interest to the present.

Turn off the radio (or flip it to some thing soothing, like classical), imagine your backbone growing tall, locate the half-way factor between enjoyable your palms and gripping the wheel too tightly, and convey your attention back to where you and your vehicle are in space on every occasion you observe your idea wandering.

Exercising. Yes, staring at TV while going for walks on the treadmill will make your workout go more quickly, but it might not do tons to quiet your mind. Make your fitness endeavors an exercising in mindfulness via turning off all displays and focusing on your respiration and where you are in space as you move.

Bedtime. Watch your battles over bedtime with the youngsters disappear when you end trying to rush thru it and honestly try to revel in the experience. Get to the same level as your kids, look in their eyes, hear extra than you talk, and savour any snuggles you get. When you relax, they will too.

CHAPTER 2
WHAT IS MINDFULNESS?

Mindfulness is the basic human capability to be utterly present and aware of where we are right now and what we're doing right now, and not too reactive or overwhelmed by using what's going on around us. While mindfulness is some thing we all naturally possess, it's extra effectively reachable to us when we exercise on a each day basis.

Whenever you deliver attention to what you're without delay experiencing by using your senses, or to your country of thinking by using your ideas and emotions, you're being mindful. And there's growing lookup showing that when you train your brain to be mindful, you're clearly redesigning the bodily structure of your brain.

What is meditation?

Meditation is exploring. It's not a constant destination. Your head doesn't come to be vacuumed free of thought, utterly undistracted. It's a one-of-a-kind place where every and each moment is momentous. When we meditate we challenge into the workings of our minds: our sensations (air blowing on our skin or a harsh scent wafting into the room), our thoughts (love this, hate that, crave this, detest that) and ideas (wouldn't it be bizarre to see an elephant enjoying a trumpet).

Understand that mindfulness meditation asks us to suspend judgment and unleash our natural curiosity about the workings of the mind, coming near our experience with heat and kindness, to ourselves and others.

How do I exercise mindfulness and meditation?

Mindfulness is handy to us in every moment, whether thru meditations, or mindful practices such as taking pauses and breathe when the cellphone rings alternatively of speeding to answer it.

Nugget: How Meditation Protects the Aging Brain from Decline

A string of recent lookup suggests ordinary meditation exercise may additionally raise intellectual flexibility and focus, presenting effective protection towards cognitive decline.

Most of us commence to misplace our keys, overlook people's names, or remedy math problems less with no trouble as we strategy middle age. This is regularly referred to as age-related cognitive decline. Years ago, scientists believed that this decline used to be inevitable, but super lookup in the previous two decades has proven that the adult intelligence adjustments with trip and training at some stage in the lifespan—a phenomenon regarded as neuroplasticity. Neuroplasticity isn't a given. Epidemiological research finds that how a brain a long time relies upon on a wide variety of factors inclusive of diet, bodily exercise, way of life choices, and education. The healthier and extra energetic one's lifestyle, the greater possibly he or she will hold cognitive overall performance over time. And meditation can also be a key ingredient for ensuring talent health and preserving correct mental performance. Here's what latest research suggests about how mindfulness meditation practice may also help preserve ageing brains match and functional.

How Meditation Encourages Neuroplasticity

To hold intellectual acuity, it's important to preserve what researchers call your neural reserve in appropriate working order. This "reserve" refers to your brain's intellectual efficiency, capacity, or flexibility. Emerging evidence suggests that the constant intellectual training that occurs in mindfulness meditation may additionally help to hold that "reserve" intact. For example, one review of the proof linked everyday meditation with positive improvements in talent function such as improved attention, awareness, better memory, and larger efficiency.

Studies are showing that daily meditation impacts each brain "states" and brain "networks." Brain nation education involves activating large-scale networks inside the brain that have an effect on a broad vary of emotional and intellectual processes. A wise example of this can be located in a current find out about published by way of a team of researchers at UCLA, who reported that experienced meditators have greater concentrations of tissue in intelligence regions most depleted via aging, suggesting that meditation practice may additionally help to minimize Genius age and protect towards age-related decline. Brain community training, on the other hand, is greater focal in that it improves precise cognitive capabilities by way of persistently activating a community related with one function, like paying attention. This is equivalent to repetitive intellectual bicep curls. Both kingdom and network coaching are believed to be important ingredients for maintaining the brain sharp.

The Agile Aging Brain

Meditation can also grant another introduced benefit—increased intellectual flexibility. For some, age can come with a pressure of thoughts, emotions and opinions, and the incapability to drift with the challenges and limitations that are phase of the life. This can be a stress source, and presumably even illness. Because most meditation practices emphasize growing an attention of thoughts, feelings, and physical sensations except growing a judgment about any experience, mindfulness mediation might also help to lessen a person's attachment to fixed outcomes, extend mental flexibility, and add to one's neural reserve.

Although encouraging, it's important to be aware that this research is in its infancy and outcomes are mixed. For example, a number of research have suggested that older meditators outperform age-matched non-meditators, or function comparably to younger contributors on a variety of interest tasks. Others have shown little or no exchange in cognitive function following a mindfulness intervention for older adults, or file that improvements are no longer maintained over time.

What we do understand is that long-term engagement in mindfulness meditation may additionally beautify cognitive performance in older adults, and that with continual practice, these benefits may additionally be sustained. That's splendid information for the tens of millions of ageing adults working to fight the terrible consequences of growing older on the brain.

Mindfulness Practice: The Basics

Mindfulness assists us to put some space between ourselves and our reactions, breaking down our conditioned responses. Here's how to tune into mindfulness at some stage in the day:

Always set aside some time. This is because you don't need a meditation cushion or bench, or any type of extraordinary tools to get entry to your mindfulness skills—but you do want to set apart some time and space.

Observe the present moment as it is. The aim of mindfulness is now not quieting the mind, or attempting to gain a country of eternal calm. The intention is simple: we're aiming to pay attention to the present moment, besides judgment. Easier said than done, we know.

Let your judgments roll by. When we note judgments arise for the duration of our practice, we can make a mental note of them, and let them pass.

Return to staring at the current second as it is. Our minds frequently get carried away in thought. That's why mindfulness is the exercise of returning, once more and again, to the present moment.

Be form to your wandering mind. Don't judge your self for anything thoughts crop up, just exercise recognizing when your idea has wandered off, and gently bring it back.

That's the practice. It's frequently been said that it's very simple, however it's not necessarily easy. The work is to simply preserve doing it. Results will compound the situation and itself.

Meditation: How best you could approach the subject

The subject termed meditation focuses on the breath, not because there is something one-of-a-kind about it, but due to the fact the bodily sensation of respiratory is continually there and you can use it as an anchor to the current moment. Throughout the exercise you can also find yourself caught up in thoughts, emotions, sounds—wherever your mind goes, clearly come lower back once more to the next breath. Even if you only come returned once, that's okay.

A Simple Meditation Practice

Sit comfortably. Find a spot that offers you a stable, solid, relaxed seat.

Notice what your legs are doing. If on a cushion, move your legs without difficulty in front of you. So this is a way to go about it: If on a chair, rest the bottoms of your feet on the floor.

Try straightening the top of your body—but don't stiffen. Your spine has natural curvature. Let it be there.

Notice what your fingers are doing. Situate your higher palms parallel to your top body. Rest the arms of your palms on your legs at any place it feels most natural that way.

Make sure you soften your gaze. You achieve this by dropping your chin a little and let your gaze fall gently downward. It's not indispensable to shut your eyes. You can surely let what seems earlier than your eyes be there without focusing on it.

Make sure you feel your breath. Also, bring your attention to the physical sensation of breathing: the air moving through your nostril or mouth, the movement of your belly or your chest.

Notice when your thinking wanders away from your breath. Inevitably, your attention will wander to different places. Don't worry. There's no need to block or get rid of thinking. When you word your idea wandering gently return your attention to the breath.

Be variety about your wandering mind. You may additionally locate your thinking wandering constantly—that's normal, too. Instead of wrestling with your thoughts, exercise watching them besides reacting. Just sit down and pay attention. As challenging as it is to maintain, that's all there is.

Come returned to your breath over and over again, except judgment or expectation.

When you're ready, gently carry your gaze (if your eyes are closed, open them). Take a second and observe any sounds in the environment. Notice how your physique feels right now. Notice your ideas and emotions.

Mindful Practices for Every Day

As you spend time training mindfulness, you'll probable discover your self feeling kinder, calmer, and greater patient. These shifts in your experience are probably to generate modifications in different parts of your life as well.

Mindfulness can help you end up greater playful, maximize your enjoyment of a lengthy dialog with a pal over a tea, then wind down for a enjoyable night's sleep. Try these 4 practices this week:

Simple Guided Meditations

1. A Simple Breathing Meditation for Beginners

This exercise can help minimize stress, anxiety, and negative emotions, cool yourself down when your temper flares, and sharpen your attention skills.

2. A Body Scan to Cultivate Mindfulness

A short mindfulness meditation practice to loosen up your physique and center of attention your mind.

3. A Simple Awareness of Breath Practice

The oldest meditation practice is also one of the simplest: Sit, and recognize you're sitting.

4. A Compassion Meditation

A loving-kindness meditation to decrease negative feelings like anxiousness and depression and amplify positive feelings like happiness and joy.

What are the advantages of mindful meditation?

When we meditate, it doesn't help to focus on the benefits, but instead just to do the practice. That being said, there are masses of benefits. Here are five motives to practice mindfulness.

Understand your pain. Pain is a reality of life, but it doesn't have to rule you. Mindfulness can assist you reshape your relationship with intellectual and physical pain.

Connect better. Ever discover your self-staring blankly at a friend, lover, child, and you've no concept what they're saying? Mindfulness helps you supply them your full attention.

Lower stress. There's lots of evidence these days that extra stress causes lots of illnesses and makes different ailments worse. Mindfulness decreases stress.

Focus your mind. It can be irritating to have our idea stray off what we're doing and be pulled in six directions. Meditation hones our innate potential to focus.

Reduce Genius chatter. The nattering, chattering voice in our head looks never to depart us alone.

WHY PRACTICE MINDFULNESS?

Some of the most famous thoughts about mindfulness are just simple wrong. When you start to practice it, you may also locate the ride pretty distinct than what you expected. There's a precise danger you'll be pleasantly surprised.

Mindful's editor-in-chief, Barry Boyce sets the document straight concerning these 5 matters humans get incorrect about mindfulness:

- Mindfulness isn't about "fixing" you
- Mindfulness is not about stopping your thoughts
- Mindfulness does now not belong to a religion
- Mindfulness is now not an get away from reality

Mindfulness Is More than Stress Reduction

Stress reduction is regularly an impact of mindfulness practice, however the ultimate goal isn't meant to be stress reduction. The purpose of mindfulness is to wake up to the internal workings of our mental, emotional, and bodily processes.

Mindfulness trains your physique to thrive: Athletes round the world use mindfulness to foster top performance—from college basketball gamers working towards acceptance of bad ideas before games, to BMX champions learning to comply with their breath, and big-wave surfers transforming their fears. Seattle Seahawks Coach Pete Carroll, assisted through sports activities psychologist Michael Gervais, talks about coaching the "whole person." As creator Hugh Delehanty illustrates, gamers analyze a combination of mindfulness, which Gervais calls tactical breathing, and cognitive behavioral training to foster what he refer to as "full presence and conviction in the moment."

Creativity emanates from mindfulness: Whether it's writing, drawing, or coloring, they all have accompanying meditative practices. We can additionally practice mindfulness to the innovative process.

Mindfulness strengthens neural connections: By coaching our brains in mindfulness and related practices, we can construct new neural pathways and networks in the brain, boosting concentration, flexibility, and awareness. Well-being is a talent that can be learned. Try this basic meditation to reinforce neural connections.

Becoming a Witness to Your Thoughts: A cursory look

In life, we are faced with a lot of shades. And if you've ever suffered from a jumble of thoughts and struggled to make feel of them all, be alive that you're not alone. Besides, everyone of us has this unsettling experience, and some of us on more occasions than others. At times like this, it's hard to make any decision, on the grounds that there's often doubt and confusion clouding sound judgment. What's a character to do? So the question is: How can you quiet the discordant thoughts and arrive at some type of clear thinking?

Meditation specialists reward the practice's potential to enable the practitioner to do just that. Not only does meditation well known that such thoughts are clamoring for attention and looking for to disrupt life, it additionally approves the practitioner to distance himself or herself from the chaos and confusion by means of developing the ability to detach and watch what's going on.

So be informed that it's this detachment and witnessing that produces a sense of calm – even amid the noise and discord. Simply put, you end up capable to stand returned and watch, to witness your thoughts besides being dominated or controlled by means of them.

Such an ability to stay apart, but witnessing it all, is the basis for development of a strong, clear mind. Be aware that it isn't that problems, issues or conflicting and competing demands will disappear. They won't. But you'll be higher able to determine a route of action as soon as you're eliminated from the power such distractions are searching for to claim over you.

WITNESS YOUR THOUGHTS: AN APPROACH WITHOUT MEDITATING

But what if you don't practice meditation? Is it nevertheless viable to stand returned and be a witness to your thoughts? If so, how? Here are some suggestions:

1. Acknowledge the thought's presence.

When a thinking that's distressing or rather charged enters your mind, renowned its presence. Always remember not to fight to quash it, because that won't work. By acknowledging the thought, you tackle its presence. This is a reminder that you are not giving it power, just witnessing it. Then, allow your thought to float to the subsequent concept and do the same.

Tip: This can also seem trivial or unimportant, in particular if you've acquired many objects on your to-do list. Yet, you ought to be inclined to renowned the thought's presence to dissipate its power. Go with the process. You'll find that it's simpler than you think.

2. Stay still, taking no instant action.

Remain nevertheless and exert no action that is propelled by using the thought, no longer now. Be aware that there will always be enough time to deal with what wishes to be accomplished as soon as your mind is clear and free of distractions — after you've stated all the distracting and conflicting thoughts and moved on.

Tip: It's difficult for action-oriented individuals to sit down still and do nothing. Quiet the promptings of your thought that inform you you're losing time. You're not. Remain nonetheless even if it feels uncomfortable. This is section of the method of learning how to be aware of your thoughts.

3. Let silence surround you.

Allow the silence inside you to fill you. Notice the sense of calmness and peace. This lets in your higher focus to sift through and discover the solutions you search for.

Tip: If you're having an hard time with letting silence surround you, don't feel like you've failed or can't per chance acquire calm and peace. Take a few deep breaths and photograph a serene and peaceable place. Imagine yourself there, entirely immersed in the experience. All exterior noise and stimuli need to progressively disperse, leaving solely silence. Sit with this silence and include it.

4. Slowly return to the present.

After permitting time for witnessing your thoughts, regularly return to the present. You have some decision to your quest and be capable to create manageable solutions. That's because your thought is clear and free of clouded and conflicting thoughts. You have helped to make stronger your mind.

Tip: Be inclined to make use of this technique each time you prefer to return to your center, to locate an oasis amid the jumble of day-to-day life. Practice these steps and you'll locate that you're higher in a position to locate clear options to your problems.

Achieve Peace of Mind and Staying Focused

For those that have been struggling with anxiety, stress, or depression then the phrase "peace of mind" would possibly sound like some thing from a fairytale. However, I can only assure you that peace aside from this means it's time to forgive others, forgive yourself, and cross on.

Don't be easily offended.

It is a lot less complicated to hold peace of thought when you let things roll off your back. And if you take offense at every little thing that other human beings do and say, you will stay in a constant kingdom of frustration. Your thoughts will feel out of manage and you will quickly lose your peace. However, if you center of attention on believing the excellent in others you are transferring your thoughts which will make finding peace lots easier.

Choose your battles carefully.

If you make it your non-public mission to correct every person who is doing something you don't agree with you are going to stay in a consistent country of strife. And it will be close to not possible to keep your thought focused on what you prefer to center of attention on. Just like parents are taught to select their battles with their children, you favor to do the equal component with the people and conditions you face daily.

For example, you might no longer agree with a conversation that is happening between your coworker and your boss, however if you are no longer section of the dialog it's first-class to remain out of it. If you pick out to contain yourself you ought to be placing yourself in a position of choosing sides, maybe even putting your job at risk, and including stress that you don't favor in your life.

Make time to journal.

Journaling is a outstanding way to release these thoughts that are bogging down your mind. You can write out your stresses and issues and then once they are out of your head, release them altogether. And be aware that some people like to rip up or burn the paper as a symbolic way of displaying that they are letting go of those thoughts.

Journaling additionally helps you to technique thru situations and see matters in a specific light. Also, take the time to write about your day, research from it, and go on from it.

Irrespective of how busy you might seem to be, always try to incorporate moments of quietude and solitude into your schedule.

Constantly being in the hustle and bustle of life is a sure-fire way to lose peace of mind and focus. This doesn't mean that you keep away from human beings at all costs, however, taking time to get away from everybody else and be in whole silence can assist you to reconciliate with yourself. If you find that you have lost all peace, you might want to take a solitude retreat. You could get away for a weekend by myself or without a doubt an afternoon. Find a quiet location to throwback to. Allow yourself to suppose about the ideas that have been rolling around in your head. Then, figure out how to deal with those thoughts. Allow yourself to recharge in the course of this time. Sometimes it can be tough to recognise what we are thinking and how those ideas are impacting us. If you are struggling to acquire peace of idea you may want to benefit from a conversation with a neighborhood therapist. They comprehend the right questions to ask to assist you get to the root of your struggle. Then, they can supply you with actionable steps to help you locate and stay in peace.

The Lesson that Transforms Meditation Practice

In short, the four elements are:

Focus.

This is the ideal, when the mind settles into the meditation, staying calm in the spaces between thoughts. It's potentially the avenue to bliss.

Mindfulness.

Sure, focal point is the last goal, however that's simpler some days than others. Sometimes, notwithstanding satisfactory intentions, our brains profession from the meditation to dinner. So we nudge ourselves back to the meditation. Then we veer off to ideas about lunch. So we lead ourselves gently again … for a few breaths. Until we locate ourselves questioning about work. And again to the meditation again. And so on. A little frustrating, however it's some of the heavy lifting of meditation. This is mindfulness, and every time we observe our thinking wandering and lead it back, we improve the mindfulness muscle.

Perseverance.

Then there are these days when even mindfulness eludes us and our minds skitter all over the place. We replay conversations. Feel our leg falling asleep. Fight the urge to fidget and quit. What's the factor of continuing? In that case, the factor is continuing. If we keep at it, continue to be with the meditation for anything duration we've deliberate even even though we're jumping out of our skin, we toughen our ability to persevere. And how can that now not be good?

Starting over.

And then there are the days when we cede to the will of the monkey, leaping up mid-meditation to do some thing we feel need to be executed that minute. It happens, and when it does, it's convenient to feel like a failure. But then, if we exhibit up again next time, willing to forgive ourselves and give it every other shot, and can do that every time we don't stay up to our intentions, without getting discouraged and self-critical, we are practicing self-compassion, another necessary tool for life.

Ways to Calm Your Mind Without Meditation

It's an unfortunate fact of the human talent that the more fatigued we are, the greater our thoughts start to race. Anxiety and tiredness work on a comments loop. be aware. So when you're battling with one, it's inevitable that you're going to have problems with the other.

While meditation is the most advantageous way to calm your mind, it's now not an option when you're incredibly tired! There is some other way to do this, which is via doing things that naturally focus your idea outdoor of yourself and guide your intelligence to launch calming neurochemicals.

The following ways to calm your thinking don't require as much intellectual electricity as meditation.

And in the brief term, they have the identical effect on our mood.

1. Do Something Complex (But Not Too Difficult).

The default mode network (DMN) is the phase of the brain that has a lot associated with the reflections about yourself. You have thoughts like: "Why do I feel lazy today?" "Should I text John lower back now or later?" "I'm starting to get hungry, maybe I need to get a snack." Meditation researchers call this "mind-wandering." It takes up a huge element of our waking life.

When we're worn-out or anxious, our minds wander more than usual, which makes us greater worn-out and anxious.

There are too many times used approaches we can constantly quiet the DMN. The first is meditation; the second is enticing in a complex task. (In fact, mindfulness coloring books are fantastic due to the fact of task complexity as nicely mindfulness.)

You can pick out something you usually do, like drawing, sports, innovative writing, or a work task and simply enlarge the difficulty slightly. For example, through drawing, you can try and draw something that is greater of a challenge, or with a sports activities or writing, you can strive setting a timer and entire a challenge in a restrained time period.

2. Always do something for people.

This is another method that can be used to get out of our personal heads when exhaustion begins to set in. It is obvious that you don't want to do anything too strenuous, however doing simple things, when focusing on others, can stop a racing mind.

You can make it an addiction to contact any person that you sense may additionally want it, or you can start volunteering or constructing something that you suppose can assist others. Focusing on the well-being of the neighborhood can also provide us reason and meaning, which can be very reinvigorating.

3. Do Something Fun and Creative.

When we are making an attempt too hard to sense higher all the effort can defeat the cause and be sort of damaging. Doing something enjoyable can help us wreck the cycle. This is because dopamine has a reenergizing impact on the fearful gadget and by way of attractive in play and creativity, we recharge our depleted energy reserves.

Ideally, you can always set a timer for fifteen minutes and just let all your ideas out on paper, and create thinking maps for how they relate to every other. Be aware that you can do this as a mindfulness exercise or simply to specific any innovative ideas you have. This helps you feel like your ideas are geared up and centered and not scattered and distracted.

Trying to do whatever artistic like painting, origami, or even lego (if you have kids) can also be effective. And fortunately, YouTube has millions of tutorials if you favor to examine something new.

4. Always get Some Exercise and Take a Long Sleep.

Exercise might also appear counter-productive when you're tired, but when we're mentally exhausted, it can occasionally start to mess with our sleep. This varies slightly relying on every individual, but is generally due to the fact exhaustion and anxiousness impact our capacity to wind down before bed, which is a imperative section of correct nice sleep. Unconscious worries can additionally wake us in the night time and cease us from getting into the deep states we need.

By exercising, eating a massive and healthful meal, and taking a long sleep, you can get the restorative effects that you need. And this isn't an invitation to oversleep, but if it's been a whilst since you bought some deep rest, it could be precisely what you need. However, it's also useful to create a pre-sleep ritual that entails calming down and not searching at any monitors for two to three hours earlier than sleeping.

5. Do Something Social.

This goes for introverts as nicely as extroverts. It's a frequent trust that introverts are drained with the aid of social interactions, however typically this happens when interacting with people they're now not comfy with.

So, if you're an introvert, make the effort be social with any individual who you always have fun with. Be informed that when we're engaged in a social situation that is fun, and no longer anxiety-inducing, we then get out of our own heads and start to recharge our batteries.

Meditation is remarkable for calming our minds, and whilst you maintain making an attempt to meditate even via difficult periods, it can be accurate to have some short-term options to help you get your power back.

Have you ever felt that with meditation? How else have you tried to quieten your mind?

CHAPTER 3

MISTAKES WHILE STARTING A MEDITATION PRACTICE

1. Believing that there is a single way that meditation has to happen.

So realizing that there are no strict policies for how meditation has to take place felt each liberating… and scary. The actuality is that you don't have to be sitting up to meditate. You don't need to be pass legged on a cushion. You don't need to close your eyes. You don't want to empty your mind. You don't have to meditate everytime at the same time or in the equal vicinity or for a unique duration of time. You don't have to use a mantra and you don't have to comply with your breath the complete time.

You are naturally a non secular being with or except these matters and it is about reaching that part of you (that connects us all) is a ways that is available and that works for you. It's much less about something you work to attain and greater about something you let yourself be, sink into, and connect with. The real work is being conscious and present that it is happening.

2. Not fully comprehending what meditation is.

You know that meditating is suitable for you. And the internet is stuffed with motives to meditate and the benefits of meditation. But what IS meditation? Remember, meditation is a word that has come to be used loosely and inaccurately in the cutting-edge world. That is why there is so tons confusion about how to exercise it. Some people use the word to mean wondering or contemplating; others use it to refer to daydreaming or fantasizing. However, meditation (dhyana) is no longer any of these.

Meditation is a technique for resting the mind and achieving a kingdom of focus that is absolutely extraordinary from the everyday waking state. It is the capacity for fathoming all the ranges of ourselves and sooner or later experiencing the center of recognition within. Meditation is now not a phase of any religion; it is a science, which ability that the manner of meditation follows a precise order, has particular principles, and produces effects that can be verified."

Though I consider that the meditative ride varies from character to person and even from day to day and minute to minute, I accept as true with that meditation includes a clear, relaxed, and inwardly centered mind. When anyone meditates, they are totally conscious and alert, however their idea is not centered on the exterior world or on the activities taking vicinity round them.

Meditation entails and still inner nation that approves the mind to become silent. When the thought is silent and no longer distracts, meditation deepens.

3. Not perception what being in a meditative kingdom feels like.

As I alluded to above, the ride of meditation varies from character to man or woman and even varies for the identical man or woman depending on the day, kind of meditation, existence circumstances, etc. Some humans feel a experience of peace and calm. Others feel pissed off and impatient. Others sense more anxiety at first. You can feel dizzy or a vibrating internal or backyard of your body. You may also experience hotter or cooler. You could sense numb or as though you are being pulled upwards. You may additionally experience as though your power is spilling out into the complete room. Or you may feel something else entirely.

Get curious about how meditation makes you sense on exclusive days. There are an endless wide variety of variable that can influence how meditation may feel to you. It's no longer static. Some people think you should feel a certain way or you did no longer achieve a meditative state. That is not true.

4. Not understanding what it capability to "achieve" a meditative state.

Some human beings trust that in order to attain a meditative state, one needs to be in a quiet room, sitting in a sure position, controlling the breath. Well, bet what? You are likely meditating every day, except knowing you're doing it.

Also, meditation isn't something to be "achieved" in the sense of some thing that is completed or checked off once you get there.

You can be in a meditative nation when you're staring into space, when you're daydreaming, when you're enjoyable in a chair, and even when you're staring at the TV. When your physique is relaxing and your thought is quiet, you naturally reap a mindful state.

5. Believing that one type of meditation is better than another.

Meditation is about being about awareness and connection with your spiritual center on a mindful level, and it doesn't count how you obtain that awareness. If you find this area via guided meditation, then do guided meditation. If you decide upon breath attention or mantras or something else altogether, do that. Be bendy and affected person with you and non-judgmental about your experience. Try to see things with a "Beginner's Mind" as though you were coming near and seeing your ride and yourself for the first time.

People meditate for unique reasons, and human's strategy meditation with distinctive desires and hopes. Some people may wish a deeper non secular connection, whilst others are seeking to research how to loosen up and enhance their cardiovascular health. Still others may be in it for a undertaking or to strive something new.

Whatever draws any individual to meditation, there are no guidelines when it comes to achieving a meditative state. The key is consciousness — becoming more conscious of when you reach this state, extra conscious of when and how many times throughout the day you acquire this state, and greater aware of what you are questioning about and doing when you attain this country and while you are there. Ultimately, consider that meditation is a practice, no longer a container to be checked or a ability to be mastered. Mistakes happen, even for advanced meditators.

The art of witnessing your thoughts: The liberating Part Of Life

It's one of these days when thousands of thoughts course through my mind. Among them self-doubt, worries, past follies, perniciously are seeking for out my intellectual energy. Feeding on each different and fueling feelings at large, these ideas spiral on in my idea by and large portray a dark and bleak future.

And again, in the ever-changing landscape of my intellectual canvas, I emerge as conscious that the ideas I give attention to are the ones that take on an intensity of brightness. Thus I are searching for to carry in occasional surges of competing high quality thoughts that colour in hope and enthusiasm into the medley. But like each other intellectual endeavor, these final — solely momentarily. Then they too fall away, simply like their predecessors.

However, in wanting to deal with the disturbance caused by thoughts of each kind, I take on the usual method of quieting the idea via breath manage and meditation. A few long deep breath helps carry in the grosser form of air to manipulate the refined form of ideas and emotions. But through experience, I understand that the hideous ideas are merely ready to pounce again.

So thru meditation, I decide to go down into the ocean, where the robust waves of ideas can no longer reach me. There I ride a depth of peace and non-permanent freedom of the silent mind. However, I discover it hard to remain down the ocean and am quickly pushed returned to the surface. But now, the turbulences of the thinking are fairly manageable and move in slower motion. Yet the waves of ideas lay simmering and waiting to accumulate mass and momentum again….

Amid this temporary silence, I come to be aware of the backdrop of my intellectual display screen towards which the film of my thinking is getting projected. By itself, this display remains blank and as a consequence any attempts to region interest on it for long fails, for there is nothing tangible to focal point on.

But the perception into the backdrop screen motivates me to probe similarly and this time, I are seeking to understand the nature of the mind that is doing what it does high-quality — thinking, perceiving, feeling, etc. Be aware that instead of going deep into the ocean, I step out of the ocean and watch the waves of thoughts. Riding high and low, these waves of thoughts lash onto the shores of my mind, the place I remain a detached observer of them all. The pervasive ideas amongst these attain out to the shores and attempt to pull me returned into the ocean. But with the power of my inquiring mind, I proceed to stay as a silent witness!

Each concept is then, like a wave, reaching out into the shores and receding again into the ocean, harmlessly and impersonally.

Once we emerge as aware of a thought, then it simply becomes an object of our attention. Meanwhile, knowing that I am feeling sad is an indicator that "I" am not genuinely sad but that I am purely aware of the feeling of disappointment passing through the mind! This goes without saying that, being aware of our thoughts and feelings helps us to apprehend that, that what we are experiencing is no longer us. It also helps us to understand that no longer the whole thing that we experience, needs to be acted upon!

By learning to watch thoughts, we grow to be patient with ourselves and our transient mental states. It will be a great notion to understand that we no longer react on an auto-pilot mode to every thought. We emerge as receptive to find out our simple essence of happiness and goodness which prevails amid the variety of thoughts.

As we turn out to be comfortable with our ideas moving in and out of our mind, just like the waves on the shores, we discover that these ideas that we give so a good deal significance to, are mainly repetitive and redundant in nature. In unmasking this entire notion processes, we are then ready to turn on and off the display of our mind — as and when we want it.

It struck me how uncommon it is to see anybody pause in the middle of the day and savor the moment in this way. two It additionally surprised me that in all of my instances again and forth to the fitness center I had never as soon as seen this little patch of nature. two

Consider the following questions for your rumination: Do you have informal situations, as you go thru your day, when you pause to be utterly present to what is within you or around you?

or do you ever set aside a few minutes in your day to deliberately engage your senses entirely and absolutely in some thing you are doing, such as eating a meal (without intellectual or different distractions pulling you away), or even something quite regular such as taking a shower or walking to your car?

What is it that you pass over in the direction of your speeding and busyness?

Informal Practice of Presence

Much has been written about the advantages of formal meditation practice, however many people are much less acquainted with the thinking of informal practice. With casual meditation exercise we seem to be for opportunities in the course of the route of our everyday day to be thoroughly present, mindful and awake. Rather than putting apart a formal time to practice meditating, one can make activities such as walking, taking a shower, washing dishes, or speaking to others as an chance for full on presence. Neuropsychologist Rick Hanson has written drastically about the benefits of "taking in the good" through searching for advantageous moments in our day that we can enrich and soak up by way of pausing to journey these suitable moments as emotions in our bodies. These can be ordinary moments that we would possibly otherwise overlook, like sipping a cup of tea, replacing a friendly glance with someone, or playing the feeling of satisfaction that comes from completing a difficult project. They can additionally be imagined moments such as calling up a time in our thinking when we felt secure or peaceful or supported, and experiencing these feelings in this moment. As we enable ourselves to trip these fantastic moments as a "felt sense" during the direction of our day, Hanson explains that this hard-wires these experiences into our brains so that we build internal resources we can later draw on.

A recent preliminary study through Dr. Barbara Fredrickson and colleagues explored the advantages of informal meditation exercise on contributors new to meditation, to see if casual exercise improves well-being impartial of formal meditation practice. Those adults that are new to meditation took part in a six-week group, both studying mindfulness meditation and loving-kindness meditation. They were encouraged to engage in casual meditation practices during the route of their day over a period of 9 weeks and to file the time spent doing so each day. Examples of casual meditation in the former group included paying interest to the bodily feeling of breathing, paying interest in the physique to a hobbies pastime such as brushing one's teeth, or consuming a meal mindfully. Examples of casual meditation in the 2nd crew covered sending sort desires (in one's mind) to oneself or others at some point of the direction of their day.

What the researchers observed was that the greater one mentioned training casual meditation on a given day, the more that man or woman said experiencing both advantageous thoughts and feelings of social integration (feeling socially related or "on the equal page" as others) on that day. In addition, these human beings who spent greater time engaged in informal meditation practices universal experienced higher degrees of fine thoughts and more emotions of social integration than human beings who spent less time engaged in informal practice. These findings have been impartial of the effects of formal meditation practice, though it should be mentioned that they were correlational in nature and this study ought to no longer prove causality. Importantly, preceding research have linked each high-quality feelings and social integration to larger intellectual and physical health, so there are implications in this study that meditation practice may want to be beneficial for one's general well-being.

Bringing Informal Practice into Your Day

While greater lookup wishes to be achieved on the outcomes of informal meditation practice, I am a massive believer in its impact. After I saw that man at my fitness center pausing to take in the little patch of nature, it was a extraordinary reminder for me to practice what I teach. So after I left the gym, as an alternative of speeding to my car, I made positive to walk over to that spot and take in the peace of the solar and grass and bog and wildlife that may want to have so easily long gone disregarded for yet some other day. After those few minutes, I drove domestic with a more peaceable and grateful heart.

I invite you to find simply a few minutes inside the path of your day or nighttime nowadays to take in yourself wholeheartedly in a moment of presence. Use as many senses as feasible to step out of your thinking-only idea and into your body, to entirely ride anything you are doing — whether or not an undertaking or a moment of pausing. Then word how you show up for the subsequent moments of your day

How to Witness: A Closer Look into your Thought

There is a way to reach the greater idea where we are all unified and related in oneness. It is here that the answers you are seeking for are available to you and your intuitive instincts in the present moment will emerge as your guiding force.

I'm truly announcing that there is a way to be sane. I'm announcing that you can get rid of all this insanity created by means of the past in you. Just by means of being a easy witness of your thought processes.

It is virtually sitting silently, witnessing the thoughts, passing before you. Just witnessing, now not interfering not even judging, because the moment you decide you have lost the pure witness. The second you say "this is good, this is bad," you have already jumped onto the idea process.

You should always understand that it takes some time to create a gap between the witness and the mind. Once the gap is there, you are in for a top notch surprise, that you are now not the mind, that you are the witness, a watcher.

And this system of staring at is the very alchemy. Because as you come to be more and extra deeply rooted in witnessing, ideas start disappearing. You are, however the idea is fully empty. That's the second of enlightenment. That is the second that you grow to be for the first time an unconditioned, sane, really free human being.

Boost advantageous restoration energy and prevent from overthinking, stress and worries. Increase your focus, concentration and sense of being in the now. Sounds of shamanic handdrum, deep chanting, rain, wind and theta brainwaves all blended into a powerful audio experience. Theta waves are related with

➤ Increased feel of internal peace and emotional balance

➤ Deep relaxation

➤ Improved memory

➤ Heightened instinct and notion

➤ Calms the chatter of your thought

➤ Increased psychic capabilities and experience of religious connection

➤ Speed healing, increased bodily recuperation

➤ More restful sleep

➤ Release really useful hormones associated to fitness and longevity

➤ Reduce mental fatigue

➤ Reduction of nervousness and stress

Mindfulness & Meditation: What's the Difference?

Nowadays, mindfulness and meditation are frequently used to imply the same things, which can be quite confusing, while not many are clear on what 'mindfulness meditation' is and how it differs from both of the above. And here's our idea:

Mindfulness is being aware. It's noticing and paying attention to thoughts, feelings, behavior, and the whole thing else. Mindfulness can be practiced at any time, at any place we are, whoever we are with, and anything we are doing, by means of showing up and being entirely engaged in the right here and now. That potential being free of each the previous and future — the what ifs and what maybes — and free of judgment of right or wrong — the I'm-the-best or I'm-no-good situations — so that we can be totally existing except distraction.

Mindfulness is the focus that arises when we non-judgmentally pay interest in the current moment. It cultivates get entry to to core components of our own minds and bodies that our very sanity relies upon on. Mindfulness restores dimensions of our being. These have never truly been missing, just that we have been lacking them, we have been absorbed elsewhere. When your idea clarifies and opens, your heart also clarifies and opens."

Mindfulness additionally releases 'happy' chemical substances in the brain; it lowers blood pressure, improves digestion, and relaxes anxiety around pain. It is easy to practice and remarkable in effect. Not a horrific deal when all that is wanted is to pay attention, which sounds like something we have to all be doing but often forget. When we do pay attention, then change turns into possible.

As pursuers of knowledge, we should always understand that mindfulness and meditation are mirror-like reflections of each other: be aware that mindfulness helps and enriches meditation, whilst meditation nurtures and expands mindfulness. Where mindfulness can be utilized to any scenario during the day, meditation is normally practiced for a precise quantity of time.

Mindfulness is the focus of "some-thing," whilst meditation is the consciousness of "no-thing."

Be careful of the fact that there are different forms of meditation. Some are aimed at developing a clear and targeted mind, recognised as 'Clear Mind' meditations. Others are aimed at creating altruistic states, such as loving kindness, compassion or forgiveness, acknowledged as 'Open Heart' meditations. Others use the physique as a capability to develop awareness, like yoga or walking; others use sound.

I ought to never nonetheless my mind. And then, as I used to be coming near my seventieth birthday, I idea the time has come. Meanwhile, part of getting older is that as the externals commence to fray so you are beckoned inward. As my thinking grew to become quieter in meditation, I located this area that appeared to be suspended at the back of my forehead, like a chandelier hanging from the top of my skull. It was once a vicinity of entire stillness.

Mindfulness Meditation is a structure of Clear Mind meditation. Attention is paid to the herbal rhythm of the breath while sitting, and to the rhythm of slow walking. This alone can have an vast impact. Ultimately, the approach is virtually an aide; it's no longer the trip itself. A hammer can assist build a residence but it's not the house.

In the equal way, meditation exercise is not an cease in itself. We can also wander off and do all sorts of other things, however stillness will constantly be there. It is a partner to have all through life, like an historic pal we flip to when in want of direction, clarity, and inspiration. There's no right way to practice, we just all do it differently. Most necessary of all, meditation is to be enjoyed!

How to Start a Daily Mindfulness Practice

1. Make it a Priority.

To start a every day mindfulness practice, you need to make a dedication to take a seat for at least 5 minutes per day. Put away any distraction, don't multitask while meditating – that defeats the whole purpose. Remember, it's simply five minutes a day. Don't make excuses, simply locate five minutes a day and make it happen!

One factor that can help to make it a precedence is to write down your intention. Research shows you're extra probably to observe thru on a purpose if you write it down and if you join with a deeper reason. Why are you doing this, and what are you hoping to get? Make sure you get out a piece of paper and write this down:

I Commit to 5 minutes of mindfulness for 30 days to create extra xxx in my life.

(fill in your personal preferred result for xxx)

Next, assume about what structures you'll need in location to make this a priority.

Is it telling your companion no longer to disturb you the first 5 minutes of each day? Setting aside time throughout your bus shuttle to listen to the meditations? Or, if you have little ones, inserting them in front of a cartoon

2. Create Sacred Space.

Decide the place you're going to meditate each day and create an inviting, comfy area for yourself. This may want to be putting up your favorite tender blanket or a candle in the nook of your bedroom, or certainly identifying you'll do the meditations on your trip to work each day on the bus. And wherever it is, make it an inviting space. Always see your self in a golden bubble of mild while riding on the bus with your headphones on, listening to the meditation mantras. Imagine your self sitting to meditate in this sacred space every morning for the subsequent month. This is referred to as "future pacing" and it makes you extra possibly to observe thru on something if you can see, feel, hear or smell your self doing some thing in the future.

3. Pick a WHEN.

In addition to developing Sacred Space and selecting a "Where," you additionally want to pick "When" you choose to meditate every day. And you'll be more successful if you choose the equal time each day and build it into your routine. I suggest doing it first issue in the morning, as lookup suggests this is when your willpower is strongest and it's additionally when your mind is clear and in a rested state. Obviously, existence happens. Sometimes you'll end up meditating at a one-of-a-kind time. But your baseline must be a time you select in enhance that you'll stick to as frequently as possible. If you're meditating in the nighttime earlier than mattress and warfare with falling asleep, you may additionally choose to try meditating in the morning or all through your lunch smash when you're less sleepy.

4. Replace Bad Habits with Good.

Creating a Ritual around this new addiction or practice is an extremely good way to make it stick. One of the best methods to create a new habit, according to research, is to change an old addiction with a new one. Do you take a look at your smartphone first issue in the morning? And if so, how does this make you feel? But if you're like most people, it makes you sense anxious and burdened out, questioning about all the matters you have to do that day and all the demands different human beings are placing on you. Instead, begin your day with a new habit with the aid of growing a Morning Ritual. At night, before you go to sleep, put a full glass of water on your nightstand. When you wake up in the morning, the glass of water is a visible reminder of your Morning Ritual. You drink the water and spend 5 minutes meditating earlier than checking your telephone or doing something else.

This convenient Morning Ritual will exchange the total tone of your day due to the fact you're beginning your day with your wants and priorities, versus responding to every individual demands. You're taking care of your body by hydrating, and your thinking by means of way of meditating. And you're being proactive as a alternative than reactive. This will help you stay grounded and founded on what genuinely things for the leisure of the day.

You'll be grateful at what making this one easy alternate will do. So be aware – don't test your telephone or take a look at the news, instead, drink a glass of water and meditate as soon as you wake up in the morning.

5. Don't Go It Alone.

Get support. Join our pal system, be area of the community, and go away a statement on the web page after you meditate. It may additionally also experience dull to make a remark after meditating, but the more you deep in, the more you'll get out of it.

Having a Buddy who is going via the Challenge with you is one of the excellent methods to get support. There is a share of the populace that barring a doubt wishes crew information to comply with by means of on things, if this is you, in reality sign up for a buddy, take phase in the community, inform your friend, your mom, or your great-uncle to test in and see how you're doing. Get the assist you need to make this a priority.

6. Let Go of Expectations.

A lot of human beings get discouraged when they first meditate, and expect they're doing it "wrong." If you're having an hard time staying still remember, this is NORMAL. Cut yourself some slack. Let go of all expectations and you'll discover this a top deal greater enjoyable. If you have a challenging time staying centered on your breath, or you leave out a day of meditating, it's ok. See if you can take a pear at as a substitute than decide yourself. There is no "right" way to meditate.

The key is to commonly come again to your breath and to the thing of view of the Observer. Imagine like you're sitting in a theatre watching the movie of your existence. Let's say your title is Sarah. You're having a difficult time concentrating. Instead of believing your notion chatter saying; "oh, I stink at this! I'm now not a applicable meditator, I'm such a spaz!" go up a degree to the balcony seats of the theatre in your private mind, and turn out to be the Observer. Look at Sarah, trying to meditate, feeling pissed off and observe her with curiosity; "Wow, isn't that fascinating, appear at Sarah beating herself up, believing she's now now not a proper meditator, how interesting, how she's creating a lot of drama about this whole meditation thing." Imagine you're staring at yourself. As rapidly as you pop up to the observer level, you create house between you and your ideas and beliefs. This is the practice. Be the Observer, get curious as an choice of judging, and you'll discover this a lot easier and extra enjoyable!

7. Be variety to yourself. two Be type to yourself. Did I mention…Be sort to yourself?

This bears repeating because it isn't reachable or herbal for most of us. My new preferred self-compassion device is this: Whenever you begin beating yourself up about how you suck at meditating, strive telling yourself; "I'm certainly a little bunny, working via my issues, attempting some component new." Forgive yourself and go on. Research indicates being structure to yourself surely BOOSTS your willpower! So don't beat yourself up if you're now no longer meditating "right". Any effort is well worth a HUGE pat on the back! The reality that you even confirmed up offers you a gold star. :). Be kind to yourself, grant yourself a gold well-known man or woman for even attempting this, and when you be aware you're being unkind to yourself, say; "I'm simply a little bunny, working by my issues," and move on.

Bonus Tip: Connect with your deeper WHY.

To truly turbo-charge your practice, see if you can join to deeper emotions and find out your deep reasons. Why are you doing this? What do you hope to get out of it?

If you're forcing yourself to meditate due to the fact you "should," it's gonna be a slog.

There's a lot of lookup on the advantages of meditation, on the other hand why, especially are you doing it? If you can find out a deeper why (for example, "I favor to be increased existing with my younger young people as an choice than having my questioning wander to all the errands I have to run." Or "I desire to be extra centered at work as an alternative of feeling constantly pulled in a million special directions"), and see your self carrying out this new liked state, you're higher in all likelihood to have a look at through. This will assist encourage you.

When you join with a deeper motivation, it's user-friendly peasy to continue to be on track.

Go massive with your questions, ask yourself; "hmm, what will my Soul get out of this?" Remember the

intention from Step 1? What is your deeper desired result? What's your xxx in this sentence?;
Blood stress is efficiently decreased through potential of mindfulness-based stress discount (MBSR) for patients with borderline immoderate blood pressure or "prehypertension

Mindfulness Leads to Drop in Blood Pressure

The learn about blanketed fifty six female and men identified with prehypertension -- blood stress that used to be once higher than desirable, on the other hand now not but so excessive that antihypertensive drugs would be prescribed. Prehypertension receives growing attention from medical docs due to the fact it is related with a large range of coronary heart disease and one of a kind cardiovascular problems. About 30% of Americans have prehypertension and can additionally be prescribed medicinal capsules for this condition.

One crew of sufferers used to be assigned to a program of MBSR: eight crew periods of 2½ hours per week. Led by using the use of an knowledgeable instructor, the training covered three indispensable kinds of mindfulness skills. Patients had been moreover stimulated to function mindfulness exercises at home.

The different "comparison" crew obtained way of existence recommendation plus a muscle-relaxation activity. This "active control" treatment crew was once no longer expected to have lasting consequences on blood pressure. Blood stress measurements had been compared between corporations to decide whether or not the mindfulness-based intervention decreased blood strain in this crew of human beings at chance of cardiovascular problems.

Patients in the mindfulness-based intervention team had large discounts in clinic-based blood pressure measurements. Systolic blood strain (the first, greater number) diminished through an frequent of almost 5 millimeters of mercury (mm Hg), in contrast to tons much less than 1 mm Hg with in the manipulate team who did now not get preserve of the mindfulness intervention.

Diastolic blood pressure (the second, limit number) used to be moreover limit in the mindfulness-based intervention group: a discount of nearly 2 mm Hg, compared to an expand of 1 mm Hg in the control group.

Mindfulness-based interventions could prevent the need for Antihypertensive Drugs Ambulatory monitoring is an more and extra used alternative to clinic-based blood pressure measurements. However, 24-hour ambulatory blood stress monitoring verified no large difference in blood pressure with the mindfulness-based intervention.

Mindfulness-based stress reduction is an greater and greater famous exercising that has been purported to alleviate stress, deal with despair and anxiety, and deal with fantastic health conditions. It has been recommended that MBSR and distinctive sorts of meditation would possibly also be useful in decreasing blood pressure. Previous research have pronounced small on the other hand large price discount rates in blood stress with Transcendental Meditation; the new find out about is the first to by and large evaluate the blood stress results of mindfulness-based intervention in patients with prehypertension.

Although the blood stress reductions associated with mindfulness-based interventions are modest, they are comparable to many drug interventions and probably giant sufficient to lead to discounts in the hazard of coronary heart attack or stroke. Further research are wanted to see if the blood pressure-lowering consequences are sustained over time.

The researchers argue that mindfulness-based interventions may additionally furnish a beneficial alternative to help "prevent or delay" the desire for antihypertensive medicinal tablets in sufferers with borderline immoderate blood pressure.

What is Mindful Yoga?

Much is identified about the benefits of mindfulness and the benefits of yoga, on the other hand what occurs when you combine the two together?

A pretty new shape of yoga referred to as Mindful Yoga, applies typical Buddhist mindfulness teachings to the bodily exercise of yoga, imparting even deeper insights into the idea and a honestly life-changing approach to your practice.

Read on to have a look at all about its benefits, precise conscious yoga poses, and aware yoga retreats to help you domesticate higher awareness, consciousness, and extended pleasant of life.

A Quick Look at Mindfulness and Yoga

Merging the exercise of mindfulness with the practice of yoga has led the way to a new and increased intensive shape of "Mindful Yoga." Mindful yoga applies everyday Buddhist mindfulness teachings to the bodily practice of yoga; it is the holistic method of connecting your thinking to your breath. Before we go further, let's start with a quick overview of mindfulness and yoga, on their own.

Mindfulness Explained

Mindfulness is knowing what you're feeling while you are undergoing it. It is moment-to-moment awareness, has the splendid of being in the now, a journey of freedom, of perspective, of being connected, now no longer judging.

Mindfulness is easy however it is complex, in that, it is a way of education yourself to honestly focal point on some factor is occurring in the present day, yet it can be one of the most transformational vehicles for non-public and religious progress. It's no wonder it's a common practice in our modern world, with athletes, organizations and health specialists alike, all claiming its splendid benefits.

Benefits of practising mindfulness include, but are now no longer restrained to: extended concentration, memory, immunity to colds and diseases, emotions of happiness and contentment; bargain in continual pain, blood pressure, stress, anxiety, and despair.

Mindfulness exercising has deep roots in Buddhist tradition, on the other hand you truely do no longer want to be a Buddhist in order to practice its teachings and techniques to your life.

Yoga Explained

The meaning of "yoga" is more intricate, as there is no single meaning of the word, however in Sanskrit the strict interpretation is "association." It is depicted as a condition of association and an assortment of procedures that enable us to interface with anything. The experience of having a cognizant association with something is a condition of yoga—an euphoric, ecstatic, satisfying knowledge.

The expression "yoga" is additionally used to portray an extensive practice and a lifestyle. It is evaluated to be at any rate 5,000 years of age, beginning in India and brought toward the west during the 1920s. Yoga has been portrayed as the old Indian study of self-acknowledgment, or the antiquated study of self-culture.

Care has consistently been a fundamental part of the physical routine with regards to yoga. The contrast between Mindful Yoga and the wide assortment of yoga practices out there is that with Mindful Yoga, the fundamental spotlight is on mind-body mindfulness, instead of arrangement subtleties and the accurate physical stance. The fact of the matter is to develop care, utilizing asana as the vehicle in which to do as such.

Carrying careful attention to any physical action makes an alarm center to whatever you are doing in that definite minute, in this way changing the development into a type of reflection. Along these lines careful yoga is viewed as a type of contemplation, as well as it is regularly rehearsed before a proper reflection sitting.

Another normal for this kind of yoga is its accentuation on watching as opposed to responding. Despite the fact that this ought to consistently be the situation in yoga, this training, specifically, places incredible significance on watching your brain and sentiments while you are showcasing the yoga present.

Most characteristically, careful yoga applies conventional Buddhist care lessons to the physical routine with regards to yoga, as an approach to reinforce mindfulness and nearness both on and off the yoga tangle. In particular, this kind of yoga applies the Buddha's Four Foundations of Mindfulness to deliberately develop mindfulness and sympathy through non-judgment, persistence, learners mind, trust, non-endeavoring, giving up, and appreciation

What is the Best Practice Approach?

The best practice way to deal with careful yoga is a methodical one, with unmistakably characterized and repeatable advances. Rather than simply "rehearsing carefully," which for the most part intends to focus on your breath and arrangement subtleties all through your training, it tends to be recommended that applying the Buddha's lessons on the four establishments of care, all through your training.

These point by point guidelines can be applied inside any posture, and by doing so efficiently, you're ready to distinguish explicit practices and roll out positive improvements. For instance, practices, for example, getting a handle on for the result of a posture, evading certain stances inside and out, or totally daydreaming from your training.

Body Scans

When you practice careful yoga, you should examine the body and be watchful for the numerous ways— some unobtrusive, others not all that inconspicuous— in which your viewpoint on your body, considerations, and entire feeling of self can move when you change stances and remain in them for quite a while, giving full consideration from minute to minute. "Rehearsing along these lines improves the inward work hugely and takes it a long ways past the physical advantages that fall into place with the extending and fortifying

The primary concern with careful yoga is to be interested and open to what you are seeing—without judgment or connection—examining your real sensations as completely as would be prudent, and afterward deliberately discharging the focal point of consideration before moving to the following region to investigate. Make sure to be interested; when the mind meanders, see any disturbance or judgment, and afterward take your psyche back to the breath and the body.

The Foundations of Mindfulness

When you apply the Buddha's Four Foundations of Mindfulness to your practice, it turns into a completely coordinated care practice. On some random day you can dedicate your training to any of the four establishments, or work through them successively.

1. Care of Body

This is the attention to the body as body; an update that the body is really a gathering of numerous parts. Skin, bones, teeth, nails, heart, lungs and every other part; each is really a little "body" situated inside the bigger element that we allude to as "the body."

In this establishment we train ourselves to watch the body part by part, instead of attempting to watch the entire body without a moment's delay, making care significantly more open.

When we take a gander at the body as made out of numerous parts, it likewise causes us to consider the to be as a body and not as "my" body or as "myself." It is basically a physical structure like all other physical structures. Since it isn't "myself," the body can likewise be classified "benevolent." This establishment encourages us to perceive that the body is fleeting, subject to damage, ailment, and demise, and along these lines not a wellspring of enduring satisfaction. In the Buddha's words, it instructs us to "know the body as it truly may be."

2. Care of Feelings

Care of sentiments alludes to both substantial sensations and feelings. So also to the body, sentiments can likewise be subdivided. Here the Buddha is guiding us to ponder "the inclination in the emotions." Whether they be charming, undesirable, or unbiased, we figure out how to watch and completely recognize our sentiments, and that they in the end consistently scatter.

Through this establishment, one figures out how to just watch unbelievably up, and not relate to them or join any judgment to them. They don't characterize what your identity is, they are essentially emotions. Considering a to be as a feeling or sensation instead of "my" feeling, we come to realize that sentiments are magnanimous. Along these lines, Buddha says we perceive reality with regards to sentiments. As it were, we "know sentiments as they truly may be."

3. Care of Mind

Care of psyche isn't alluding to the reasoning personality, rather, it is progressively similar to cognizance or mindfulness. Once more, we talk about the psyche as though it were a solitary article, yet it is really a progression of specific occasions of "mind as a top priority."

This establishment of care instructs us that awareness emerges from minute to minute, based on data waking up, just as from inner mental states. The psyche all alone can't exist, just certain perspectives that show up, contingent upon inner or outer conditions.

When we give close consideration to the manner in which each idea emerges, and after that passes away, we increase some understanding that we are not our musings. We learn not to connect our character to our contemplations and we come to know "mind as it truly may be."

4. Care of Dharma

"Dharma" is a Sanskrit word that is as hard to characterize as "yoga." It can basically be depicted as "characteristic law" or "the manner in which things are."

This establishment of care is once in a while called "care of mental articles." With this instructing, we discover that everything around us exists for us as mental items; signs of the real world. They are what they are on the grounds that that is the way we remember them.

Care of Dharma is to rehearse attention to the between presence of all things, and mindfulness that they are transitory, without self-substance, and molded by everything else.

Beneath we diagram a portion of the fundamental advantages of rehearsing care on the yoga tangle.

1. A profound feeling of mindfulness/opening into oneself

As a rule, the act of care brings about an extension of your point of view and of your comprehension of what your identity is (Kabat-Zinn, 2005). With careful yoga, we figure out how to turn out to be adroitly mindful of routine examples of reactivity. For instance, do you hold your breath when diving deep into a turn? Do you become unsettled or irate during testing stances, and wish for them to be finished?

This sort of sharp personality body mindfulness turns into a device for change outside of the yoga practice, since it is through mindfulness that we develop our capacity to see—and be with—things as they seem to be. Preparing our mindfulness causes us to move away from attributes than are keeping down our development, for example, protection from what is, playing the person in question, and responding to things rather than reacting to them (Dodd, n.d.).

2. Causes one to confront the difficulties of regular day to day existence/show less reactivity

Careful yoga practice empowers tolerance and disheartens reactivity on the tangle, which thus offers ascend to more persistence and less reactivity off the tangle. This can be found in all aspects of one's life, including work, connections, public activity and relaxation exercises (Moss, 2018). This expanded feeling of tolerance can make clashes and showdowns simpler to explore, likewise with training, we figure out how to stop and reflect before we respond, as indicated by our examples.

3. Acknowledgment

Through the careful yoga practice, we figure out how to give up and acknowledge circumstances for what they are at that time. Bringing this into regular daily existence can be extraordinarily important, as when we acknowledge an apparent negative circumstance for what it is, we start to kill it, and all the more effectively travel through it. Acknowledgment is even known to help those with sorrow, for instance, as when you start to acknowledge your downturn you begin to remove control from it, and furthermore understand that it is simply thought and feeling, it isn't you.

Rehearsing acknowledgment on the tangle sets you up for reality, as you genuinely don't get the chance to pick what will occur straightaway. Careful yoga instructs you to move with the punches.

4. An increased feeling of sympathy and non-judgment for oneself as well as other people

Expanded empathy, generosity, and comprehension, are everything that we can remove the tangle and convey into our ordinary presence, through standard routine with regards to careful yoga. As careful yoga builds your mindfulness and comprehension of reality—of body, sentiments, mind, dharma—it extends your acknowledgment of essential goodness in yourself and in others.

Explicit "heart opening" presents all through the yoga practice likewise mean to help a solid, open heart (this is in the passionate sense, not the physical heart). As the heart chakra is identified with our capacity to give and get love, customary careful yoga practice mends enthusiastic blockages and relinquishing negative convictions.

5. Develop your own yoga practice

Another advantage of careful yoga is that it can develop, and begin to carry all the more significance to your own yoga practice. For a few, after numerous long periods of training, yoga can turn out to be a piece of a day by day agenda, or simply a type of activity. At the point when the training begins to progress toward becoming something you are doing through routine development and not through cognizant idea, it is never again yoga.

Careful yoga by its very nature, turns you off of "autopilot," and opens you all the more profoundly into your training. It can likewise go about as an extension between the act of asana and the act of contemplation, for the individuals who don't have a ton of involvement in or comprehension of reflection methods.

Why Yoga and Mindfulness Go Together

Yoga and care go together on the grounds that the point of both is to accomplish a more significant level of association, mindfulness, or association, between the psyche, body, and soul. Indeed, yoga without careful mindfulness can't be yoga. Both yoga and care intend to calm the brain, so as to develop a more profound association with and comprehension of oneself. The two of them instruct you to tune into your breath, focus on real sensations, and figure out how to acknowledge reality all things considered at that time.

Care is something that we develop through yoga practice. The yoga studio likewise happens to be the ideal setting for figuring out how to turn out to be progressively careful, since it is loaded with conditions that are outside our ability to control. A few days you may feel fretful or exhausted, or unsettled by the clamors originating from outside the yoga studio or maybe from the individual on the tangle beside you. Careful yoga trains you to reframe these conditions and feel less responsive towards them.

In conclusion, yoga practice is something that readies the body for careful reflection. The two have consistently been inseparably associated, with a physical yoga practice just prompting improved care, and an ordinary care/care reflection practice just prompting a more grounded yoga practice. On the off chance that you investigate Patanjali's eightfold yogic way, you see that "unity" is the last objective of careful contemplation.

So yoga and care are not only two things that go together well, they are really two pieces of an entire, antiquated shrewdness model for accomplishing a more significant level of awareness.

Four Mindful Yoga Poses

Careful yoga is a sort of yoga frequently rehearsed before reflection. Similarly as there are sure represents that stretch as well as fortify your body, and represents that give you vitality, there are likewise represents that set up your body for contemplation. These careful yoga postures are intentionally straightforward, as they help to hinder your breath just as your body, calm the psyche, and obviously, elevate your mindfulness.

1. Tadasana – otherwise called "Mountain Pose"

This posture is the establishment for every single standing stance. It is so apparently basic that it is regularly not rehearsed carefully. It is a fantastic stance to help carry attention to all zones of the body, just as the brain, to check whether it is straying.
Prompts:

Stand up with your arms at your sides. Press each of the four corners of your feet into the ground, circulating your weight equally between the two feet. Envision your pelvis as a bowl with its edge level, both side to side and front to back. Lengthen the spine, keeping the lower ribs from sticking out, tenderly lifting the chest and opening the heart. Loosen up the shoulders down your back. Keep your jawline parallel to the floor and your ears focused over your shoulders.

2. Vrikshasana – otherwise called "Tree Pose"

The great adjusting stance, Tree Pose helps center your psyche around discovering balance on one standing leg. This is another straightforward represent that tends to give the mind a chance to stray. Too, since it is an adjusting represent, the loss of parity may make one experience sentiments of annihilation or judgment, should they be not able keep up the parity.

Signals: (stance to be finished on each side)

Standing with your arms by your sides, begin to move your weight to your correct foot. Breathe in while lifting the contrary leg, pivoting it remotely. Utilize your left hand to help control the bottom of your left foot onto your inward right thigh. Get your hands to your chest Prayer position.

Your left foot ought to press solidly into your correct thigh, and right thigh squeezing immovably into your left foot. Keep up this posture while taking in and out.

3. Anjaneyasana – otherwise called "Low Lunge"

Low Lunge is an extending stance which improves parity, focus and center mindfulness. During this posture, it isn't unexpected to lose cognizant consciousness of the breath, or might bring out a craving for the posture to be finished, making it an incredible exercise in care.

Signs: (stance to be finished on each side)

Beginning from Downward-Facing Dog Pose, step your correct foot forward and place it close to your correct thumb, arranging your correct knee over your correct lower leg. Let your left knee to the cold earth, guaranteeing to put it behind your hips. Raise your middle and clear your arms over your head, palms confronting each other, biceps close to your ears.

Enable your hips to settle advances and down until you feel a stretch in the front of your left leg and psoas muscle. Draw your tailbone down, extending your lower back and connecting with your center muscles. Start to draw your thumbs into the back plane of your body as you reach up with your heart, moving your look upward for a gentle backbend.

4. Supta Baddha Konasana – otherwise called "Leaning back Bound Angle Pose"

An exemplary therapeutic stance, this is an incredible closure pose for careful yoga work on, going about as a segway into contemplation as it brings mindfulness internal. In this stance, the brain may begin to meander because of physical inconvenience in the inward thighs and crotch.

Prompts:

Beginning from Corpse Pose, bring the bottoms of your feet together, and let your knees fall open. Envision that your internal crotches are sinking into your pelvis. Broaden your arms out close by, calculated at around 45 degrees from the sides of your middle, palms looking up. Begin to loosen up your face, chest, shoulders, hips, and feet. Enable your knees to drop further, as you go further into the posture.

Care how skills

What you should do to be careful has just been clarified in a past post. Watch, depict, and take an interest are three distinct methods for taking part in life in a careful way. To make those encounters all the more dominant, you need the "How Skills," or guidelines on how/the manner in which you are to rehearse the "what abilities."

One-mindfully

One-Mindfully is something contrary to performing various tasks. For a large portion of us, most of the day we complete a few things on the double. Our way of life appears to esteem this "aptitude," and a considerable lot of our occupations necessitate that we do this at any rate a segment of the time. In spite of the fact that it feels we are getting progressively cultivated when we are accomplishing more things all the while, is really happening that we are doing a great deal of things inadequately. Having our consideration spread along these lines, our mind skips from undertaking to task, from subject to point. This is hazardous for various reasons. When we train our brain to skip around along these lines, it is more earnestly to perceive when we are diverted. On the off chance that one of the spots your brain goes when you are diverted is stresses over the future, or past excruciating encounters, you are progressively helpless against a negative move in your state of mind. Doing each thing in turn with intentional, centered consideration makes it simpler to perceive when our psyches have meandered. We are then increasingly ready to turn it back toward the job needing to be done.

Making a routine with regards to doing just a single thing, and doing it completely can be transformative. Numerous individuals see the time they spend stressing or ruminating is altogether chopped somewhere near trying to do each thing in turn. Frequently individuals find that exercises they used to discover baffling interpretation of an alternate quality, and are here and there even pleasant. For example, a great many people loath sitting in rush hour gridlock. For them, tuning in to the radio appears to be a basic interruption. For other people, browsing email, having breakfast, putting on cosmetics all make traffic time appear to be increasingly middle of the road. In any case, in the event that you tried different things with killing the radio and constrained all interruptions, sitting peacefully, carrying the brain to sitting or breathing, you may discover these interruptions are a bit much. You may considerably find that the quiet and straightforwardness of sitting in your vehicle is an invite break from the hecticness of present day life. By purposely doing only this one action carefully, you will perceive when your mind meanders to a horrendous obligation at work, or a distressing circumstance you foresee later in the day. As opposed to preparing yourself for stress and nervousness right to work, you can utilize the chance to rest and recover. Doing things one-carefully enables you to establish the pace for what you are doing, and take part in it in a way that is remedial.

NON-JUDGMENTALLY

Non-judgmentally alludes to the manner by which you depict things in your mind when rehearsing care. It has been found through broad research, to be one of the most significant segments of persuasive conduct treatment. Judgment alludes to pondering something in worth terms, or thinking as far as either positive or negative. Decisions can be a useful shorthand when we're settling on speedy choices, for example, regardless of whether to purchase the ruined banana or the ready banana. Decisions are useful for this situation, since we realize a terrible banana is one that would be undesirable to eat or make us wiped out. In any case, there is nothing that is inalienably "awful" in the banana, so one might say, there is no "disagreeableness" we can point to in the banana itself. The judgment extremely just exists in the brain. We can point to the ruined parts, the staining, the soft pieces. However, there is nothing we can point to as inalienably "terrible." Someone else may pass judgment on a similar banana to be "great" if the objective is to discover compost without squandering eatable nourishment. Or then again, in case you are making banana bread, a delicate, dark colored banana is a "decent" banana to utilize. Great and terrible extremely just exist in the psyche of the viewer.

So how does judgment go into our discourse of care? All things considered, if part of being careful is interfacing with reality instead of our musings about the real world, holding decisions gets us further from this objective. One of the objectives of care is to enable us to draw nearer to what is really occurring, as opposed to only associating with the musings we have about what's going on. As decisions extremely just exist in our brains, they don't push us toward a careful encounter. Since feeling dysregulation is generally activated by the implications individuals make of circumstances as opposed to the genuine circumstances themselves, the non-judgmental part of care enables individuals to control their feelings by returning them in contact with the circumstance.

On the off chance that you have a dread of encountering nervousness, the minute you sense a side effect of tension, you presumably place a wide range of decisions on the experience. "This is horrendous." "I can't stand this." "I am powerless for inclination this." All of these worth explanations serve to expand negative feelings about the uneasiness, presumably causing expanded tension, just as disgrace, outrage, and so forth. Rather than purchasing in to these decisions, on the off chance that you were to rather carefully portray them, non-judgmentally, you may stay away from this descending winding. "Seeing snugness in my chest. I notice I'm having considerations about not having the option to deal with uneasiness. I see my heart thumping." You won't really quickly wipe out the nervousness, however by really depicting what's going on without judgment, you contact the feeling without the majority of the undue enduring you may typically encounter when focusing on the decisions rather than the genuine circumstance. Taking this goal point of view, depicting "only the realities," enables us to expand our ability to endure troublesome minutes, and therefore, demonstrate to ourselves they we can deal with them.

Successfully

Successfully intends to be eager to do what attempts to accomplish your goal. Instead of concentrating on what is "correct" or what you "merit," viability is tied in with playing by the guidelines managed by the circumstance. In the event that you believe you are unfairly pulled over on the road, you can attest your privileges, educate the cop on where he/she isn't right, and compromise case. Those are largely methods for responding to the circumstance. Furthermore, if your solitary goal is one of social equity and protecting the constitution, those practices might be the viable ones. Nonetheless, if your goal is more to escape paying a ticket, the viable activity in this circumstance would most likely be to be amiable, apologize, approve the official's point, and so forth. It may not be the "reasonable" thing, however it is the powerful thing.

Being compelling is a care expertise, since it requires a careful method of working. It is a position of eagerness, and one that acknowledges the present circumstance so as to viably move through it. One meaning of care is acknowledgment of the present minute. Adequacy encapsulates both tolerating the present minute, and responding to it in a liquid method to arrive at your objectives. Adequacy is tied in with accomplishing your goal not regardless of the present circumstance, but since of the present circumstance.

This isn't to imply that that you should forfeit your qualities in the administration of doing what works. That isn't compelling. What viability is, is being eager to do what works when the expense is middle of the road, as opposed to unbendingly holding to some perfect that is "ideal." There is an old articulation that you can "right" yourself "ideal" out of a relationship. Being correct is decent, yet in the event that you penance everything in the administration of being correct, you wind up losing a great deal. It is caught by the similarity of being on the road where as far as possible is 65, and the individual before you is going 45. You can decline to acknowledge this circumstance, sounding, riding the individual's tail, reviling and fingers, notwithstanding demanding proceeding to drive 65 as you furrow into the vehicle. Or on the other hand you can take a full breath, move to another lane, and proceed onward. What appears to be increasingly viable?

CHAPTER 4

WATCHING

CONSIDERATIONS IN

CONTEMPLATION

In the event that you can watch your contemplations without getting related to them, at that point half of your issues won't be there. Numerous issues in life are simply made by psyche and its considerations.

One of the fundamental rule in watching considerations is your non-contribution with them. A great many people get include with the reasoning procedure since they accept that it's their musings and it's their reasoning procedure. Be that as it may, no idea have a place with the spirit. When you experience your source (or focus or soul) in snapshots of rapture or no-psyche or delight, at that point where every one of these musings have gone?

Insight of sages says that no idea have a place with the spirit. Every one of the considerations are at mind level just that is at the outskirts. In any case, at the middle or the wellspring of your being (soul) there is no idea as there is outright quietness, stillness and delight plaguing at your inside.

To encounter that happy and quiet condition of your being, you have to initially watch the considerations going on in your psyche. Gradually as you quit engaging with the reasoning procedure then your mind will begin backing off. Since mind benefits from your vitality. More you figure, more it will wind up dynamic. As you quit getting include in speculation then it doesn't get vitality from you and its force starts backing off. As your mind starts backing off, you will begin drawing near to your internal focus. So this aloof viewing of musings is the route to your being.

genuine article as it extends the quietness inside and you become more acquainted with your internal identity. Keep in mind, not to get energized as your contemplation extends. Additionally observe any inner self inclination emerging in you. You need to turn into an observer to every one of the contemplations or feelings emerging in you. You can't be incomplete that you will just watch wrong musings and will get related to great or satisfying considerations. Observe each idea which rings a bell with no inclination.

6. Work on viewing the considerations as much as you can

As you continue viewing the contemplations, at that point gradually over some stretch of time your seeing focus will create. Presently you can watch your considerations while remaining in an open line or while strolling or doing some other everyday undertaking. This resembles you have graduated to the following stage. For this to occur, attempt to watch your contemplations at whatever point you get the reality to do it. Practice as much as you can. You will commit errors however don't stress. Continue watching the brain as regularly as possible. Check this post of 51 hints for amateurs in reflection.

7. Watch the watcher

As your seeing focus will grow all the more then you will see that there is a middle inside you which is continually viewing everything. Presently you watch this inside who is viewing everything. This is the trickiest part and accompanies parcel of training and is for cutting edge meditators.

Scarcely any tips for watching considerations:

1. Cut down on your understanding propensities. Try not to understand paper or magazine. Just read what is sufficient or required for your occupation.

2. Quit staring at the TV, film or surfing web. Since whatever you read in web or in paper remains in your psyche. it gives a force to the musings. Something very similar comes in your fantasies moreover. So cut all the psychological junk which you are taking inside you unwittingly.

3. Rest soundly. In the event that you can't rest profoundly, at that point you can't think profoundly. Check this post on the most proficient method to rest profoundly.

4. Try not to be aspiring or vain in reflection. Appreciate the reflection.

5. Try not to be not kidding in contemplation yet be genuine in your training. On the off chance that you are getting to be not kidding, at that point watch this conduct of yours. Subsequent stage from watching contemplations is to watch your feelings. So attempt it with various feelings you get while rehearsing contemplation like fatigue, blame inclination, rush to prevail in reflection, etc.

6. At beginning phases of reflection it builds up a contemplation space in your home.

7. It additionally helps a great deal in the event that you are standard in reflection practice.

8. Have tolerance and assurance.

9. Give your 100 percent to reflection. Make it your top need throughout everyday life.

10. Peruse some great reflection books or go to any contemplation camp or visit any ashram where reflection is polished. Bunch vitality and similar otherworldly companions keep you persuaded and furthermore you gain from one another encounters.

11. Figure out how to acknowledge quietness and aloneness throughout everyday life. These two characteristics will go far in developing your contemplation practice.

Guided Meditation Scripts

Utilize these guided reflection contents to quiet the brain and loosen up the body. Contemplation is the demonstration of centering the brain to unwind, improve inward mindfulness, and make positive mental or physical changes.

You may see that a large number of the unwinding practices here fit into more than one class. A portion of the contemplation contents could likewise be delegated guided symbolism, uneasiness alleviation unwinding, rest unwinding, or different sorts of unwinding system. A portion of the contemplation contents on this page can likewise be found on these different pages, yet they are sorted out here as per the reason and kind of reflection included.

In the event that you are searching for an essential prologue to reflection, start with the fundamental contemplation contents underneath for a prologue to how to ponder. As you become acquainted with thinking and begin to build up the expertise to center the brain, you will effortlessly have the option to utilize reflection strategies to roll out positive improvements and to adapt new aptitudes.

A Guided Breathing Meditation to Cultivate Awareness

This training is a breathing contemplation. We center around breathing not on the grounds that there's anything unique about it but since that physical vibe of breathing is consistently there. All through the training, you may end up got up to speed in considerations, feelings, sounds—any place your psyche goes, basically return again to the following breath. In case you're occupied the whole opportunity and arrive back just once, that is flawless.

1) Sit serenely, finding a steady position you can keep up for some time, either on the floor or in a seat. Close your eyes in the event that you like, or leave them open and look descending toward the floor.

2) Draw thoughtfulness regarding the physical impression of breathing, maybe seeing the constantly present rising and falling of your belly or chest, or maybe the air moving in and out through your nose or mouth. With every breath, focus on these sensations. On the off chance that you like, rationally note, "Taking in… Breathing out."

3) Many occasions over, you'll get occupied by musings or emotions. You may feel diverted as a rule. That is ordinary. There's no compelling reason to square or kill thinking or whatever else. Without giving yourself trouble or anticipating anything unique, when you find that your consideration has meandered, see whatever has occupied you and afterward returned to the breath.

4) Practice stopping before making any physical changes, for example, moving your body or scratching a tingle. With expectation, move at a minute you pick, permitting space between what you experience and what you do.

5) You may discover your mind meandering always, made up for lost time in a hurricane—that is typical, as well. Rather than grappling with or drawing in with those considerations to such an extent, work on watching, taking note of any place your consideration has been, and afterward coming back to the physical vibe of relaxing.

6) Let go of any feeling of attempting to get something going. For these couple of minutes, make a chance to not plan or fix or whatever else is your propensity. Apply enough exertion to continue this training, however without causing yourself mental strain. Look for equalization along these lines; on the off chance that you wind up for the most part wandering off in fantasy land and off in dream,

dedicate some additional push to keeping up your core interest.

7) Breathing in and breathing out, return your thoughtfulness regarding the breath each time it meanders somewhere else.

8) Continue to work on seeing without expecting to respond. Simply sit and focus as best as you are capable. As hard all things considered to keep up, that is all that there is. Return again and again, without judgment or desire.

9) When you're prepared, tenderly open your eyes. Notice any sounds in the earth. Notice how your body feels at the present time. Notice your contemplations and feelings. Putting everything on hold, choose how you'd like to proceed with your day

Guided Therapeutic Imagery

Guided restorative symbolism, a method where emotional well-being experts help people in treatment center around mental pictures so as to bring out sentiments of unwinding, depends on the idea of mind-body association. Mind-body association maintains the connection among body and brain as one significant factor in an individual's general wellbeing and prosperity. In guided restorative symbolism, an individual can approach mental pictures to improve both enthusiastic and physical wellbeing.

HISTORY: GUIDED THERAPEUTIC IMAGERY

Different types of guided symbolism have been utilized for quite a long time, as far back as antiquated Greek occasions, and the procedure is a built up methodology in Chinese medication and American Indian conventions just as other mending and religious practices. Jacob Moreno's system of psychodrama, created during the 1940s, can likewise be connected to guided symbolism, as the institution of the individual in treatment's interesting concerns can be comprehended as a strategy for coordinating an individual's very own symbolism. Truth be told, Hans Leuner, who further created psychodrama, called the methodology guided full of feeling symbolism.

During the 1970s, Dr. David Bressler and Dr. Martin Rossman started building up help for guided symbolism as a viable methodology for the treatment of ceaseless torment, malignant growth, and different genuine sicknesses. Their work drove them to help establish the Academy for Guided Imagery in 1989. All through the 80s, various wellbeing promoters and experts started to distribute materials investigating the positive effect of guided symbolism on wellbeing concerns both mental and physical. Ulrich Schoettle, Leslie Davenport, and Helen Bonny were a couple of such people.

Right now, guided symbolism is a set up methodology in reciprocal and elective medication, and examinations show it is every now and again accommodating when utilized as a major aspect of the restorative procedure.

GUIDED THERAPEUTIC IMAGERY TECHNIQUES

Guided helpful symbolism is a procedure utilized in a wide scope of remedial modalities and settings including gathering and individual treatment. When taken in, the procedure can likewise be drilled freely, without the bearing of an advisor. Guided symbolism contents can be discovered on the web and in self-improvement guides. Numerous people may get advantage from rehearsing guided symbolism all alone, however looking for guidance from a prepared proficient before endeavoring to utilize guided symbolism alone is normally prescribed. Guidance in the strategy can enable people to acquire most extreme impact from the mediation.

Commonly a specialist utilizing this methodology will give verbal prompts to coordinate the focal point of the symbolism, frequently promising the member to see different tactile parts of the scene. An individual in treatment may, for instance, be approached to imagine a tranquil spot, incorporating into this vision any fragrances, sounds, and surfaces present. Along these lines, guided helpful symbolism grows past representation since it includes each of the five detects. Guided symbolism is intended to affect the body just as the psyche, and breathing commonly turns out to be increasingly slow controlled during the procedure while muscles unwind, making a condition of quiet and unwinding. A few specialists may utilize music as a major aspect of the strategy.

The procedure of guided helpful symbolism has a few likenesses to different methods intended to conjure a condition of unwinding, for example, spellbinding.

The two methods include some perception, an attention on the inward mental experience, and a casual perspective. Be that as it may, entrancing will in general spot more spotlight on proposal while guided symbolism underlines the faculties. At the point when utilized restoratively, trance can use the casual state to enable an individual to turn out to be progressively responsive to new thoughts and convictions. Guided symbolism attempts to join an individual's faculties so as to more readily immediate and center consideration around a specific territory of concern, envisioning an ideal result for that worry.

ISSUES TREATED WITH GUIDED IMAGERY

While at first viewed as close to an option or correlative methodology, the methodology's demonstrated adequacy has accumulated help as of late. Guided restorative symbolism is presently generally utilized and bolstered by research. The procedure is generally utilized for pressure the executives, with the individual in treatment urged to picture a spot that ingrains a feeling of unwinding.

Research shows guided symbolism to be useful in the treatment of various concerns, including:

· Stress

· Tension

· Gloom

· Substance misuse

· Sorrow

· Posttraumatic stress

· Relationship issues

· Lessened self-care

· Family and child upbringing issues

Notwithstanding enthusiastic and social issues, guided symbolism is likewise frequently utilized by medicinal experts to address torment the board, hypertension, and the decrease of undesirable practices, for example, smoking. Guided symbolism is additionally regularly utilized among competitors so as to upgrade execution. Guided symbolism strategies are commonly used to target explicit issues. An individual with malignant growth, for instance, may utilize guided symbolism to envision sound cells and solid, amazing organs.

Preparing for guided therapeutic imagery

The Academy for Guided Imagery offers proficient accreditation in guided helpful symbolism, or Interactive Guided Imagery, as it is likewise known. Intrigued experts must finish 150 hours of preparing, 33 hours of free investigation, and be authorized to rehearse as a psychological well-being proficient. Wellbeing instructors, individual mentors, body workers,and advisors may likewise seek after preparing in this technique.

Preparing, which comprises of three levels that must be finished inside two years, is offered through home-study modules and online gathering study workshops. Extra proceeding with instruction trainings are additionally accessible through AGI's site.

Restrictions of guided therapeutic imagery

Despite the fact that the utilization of guided restorative symbolism is upheld by research, a few investigations recommend it can prompt false recollections. Be that as it may, there are ordinarily different elements adding to the recuperation of false recollections, for example, bunch weight, character elements, and individual encounters.

Guided symbolism may not work for each person, and a few people may like to address their worries with different methodologies.

This system is commonly viewed as safe for use by a great many people, regardless of whether they look for the help of a psychological wellness expert or utilize guided symbolism all alone. The underlying direction of a specialist is energized, and when an individual encounters a genuine concern, the help of an emotional wellness expert is constantly suggested.

Guided symbolism is an unwinding strategy that utilizations positive mental pictures to impact how you feel. It can improve your customary Parkinson's treatment. Be that as it may, it doesn't supplant conventional treatment.

Guided symbolism is an antiquated practice that incorporates straightforward representation. It is a protected and basic procedure.

Guided symbolism centers around pictures. Be that as it may, this kind of symbolism encourages you saddle every one of your faculties - locate, taste, sound, smell, and sensation. This causes you associate with your internal assets for improving wellbeing.

With guided symbolism, you utilize your creative mind to make unwinding or positive pictures and encounters. Your body translates these as genuine. So this can likewise have an undeniable effect on your physical wellbeing.

How would you do guided symbolism?

You can do guided symbolism in the solace of your home. Or on the other hand, to begin, you can see an expert who is affirmed in performing guided symbolism.

A specialist may urge you to initially attempt to discharge strain. To begin, it can concentrate on your breathing and pulse.

Guided symbolism

Guided symbolism is an engaged practice that includes every one of the five faculties to touch off positive recuperating messages all through the brain and body. The training is frequently traded with perception, self-spellbinding and guided reflection, yet it has its very own arrangement of systems. The advantages of guided symbolism are immense — there is inquire about that demonstrates the training can diminish dread and uneasiness, reduce the recurrence of cerebral pains and has been demonstrated to diminish mental misery in malignancy patients. Also, it's a training that can be acquainted with your at-home care routine whenever.

What is guided symbolism?

With guided symbolism, you use the majority of your faculties — vision, taste, sound, smell, and contact — to construct pictures in the mind that your body feels are as genuine as outer occasions. This doesn't imply that during the training in your "continuous" physical body you will smell, hearing and tasting objects, however your mind will picture the makings of each sense, versus increasingly customary guided reflection that is centered absolutely around the psychological state without the expansion of entire body detects. Guided symbolism can really invigorate changes in pulse, circulatory strain and respiratory examples, on account of the profound, physical personality body association.

Consider it a significantly more intensified adaptation of having a nourishment longing for built from memory, at that point seeing your salivary organs become dynamic. Your psyche and body are interfacing over a picture created in your mind that has contacted every one of your faculties. Presently, imagine a scenario in which you can imitate that for stress the board and relief from discomfort.

How is guided symbolism unique in relation to representation? Perception is the point at which an individual spotlights absolutely on visuals. Guided symbolism develops an inundated perspective all through the whole body by picturing each of the five detects modifying. How does this vary from entrancing? As a general rule, spellbinding requires a member and a trance inducer. The trance inducer acquaints recommendations with the member to help enter the subliminal personality. With guided symbolism, you are utilizing the sole intensity of your own creative mind.

IN ALIGNMENT: HOW TO MAKE YOUR INTENTION MATCH YOUR ATTENTION

What does the word expectation mean? I'm certain we've all heard it or been to a yoga class where the teacher approaches us to set an aim for the class. Dr. Wayne Dyer says that aim is, "A solid reason or point, joined by an assurance to deliver an ideal outcome." One of my goals is to consistently rouse others to roll out little improvements toward the beginning of the day that have the ability to impact the manner in which they work for the duration of the day and eventually how they live. Changing my morning has made a huge difference for me here, so it's my goal to help other people do likewise! Sounds basic, isn't that so? How about we burrow somewhat more profound.

HERE ARE SOME EXERCISES TO GET IN STRONGER ALIGNMENT WITH YOUR INTENTION

Make a move: What is one move thing you can make today to get these two things in closer arrangement? This might be an option that is more profound than what you have going on today or this end of the week. Sit in contemplation or stillness for two or three minutes and truly consider where arrangement and misalignment falsehood identified with your aim and consideration. What would you be able to placed into movement at this time to unite them?

Journaling Exercise: These five stages are taken from The Power of Intention, I exceptionally prescribe this book. For the present, simply do some journaling and reflection on every one of these five territories identified with aim. Where do you have solid regard for help that region? Which classification could utilize some more consideration?

1/Visualize the Power of Intention: Allow the seven words that speak to the essences of aim to embellish your representation of the forces of goal. Imaginative, kind, adoring, lovely, growing, copious and responsive.

2/Be Reflective: A mirror reflects without bending or judgment. Consider resembling a mirror and reflect what comes into your existence without judgment or conclusions.

3/Expect Beauty: Expecting benevolence and love alongside excellence to be a major part of your life by profoundly adoring yourself, your environment and by showering love for all of life. There's continually something to delightful to be experienced any place you are.

4/Meditate on Appreciation: The intensity of aim reacts to your valuation for it.

5/Banish Doubt: When uncertainty is expelled, bounty twists and the sky is the limit.

Drawing in Anything You Want Through Focused Intention

There are three primary columns that structure the law of fascination (LOA) on which the procedure is based. First is want, which originates from difference, as we have talked about in changing your intuition to view negative life circumstances as potential chances. You normally request things that you have not yet experienced, and you additionally request change when something feels awful or interestingly with your longing.

The second LOA is consideration. Wants lead to consideration, which can likewise be called a goal. Consideration gives you a push to assemble all the vitality that goes in cognizant showing of the craving.

The third column is conviction. Convictions are what reinforce your aim - and on the off chance that you have a firm faith in the appearance procedure, the procedure goes as easily as a marshmallow liquefying on your tongue. There can be no opposition in the way of convictions - that is the key.

Feelings assume a job here. Despite the fact that they don't really create the wants, they are solid pointers of where you are going with your aim sign. They approve what you think or what you look like at things. Since feelings don't make things, you can progress nicely, hypothetically, notwithstanding aiming from an impartial, unfeeling state. That could place you in the nirvana achievers association. Being in a condition of nonpartisan feeling is troublesome.

A lot simpler is:

Seeing whatever feelings you have in the now

• Embracing them all

• Focusing on the positive ones for better outcomes

• Determine what you do ask for from the entire experience - in the event that you can include energy you will fan the flame

Watch your feelings right now - on the off chance that they are incredibly negative, you are not moving toward what you need in your life. Having a lot of antagonism out of differentiation is a pointer to what you don't need. Positive feelings, conversely, will frequently fill in as a pointer toward what encounters you need to show, nor being washed away interestingly nor going excessively outrageous on the angle of negative inclination. These, when in equalization, are an indication that you are utilizing contrast in the most ideal manner you can.

When you understand that you are a being of profound vitality, the wants that are worked up inside you will be consistently replied by the universe. You want it, and the need is replied - a procedure everlastingly rehashing. To accomplish this condition of want satisfaction, we have to fret about the awareness with which we go to every minute and how our brains procedure those minutes. On the off chance that we bring opposition, at that point we square satisfaction of our wants.

Our feelings and sentiments are our guide. These moment groupings of occasions are crammed with data. This data comes as sentiments, for the most part negative, yet sentiments and feelings that currently progressed toward becoming images or central procedures for my future considering life. As you watch these contemplations, you start to see synchronicity. You would then be able to start to see relationships to how musings show themselves into our physical reality.

Negative circumstances relabeled as complexity currently become the mile marker for an adjustment in deduction, a turn in one's wants versus an awful or static occasion. The rotate in speculation prompts an adjustment in conduct, which leads toward indication of another result. I adore differentiate - it brings me into the dynamic procedure of stream versus resistive reasoning that holds us solidified. Complexity can feel awful now and again, yet it is from differentiation that we make development and development.

Differentiation has shown me a ton. It instructed me to want, to request things yet un-showed. It continued visiting me with the look of new things that I can put a cognizant goal on. I had such huge numbers of choices! I adored it. It gave me the rush of effectively showing my desires, little and huge. It likewise instructed me that marking a craving as large or little is as a general rule only a proportion of the fact that you are so prepared to acknowledge the wants showed. It gave me kind of an estimating tape to keep a beware of my obstruction, to enabling things to come in my life and a record of my cognizance.

On the off chance that you need to start to change something in your life, change the way in which you take a gander at it. See differentiate or a terrible life circumstance as a chance to turn, to move toward a path of your new want. Use differentiate as a seed for change. When you see what you don't care for, start to scan for an aim, pronounce a way and after that enable the universe to take the necessary steps - isolate from the result.

Contemplation Can Strengthen Your Intentions

Defining objectives and imagining your deepest longings is a typical practice toward the start of each new year. Maybe you, similar to a large number of others, have made a New Year's Resolution. For those of you who did, how's it going? In case you're seeing it's beginning to falter, you are not the only one. A University of Scranton research study expresses that for all the sincere goal, just a little division of us, a negligible 8% truth be told, keep our New Year's objectives long haul. Resolve is just insufficient for the greater part of us.

So what's the mystery of the individuals who do succeed? Forbes Magazine reports that two stages are key in showing a longing.

Keep the expectation straightforward and keep the rundown short.

Remain Focused.

At the end of the day, set little, explicit, achievable objectives and keep your focus on the big picture. Pick a certain something, at that point focus on that for 21 days. 21 days is the by and large endless supply of time it takes to altogether build up another propensity or thought design.

Obviously, obstructions and difficulties emerge endeavoring to defeat our responsibility.

Getting occupied is one of my own impediments to meeting my objective. I basically overlook amidst contending needs and day by day requests. Therefore, I think that its supportive to record my determination in some fun vivid way and afterward post it in an obvious spot where I will peruse it consistently after waking and just before I flip off the light during the evening. I have to keep my dedication dynamic in my psyche as contending needs as often as possible spring up. When I'm mindful that I'm not seeing the updates any longer, I revise and after that post them in another spot.

Another associate to showing a purpose is to consolidate it into a contemplation practice. In what way, you may inquire? Quite a while in the past, a companion shared some insight that his dad gave him upon his graduation from school. He stated: "Child, the mystery of a fruitful life is basic. Center, you win. Dissipate, you lose." I've contemplated those words many occasions throughout the years and have seen reality inside my life and my reflection practice. Basically: that which I practice reliably, I show signs of improvement at.

This is particularly obvious when making way of life changes to improve one's wellbeing. It takes duty and center and I would include Support. Backing as proposals by medicinal services suppliers, loved ones.

The organization you keep, is a lot more grounded than self discipline. Get a pal to go on strolls with, try making solid suppers with, and start an intercession practice. You'll be astounded at how much these will help in achieving your objectives.

There are numerous approaches to ponder however most teach you to concentrate on some article or "mental grapple". Perhaps the least demanding thing for me to concentrate on is you're my breath streaming in and out. It's consistently with me and it gives my mind something to focus on while going around my monkey mind from meandering into old examples and mental prattle. It has a quieting impact. At the point when my breath is unfaltering and quiet, I feel progressively present. When I am available, I settle on better decisions – including conduct and way of life changes expected to help my goals.

Here's a short contemplation to go after yourself… in some simple advances:.

Set aside all interruption. (telephone on quietness, PC screen off, and so on.)

Sit serenely and sit up tall. (Drooping prompts napping)

Delicately close your eyes.

Output your body, make alterations should have been increasingly agreeable.

Take a full breath, at that point let it out as a moan.

Delicately grapple your consideration on every inward breath and exhalation for 5 to 6 breaths.

Consider something you truly need in your life (inhale just clean air – for example quit smoking, dispose of prepared nourishments, walk a mile daily, ruminate for 5 minutes every morning, be increasingly patient and kind to your children/life partner/and so on..)

Dial in your expectation until you can obviously envision it. Feel it. Be it-as though it is now valid. Concentrate on this for 30 seconds. In the event that your mind meanders, just start once more.

Prepare for the delicate unfurling of shrewd quiet inside. End the contemplation with a short proclamation of appreciation and attestation. For instance: "I pick wellbeing and imperativeness." Or essentially "Great job (embed your name)."

Change steadily and discreetly once again into your day.

Keep in mind: what you practice, you reinforce.

A Basic Mindfulness Meditation Script for Social Anxiety Disorder

Coming up next is a care contemplation content that you can use to help beat social tension issue (SAD).

This content depends on fundamental reflections, and those for adapting to nervousness. Pick a calm spot and time to rehearse your contemplation. You may likewise wish to set a clock to flag the finish of your reflection; somewhere in the range of 20, up to 40 minutes is an ordinary length for training.

In the event that you would like to tune in to the content, you could likewise consider recording yourself perusing the entry beneath and afterward play it back to yourself through earphones.

Start your reflection by picking a position. Sit in a seat with a caution however agreeable stance, back straight, hands resting in your lap and feet level on the floor.

Ensure that you're adjusted and not stressing. Slacken any tight attire and close your eyes.

Step by step see the stillness of your body. Loosen up your stomach, chest and shoulders, and start to concentrate on your breath.

Take in profoundly through the nose, enabling the air to stream down to your stomach, and afterward discharge.

Rehash the breath, enabling the air to tenderly move through. Notice a feeling of quiet as you inhale out. Discharge strain and worry as you bit by bit locate an agreeable cadence for your relaxing.

As you take in and out, see any considerations or sentiments that you have.

You may begin to stress over the future or consider the past—it's typical for your brain to meander. A few emotions and musings may be troubling, yet give a valiant effort to watch and not pass judgment.

Make a note of the idea or feeling and what it is: perhaps you stressed over an up and coming get-together or thought about a discussion that went poorly well.

In the event that a negative idea or feeling catches your eye, make a note of it and after that arrival to concentrating on your breath. It's normal for your psyche to meander to your social and execution fears, however make an effort not to be reproachful of yourself.

Notice the idea or feeling, however don't tail it, and don't give your mind a chance to seek after it. Perceive that it's just an idea: it's what your psyche does. You can see it and after that let it go.

Imagine yourself at the sea shore, lying on the warm sand.

A reviving breeze blows in and you feel loose. Envision your musings and sentiments resemble the breeze blowing or the waves rolling, and proceed with your breathing, letting everything become the breeze and the waves.

Feel how the waves travel every which way. Stay cool, and let your considerations move and change. Relax.

Purposefully infer a circumstance that you dread. Envision yourself conversing with outsiders or giving a discourse.
Sit with the awkward contemplations and emotions that this circumstance brings, and essentially let them be, without standing up to.

Unwind and let the contemplations and emotions bit by bit break down. Obstruction will make the pain remain, while acknowledgment will enable the cynicism to disseminate.

Keep in mind that you will consistently encounter some uneasiness; it's incomprehensible for it to totally vanish. Rather than opposing, figure out how to respect your considerations and emotions, acknowledge them, and after that vibe how they coast away.

When you do wind up in a snapshot of bliss during your day, seize it, keeping the inclination in your mindfulness.

Tally to 15 seconds, enabling your cerebrum to begin setting up and fortifying new pathways. The more you utilize these pathways, the more profound the depressions become. Upbeat contemplations will in the end fill those notches.

Continuously, when you are prepared, take your consideration gradually back to your breath. At that point, move to your body and your environment. Move delicately, open your eyes, and stretch.

Straightforward Steps to Start Practicing Guided Imagery for Anxiety Relief

Guided symbolism for social uneasiness includes the utilization of perception methods to enable your body to enter a casual state. At the end of the day, you close your eyes and envision the sights and hints of a spot that you find unwinding.

Kinds of Guided Imagery Visualizations

The most widely recognized representation includes a tropical sea shore, warm sun, and alleviating hints of the sea. On the off chance that you find, in any case, that some other envisioned scene is increasingly suitable for you, for example, sitting before a thundering flame on a stormy night, definitely, utilize that setting.

The sort of scene isn't significant, what is important is that you envision each sight, sound, and smell and transport yourself to that spot.

How Guided Imagery Can Help Social Anxiety

Guided symbolism can help with your tension by enabling you to oversee negative feelings. Notwithstanding the models given above, it can likewise be utilized to imagine positive results in different social and execution circumstances. As opposed to imaging the most exceedingly terrible, guided symbolism allows you to encounter the most ideal result before entering a circumstance.

Instances of How Imagery Can Be Used for Anxiety

A performer who has execution nervousness could utilize symbolism to envision conquering tension to perform at a specific level.

A competitor living with execution nervousness could imagine a challenge and sentiments of unwinding as opposed to uneasiness.

An entertainer with execution uneasiness could imagine going through a scene loaded with certainty and without nervousness.

An understudy with execution uneasiness could envision giving an introduction without tension.

A socially on edge individual could envision setting off to a gathering and having a decent encounter.

Case of a Guided Imagery Visualization

In the accompanying case of guided symbolism for uneasiness, the well known sea shore setting is utilized. On the off chance that you prefer an alternate setting, essentially supplant the subtleties recorded underneath with those pertinent to the situation you are utilizing.

Significant: If you live with an ailment, if you don't mind counsel with your primary care physician before starting any sort of unwinding preparing exercise.

1. Locate a Quiet Place Free From Distractions

Lie on the floor, or lean back in a seat. Extricate any tight attire and evacuate glasses or contact lens. Rest your hands in your lap or on the arms of the seat. Pick a period and spot where you realize you are not liable to be interfered.

2. Take a Few Slow Even Breaths

On the off chance that you haven't as of now, put in no time flat rehearsing diaphragmatic relaxing. Inhale profoundly down into your stomach, like how you would do in a yoga class. This kind of breathing will assist you with relaxing much more.

3. When You Are Relaxed, Gently Close Your Eyes

Envision yourself lying on a delightful segregated sea shore. Picture delicate white sand around you and perfectly clear waters with delicate waves that lap at the shore. Imagine a cloudless sky above and palm trees influencing in the breeze behind you. Keep on keeping your eyes shut and picture this excellent tropical scene.

4. Take in and Smell the Scent of the Ocean and Tropical Flowers

Notice the sound of the waves tenderly moving onto shore and winged animals in the trees behind you. Feel the warmth underneath you and the warm sun on your skin. Notice the flavor of a reviving tropical beverage as you carry it to your mouth. Don't simply picture the scene—contact it, taste it, and smell it as much as your creative mind will permit.

5. Remain in This Scene for whatever length of time that You Like

Notice how loose and quiet you feel. Appreciate the sentiment of unwinding as it spreads all through your whole body, from your head to your toes. Notice the distance away you feel from tension and stress. Proceed in this phase of the guided symbolism process for whatever length of time that you like. You ought to step by step see how quiet and loosened up you feel.

6. Slowly Count Backward From 10

Open your eyes, feel loose however alert. You have come back to your environment, however a quiet state will have supplanted any uneasiness or stress that you initially felt. Presently, take a shot at making an interpretation of this smoothness into the remainder of your day.

Utilizing Guided Imagery Recordings

You may think that its difficult to practice guided symbolism simply utilizing a composed content like the one above. Notwithstanding adhering to these composed guidelines, you may consider utilizing a voice recording, for example, the free MP3 sound document offered by McMaster University with bearings on rehearsing guided symbolism.

Utilization of a sound chronicle will enable you to completely unwind and focus on the method. You could likewise record yourself perusing a guided symbolism content that you've made yourself.

A Word From Verywell

Guided symbolism is one type of unwinding preparing that you may discover accommodating for social nervousness. In any case, if your uneasiness is extreme and you have not gotten proficient treatment, for example, intellectual conduct treatment (CBT) or medicine, it is imperative to contact your primary care physician or a psychological wellness proficient for determination and an arrangement for showing signs of improvement.

While self improvement techniques can be utilized for mellow to direct uneasiness, progressively extreme tension frequently requires conventional treatment procedures.

Practice Deep Breathing for Anxiety

Diaphragmatic breathing, or profound breathing from the stomach as opposed to the chest, is an approach to unwind and lessen uneasiness of different sorts. In spite of the fact that we are largely fit for breathing thusly, not many of us do as such in our regular day to day existences.

Significance of Deep Breathing

Profound breathing causes you to maintain a strategic distance from the "battle or-flight" reaction to upsetting circumstances. In these circumstances, your body's programmed frameworks are on high alarm and sign your heart to pulsate quicker and breathing rate to increment. By deliberately getting to be mindful of your breathing and managing its profundity and rate, the probability of spiraling into a frenzy or nervousness assault is brought down.

The most effective method to Practice Diaphragmatic Breathing

Note: If you live with an ailment, counsel with your primary care physician preceding starting any kind of unwinding preparing exercise.

It's ideal to rehearse this breathing example while you are in a loose and safe condition at home. Along these lines, you will be bound to utilize this strategy when looked with circumstances that trigger manifestations of social nervousness issue (SAD) or different issues with tension.

The following are the means to take to rehearse profound relaxing:

Locate a peaceful spot free of interruptions. Lie on the floor, or even lean back in a seat, release any tight apparel and expel glasses or contact lens. Rest your hands in your lap or on the arms of the seat.

Spot one hand on your upper chest and the other hand on your stomach. Breathe in, taking a full breath from your mid-region as you tally to three. As you breathe in you should feel your stomach ascend. The hand on your chest ought not move.

After a short respite, gradually breathe out while tallying to three. Your stomach should fall down as you breathe out. In the event that you wish, you can say an expression as you breathe out, for example, "quiet."

Proceed with this example of musical relaxing for five to ten minutes until you feel loose.

Notwithstanding adhering to these guidelines, consider tuning in to a voice recording, for example, the free MP3 sound document offered by McMaster University, which incorporates headings on rehearsing diaphragmatic relaxing. Utilization of a sound chronicle enables you to completely unwind and focus on the system without adhering to composed guidelines.

Impediments to Practicing Deep Breathing

In the event that you find that you come back to shallow breathing in spite of rehearsing profound breathing, it may be the case that you need more practice in various circumstances. Take a stab at taking a yoga class that supports profound breathing or pursue a care reflection course. Utilizing different techniques that join profound breathing will give you more opportunities to practice and start to ace the specialty of breathing from your stomach.

Artists and Deep Breathing

Artists are educated to inhale profoundly while singing to improve the sound of their voice and to keep a melody without breaking in the center. In the event that you are an artist or performer who plays a breeze instrument and live with social uneasiness, you may profit by rehearsing profound relaxing. Breathing profoundly from your stomach area while performing will counteract hyperventilation or the inclination that you can't slow down.

Other Relaxation Exercise Techniques to Use With Deep Breathing

· Dynamic muscle unwinding

· Guided symbolism

· Autogenic preparing

· Yoga

· Contemplation

· Body filter

In the event that profound breathing alone doesn't appear to improve your uneasiness, consider finding out about and rehearsing these different methods. You may even locate an on the web or nearby advisor who can manage you through these kinds of activities.

For an accommodating mentor in your pocket, there is additionally "Woebot," a visit application that can manage you through unwinding practices just as assistance you challenge negative idea designs.

A Quick Five-Minute Breath Exercise

Not certain how to execute profound breathing into your day by day life? The following is a speedy routine you can rehearse every day to remind you to inhale thusly:

Set your telephone to go off once per day at a helpful time.

At the point when the alert goes off, practice profound relaxing for five minutes.

After the five minutes are up, check whether you feel increasingly loose and less on edge.

After some time, it should turn out to be increasingly normal to inhale along these lines constantly.

Breathing profoundly from your stomach is an educated ability. In spite of the fact that as infants we as a whole do this intuitively, when you live with nervousness it can feel hard to inhale along these lines in a snapshot of frenzy. In the event that subsequent to rehearsing profound breathing despite everything you feel serious nervousness, consider counseling a psychological wellness expert or therapeutic specialist for appraisal and suggestions for treatment.

CONCLUSION

We've all heard that reflection prompts more prominent mental lucidity, lower levels of pressure and diminished uneasiness. Yet, how does contemplation advantage the mind? Studies have demonstrated that care practice achieves positive physiological changes that make the association among contemplation and the cerebrum considerably progressively significant.

In ongoing decades, contemplation has turned out to be progressively ordinary. Individuals are investing energy working with their brains, following their breath and figuring out how to welcome the intensity of the present minute. Reflection gatherings are springing up all over – in schools, networks, senior focuses and past. It's moved toward becoming so standard that even the business network has joined the development is fixated on reflection, and there's new proof it improves the mind."

Research in the field of brain science has affirmed what each meditator knows: reflection is useful for body and soul. Science is currently ready to strengthen the cases by demonstrating how contemplation physically impacts the remarkably unpredictable organ between our ears. Ongoing logical proof affirms that reflection sustains the pieces of the cerebrum that add to prosperity. Moreover, it appears that a customary practice denies the pressure and uneasiness related pieces of the cerebrum of their sustenance.

www.ingramcontent.com/pod-product-compliance
Lightning Source LLC
Chambersburg PA
CBHW031100250726
48655CB00004B/1517